RUNNING THE SHOW

SHOW

21 YEARS OF LONDON WEEKEND TELEVISION

DAVID DOCHERTY

Boxtree

For my mother

First published 1990
© David Docherty

Jacket design by Paterson-Jones
Design by Sarah Hall
Typeset in Linotron Plantin by Cambrian Typesetters, Frimley
Printed and bound in Great Britain
by Richard Clay Limited, Bungay, Suffolk

for Boxtree Limited
36 Tavistock Street
London WC2E 7PB

British Library Cataloguing in Publication Data
Docherty, David, 1956–
Running the show: 21 years of London Weekend Television.
I. London. Commercial television services. London Weekend
Television
I. Title
384.55409421

ISBN 1–85283–103–0

CONTENTS

ACKNOWLEDGEMENTS

Those who gave interviews for the book included (in rough historical order): David Frost, Aidan Crawley, Michael Peacock, Clive Irving, Tom Margerison, John Bromley, Kenith Trodd, David Montagu, Lord Campbell of Eskan, Lord Weinstock, Frank Muir, Doreen Stephens, Humphrey Burton, John Page, Shirley Bennett, Joy Whitby, Eric Flackfield, Roy Van Gelder, Stella Richman, Humphrey Barclay, Barry Took, Skip Humphries, Bert Hardy, Sue Stoessl, Ron Miller, Alan Evans, Judith Thomas, Peter Coppock (for whose patient help I am particularly grateful), Warren Breach, Peter Cazaly, Les Rowarth, Keith Pitts, Lord Aylestone, Sir Brian Young, John Freeman, Michael Grade, David Bell, John Birt (who put forward my name), Colin Freeman, Nick Elliott, Jane Hewland, David Cox, Rod Allen, Janet Street-Porter, Brian Tesler (who said yes), Melvyn Bragg, Greg Dyke, Alan Boyd, and Christopher Bland. I am extremely grateful to John P. Hamilton for his guided tour of LWT's archives, and to all of those who gave me off the record briefings. I am sure his colleagues would like this book to be in memory of Cyril Bennett.

Barry Cox put up with my impossible deadlines and lame excuses over the past year. He has been patient and courteous and more than helpful. Anthony Smith and Colin Shaw read and re-read my chapters as I tried to shape them. Both are well aware how much I appreciate their help.

Personal thanks go to the Board, the staff and my colleagues and friends at the Broadcasting Research Unit, where I began the project (especially Steven Barnett, David Morrison and Michael Tracey), and to David Houghton, Katherine Lannon, Clare Reynolds and Shivaun Meehan at the Broadcasting Standards Council, where I completed the book. Colin Shaw, the Council's Director, apart from acting as my sounding board, persuaded the Council to allow me a considerable amount of time to write the book. I owe him a great deal.

Finally, I have bored so many people with stories about this book over the past two years that I must thank them for their patience.

PREFACE

FROG PERSPECTIVES

'Just tell the truth,' said John Birt when I asked him how best to begin the history of London Weekend Television. Easier said than done. I had to make several choices as to which truth I wished to tell. Was I to follow Machiavelli and strip away the pretensions of public service broadcasting. Was I to expose the hypocrisy, greed and venality of broadcasters? Was I to bestow my opinionated approval on the few men and women honest enough and tough enough to dispense with the absurd emotionalism of an outmoded and elitist philosophy? After all, I reasoned, many of the broacasters and programme-makers who are self-styled educators of the nation have trouble making sense of the Green Cross Code. However, for all of its faults, ITV has consistently produced programmes which are among the best which advertising-supported television has yet offered. Furthermore, ITV was, for at least ten years, a match for the BBC, and the Corporation, for all its manifest elitism and arrogance, is widely recognized as the premier public service broadcasting organisation in the world (not least at the BBC). Moreover, I admired many of the broadcasters about whom I was writing and who were clearly committed to a broadcasting philosophy which demanded more of them than a slavish following of the ratings. Was I to defend this system? The temptation to make a small contribution to safeguarding the future of ITV by whitewashing the past was strong. However, little purpose would have been served by such a servile report; its bias would have been plain for all to see.

As well as choosing my frame, I had to select the people about whom I wanted to write. History requires a decision as to what should be left out of the account. In my mind I had to make a choice between a history which concentrated on the technicians, camera-men, script writers, directors etc. – a story of what it was like day to day to work for LWT – and an account of what it was like to *run* a commercial television company. I chose the latter for two reasons: first, the book was written in interesting times; the broadcasting policy of Margaret Thatcher's Conservative Government was, throughout the book's gestation, pushing through immense changes in ITV. Secondly, the story I wanted to tell about the tension inherent in ITV's balancing of public service commitments and the profit motive entailed that the focus of this history is LWT's programme division and the senior executives who devised the strategies which produced the programmes.

This is not then a systematic history of LWT. The stories of the production and finance divisions will, I am sure, be told elsewhere when an overall assessment of ITV is produced to match that of Asa Briggs history of the BBC.

There is another type of story; one which I was commanded to write by people in various bars and restaurants around the television conference circuit. When my fellow drinkers heard that I was writing this history, they ordered me to 'stick the knife' into several of LWT's past and present executives. This request may have come from people who had fallen foul of said executives; but, for many television people, gossip is the stuff of history. I fail to see the point in warming up old industry scandal and slander which, for the most part, is of interest only to insiders. Instead, I have assembled an account of how money, philosophy, ambition and politics have combined to produce LWT; moreover, I have sought to expose the paradoxes and contradictions of commercial public service broadcasting and to pick my way through the intricate checks and balances within ITV.

   This is an old-fashioned history. I have tried to understand, and not blithely to condemn, protagonists in stories. I have adopted what Nietzsche calls a frog perspective. I have inserted myself at the bottom left hand corner of scenes and events and asked: What reasons did such and such a person have for his action? How did he come to believe that his action was justified? What was it in his personality, or in the situation, that made one action seem reasonable, justifiable and moral, and another act appear as the antithesis of these virtues? Such questions and frog perspectives protect the interrogator against arrogance. Instead of censuring actions as petty and self-serving, I have put them into their financial, political, personal, bureaucratic and cultural contexts. I have not stood above the process by which people came to a decision and, with the benefit of hindsight, arrogantly handed down a verdict. Interpretations and verdicts are for the reader.

— 1 —
HOW TO MARRY THE ITA

'Better authentic Mammon than a bogus god.'
Louis Macneice, Bagpipe Music

For around thirty years, the 1960s office block which housed the Independent Broadcasting Authority (IBA) stood as a monument to the unknown bureaucrat.[1] Functional, anonymous and unpretentious, it was overshadowed by the sprawling ostentation of its neighbour, Harrods. People rushed past the IBA's modest front entrance without a second glance, and yet the Authority played a considerable role in their lives: for over a third of a century it partnered, irritated, regulated, guided, educated, scolded and cajoled the television companies which collectively comprised the Independent Television network (ITV). This alliance created a commercial television system which, by and large, cared as much about quality and originality as it did about profit and ratings.

In 1954 the IBA's predecessor, the Independent Television Authority (ITA), was established to regulate the embryonic commercial television system. The Authority was a classic example of British institutional engineering; it was a compromise between unfettered competition and government control. Moreover, it exercised control over a medium which reached into the heart of people's homes. Most Parliamentarians agreed that television was a powerful force for good or ill; it could enlighten minds, enlarge experience and provide pleasure or, in its darker manifestations, become a medium of propaganda and a subverter of culture.[2] Therefore, although Churchill's Conservative government was committed to introducing an advertising-supported television service in competition with the BBC, it had to meet the fears of many Conservatives and most Labour politicians that the new service would play on coarse instincts and bad taste.

A free market solution, which relied on self-regulation by the commercial television companies, was not offered as a serious solution. In the mid-1950s, fashionable political alternatives were variations on a collectivist theme; consequently, an appropriate bureaucratic compromise had to be found which would break the BBC's monopoly on broadcasting while securing the public interest. This problem was resolved by adapting the institutional model of the public corporation.[3] These organizations – of which the BBC was one – were appointed by, and answerable to, government, but were functionally, if not actually, autonomous.

The ITA's constitution was similar in form to other public corporations such as the National Coal Board, and its members, appointed by government, were drawn from the pool of schoolmasters, retired civil servants and former politicians – known collectively as the great and the good. The ITA had one significant advantage over many other public corporations: because it owned and operated transmitters, on which it leased time to programme providers, it was financially independent of government. This autonomy was to be important over the years.

The Authority was charged by Parliament with drawing up rules on advertising and monitoring their application; ensuring competition between a number of different programme providers; and securing a proper balance in the range and quality of the output of those holding ITA contracts. Thus it encouraged competition while shackling its wilder excesses.

To varying degrees, and in various ways, the Authority and its staff became entangled in the day-to-day affairs of its franchise holders. However, the real power lies in awarding contracts, which it did on four occasions: 1954, 1964, 1967 and 1980.[4] These were moments of ultimate power during which the Authority became a dangerous organizational demiurge placated only with promises and attention, respect and honour. The Authority wrenched contracts from their astonished holders; transferred cities, towns, and regions from one franchise to another; and forced infuriated companies to merge or to separate. The Authority was an ever-present reminder of business mortality.

At the end of the third franchise round, in the summer of 1967, John Spencer Wills, the Chairman of Rediffusion – London's weekday ITV contractor and one of the ITV network's longest-serving and largest companies[5] – waited to hear his company's fate. Wills was a tough and resolute businessman. In the summer of 1956, in the first year of Rediffusion's contract, the company's losses threatened to break his career. Between September 1955 and July 1956 Rediffusion lost almost £3 million (and was to lose another £2 million – before going into profit). By the end of that summer his partners, Associated Newspapers, who published the *Daily Mail*, were profoundly anxious about the security of their investment. One evening, in August 1956, Wills was invited to dinner by Lord Rothermere – the Chairman of Associated Newspapers – after which Wills was asked curtly if he would buy Rothermere's shares. Wills refused to shrivel before this treatment and he informed Rothermere that he would only recommend that his Board buy the shares if they were offered at a 25 per cent discount. Rothermere grunted his assent and the deal was struck. Wills persuaded the Boards of Rediffusion, and of the parent company, British Electric Traction, to pay £1.65 million for the purchase of 200,000 shares and a further £2 million for unsecured loans and loan stock. This signal of confidence in Rediffusion's future did much to shore up the other ITV companies, which were weighed down by heavy start-up costs and sluggish growth in advertising revenue. Many might have cut and run if not for Rediffusion's continued existence. The ITA, in Wills' opinion, owed him a great deal.[6]

Wills' coolness during this period of intense financial pressure was legendary. However, although he was delighted at Rediffusion's subsequent prosperity, and pleased with the company's programmes, he was slightly anxious about its future. On 5 May 1967, Wills had attended an interview with the ITA during which he, and his company's senior executives, were quizzed and, to his mind, interrogated. Wills had never concealed his contempt for what was, in his opinion, a peculiar and unjust system of running ITV. British Electric Traction, of which Wills was chairman, possessed contracts for other public services – such as air and bus routes – and he could not see why, when these arrangements were renewed without mystery and rigmarole, Rediffusion had to go to such extraordinary lengths to retain its London television contract. This was the second time in three years that Wills had to re-apply for the franchise and, finally, when he could stand the grilling no longer, he let it be known that he expected the Authority to stop dithering.

Some members of the Authority were clearly furious at this outburst. Wills was nonetheless astonished when, in the middle of June, the ITA decided that Rediffusion should merge with another company – ABC, which previously had served the North and the Midlands at the weekend. Moreover, to pour salt in the wound, ABC was awarded a controlling interest in the new company. Wills was further dismayed to discover that the new weekend franchise for London was to be offered to the London Television Consortium – a virgin company which was led by one of his performers, a Conservative MP, and the Controller of BBC1 – respectively, David Frost, Aidan Crawley and Michael Peacock.

This was a seminal event in the history of ITV, and it remains one of the Authority's most extraordinary and controversial decisions. A much-touted explanation is that after Wills had alienated the ITA, the members of the Authority were charmed by the intelligence, freshness and promise of Peacock and Frost. There is a great deal more to the ITA's decision, however, than a fit of pique, a clash of personalities, or the passing of the old guard; it represented a struggle for control over the running of independent television. The clash signalled the Authority's determination to usher in a new age; one in which commercial broadcasting would fully contribute to the maintenance and development of public service broadcasting. Rediffusion came to represent discredited ITV values at the point when the London Television Consortium – which became LWT – exploded on to the scene to promise new hope that the ITA could create the conditions for a genuine public sevice.

Creating Public Service

ITV fitted the 1950s like a comfortable duffle coat. When it broadcast the first advertisement at 8.12 pm, 22 September 1955, it celebrated and evoked the character of post-rationing Britain. ITV, which aimed to be popular television for the new working class, arrived at just the right moment. The working class was on the move. Families which had, for a century or more, lived cheek-by-jowl in the warren of streets which linked the cities of the industrial revolution, were breaking up and spreading across the rebuilt cities and towns of the 1950s. As a result of the Housing Acts of 1946 and 1949, and the New Towns Act of 1946, the number of new houses increased from 55,000 a year in 1946 to 227,616 in 1948, and reached a high point in the early 1950s when 300,000 homes a year were being completed.

There were two simple reasons why this policy broke the back of the working-class extended family. First, many of the houses were built around the outside of towns and cities. Secondly, housing departments forced families to accept homes on different estates, often many miles apart. As it was extremely difficult and expensive to travel, the intricate bonds which united extended families simply unravelled.[7]

The new homes needed to be furnished and made comfortable, and the 20 per cent increase in the standard of living between 1948 and 1955 provided sufficient disposable income to trigger the inexorable spread of consumer durables: washing machines, refrigerators, vacuum cleaners, telephones, and, above all, televisions, became commonplace.

Commercial television, which embraced and symbolized the values of affluence and consumerism, appeared to confirm that the old, dull, poor Britain of Depression and of rationing was on the run. However, the values of the old world were buried deep in the character of the new. The 1950s, as Germaine Greer has recounted, were simply 'ten years of foreplay'. It may have appeared serious when kids were ripping up seats during Bill Haley's *Rock Around the Clock* (although Haley's kiss curl should have given away the game), or when 'angry' young playwrights and authors fulminated against bourgeois values, but normal service was resumed without too much disruption. It was difficult to hear the crack of doom in the voice of Cliff Richard who, after all, wanted to remain a bachelor boy simply because he enjoyed living with his mother.

By the early 1960s, however, a real cultural conflict was brewing. Phillip Larkin identified the *casus belli* in his poem 'Annus Mirabilis':

> So life was never better than in 1963
> – But just too late for me –
> Between the end of the Chatterley ban
> And the Beatles' first LP

Several highly volatile ingredients combined to produce a potent cocktail. The Conservative Party covered itself in disgrace when John Profumo, the War Minister, lied to the House of Commons about his illicit relationship with a woman – Christine Keeler – who had also shared a bed with a Russian diplomat. The anachronistic identity of the Conservative Party was further enhanced when Alex Douglas Home succeeded Harold Macmillan to the premiership in 1963. Home was one of the more decent men to hold this position; however, as an old Etonian, Oxonian and a 14th Earl he was hardly the epitome of the modern world. If the Tories seemed wedded to the past, the Labour Party was embracing the future with the breathless enthusiasm of Dan Dare. It spent money updating its image; digested the implications of Anthony Crosland's *The Future of Socialism*; and, in Harold Wilson's celebrated phrase, yoked itself to the 'white heat of the technological revolution'. At the 1963 party conference Judith Hart, an outspoken left-winger, declaimed, 'socialists and scientists together can make their dreams a reality.'

Some aspects of British culture were becoming distorted, as if in a fairground mirror. Religious symbols, previously a relatively fixed point in the national consciousness, even among those without a formal religious affiliation, were threatened from within the very heart of the English national church by Bishop John Robinson, whose book, *Honest to God*, announced that God had unaccountably gone on holiday without leaving a forwarding address. Robinson's book merely summed up various theological arguments which had been familiar for at least a century, but it became a *cause celebre*, and the ensuing inconclusive debate suggested that uncertainty was the defining characteristic of a church unable to adjust to the modern world.

Other institutions were similarly transformed: higher education, for example, which previously had been the preserve of a small elite, expanded rapidly and grammar school boys began to comprehend that they were a class whose time had come. Marriage and fidelity were challenged when sex, with a joyous whoop and pharmacological support from the contraceptive pill, claimed top billing as *the* historical force for change. '[W]elcome to the post-pill generation' exulted a character in one of 1960s most powerful novels, John Updike's *Couples*.

Change, the new class proclaimed, was necessary and good in itself.

The musicians, playwrights, painters, journalists, philosophers, hair-dressers and sociologists who dominated and seemed to direct these changes were restless and iconoclastic and they attracted as much hatred as they won adulation. However, the anti-Christ, as far as many people were concerned, lurked on the third floor of the BBC's Broadcasting House – Hugh Greene, the BBC's director-general. Mary Whitehouse, a schoolteacher who orchestrated a public campaign against the BBC, accused Greene of being 'responsible for the moral collapse in this country.' She was not an isolated voice moaning in the wilderness; in 1966, 335,355 people signed a petition endorsing her protest.

Greene courted controversy; he delighted in riding in the whirlwind and directing the storm. He summarized his beliefs to the Commonwealth Broadcasting Conference of 1963: 'We think it is an important part of our duty . . . to question authority rather than to accept it, to ask in fact whether the Emperor has any clothes.' Greene, as much as anyone in the early 1960s, flowed with and helped direct the spirit of the age. He was a headstrong, individualistic, modernizing, cantankerous, self-centred visionary.

Commercial television, by contrast, appeared oblivious to the apparently radical transformation flowing around it. By the time of the Beatles' first LP the programmes on some of the ITV stations were little different from those with which they had begun in the mid-1950s. Rediffusion, for example, persevered with game show formats, such as *Take Your Pick* and *Double Your Money* which, although popular, did not endear TV to the cultural establishment, the new left, or the grammar school boys. Consequently, the 1960s were open season on ITV. It was lampooned, vilified, and censured by educationalists, sociologists, philosophers and literary critics. These criticisms could have been shrugged off as sour grapes on the part of a middle class which hated the sight of the working class enjoying themselves. This view was prevalent in an ITV network dominated by powerful men, such as Lew Grade of ATV and the Bernsteins at Granada, who delighted in popular entertainment, and by others who took the cynical view that as the working class bought the bread, milk, and soap powder which were advertised on ITV, the network should broadcast programmes which were guaranteed to bring in large numbers of such viewers. Neither the cynics nor the entertainers could, however, ignore a government committee on broadcasting which synthesized many of the criticisms aimed at ITV from elsewhere.

The 1954 Television Act had allotted a term of ten years to the ITA. It was widely assumed, however, that a government committee on broacasting would review the successes and failures of this experiment. In 1960, Harold Macmillan's government set up such a committee under the chairmanship of the industrialist, Sir Harry Pilkington. Its terms of reference were:

To consider the future of the broadcasting services in the United Kingdom, the dissemination by wire of broadcasting and other programmes, and the possibility of television for public showing. To advise on the services which should in future be provided in the United Kingdom by the BBC and the ITA.

To recommend whether additional services should be be provided by any other organisation.

To propose what financial and other conditions should apply to the conduct of all these services.

The committee contained such luminaries as Peter Hall – subsequently director of both the RSC and the National Theatre – and a future director of London Weekend Television, Sir Jock Campbell (who resigned from the committee during its first year). Its guiding lights were Richard Hoggart – the author of *Uses of Literacy* – and Denis Lawrence, the committee's secretary and a civil servant in the Post Office.

The committee's report was delivered in 1962 and it constituted a stinging rebuke to independent television. ITV's evidence to the committee was chaotic, discordant and disorganized, particularly when compared to the authoritative and literate presentations by the BBC. The committee argued that broadcasting should 'give people the best possible chance of enlarging worthwhile experience', and, consequently, it gave short shrift to the opinion expressed by some ITV men that broadcasting should simply provide the public with programmes for which they have expressed a preference. The report stated:

It seems to us that 'to give the public what it wants' is a misleading phrase: misleading because as commonly used it has the appearance of an appeal to democratic principle but the appearance is deceptive. It is in fact patronising and arrogant, in that it claims to know what the public is, but defines it as no more than the mass audience; and in that it claims to know what it wants, but limits its choice to the average of experience. In this sense we reject it utterly. If there is a sense in which it should be used, it is this: what the public wants and what it has the right to get is the freedom to choose from the widest range of programme matter. Anything less than that is deprivation.

The committee summed up its philosophy thus:

The point was made neatly to us as follows: 'Those who say they give the public what it wants begin by underestimating public taste, and end by debauching it.'

The howls of protest and dismay could be heard from ITV's most southerly region, Westward, to Grampian in the far north of Scotland. In Brompton Towers, the ITA's terrible despondency was almost tangible.

Twenty years later, Bernard Sendall, who was Deputy Director General at the time, wrote of the committee: 'collectively, they displayed a general puritanical spirit. More than one of the statements that appear in their report, and to which they put their names, seem to betray an air of almost arrogant moral superiority which as individuals they would no doubt be most eager to disown.'[8]

Sendall's reflections on Pilkington shed light on the ITA's enthusiastic response to the LWT consortium. He pointed out:

> the proportion of serious programmes was, even before Pilkington reported, virtually as high as it has ever been, before or since; but their impact on the intelligentsia – all light rather than heavy viewers – had been minimal. It seems obvious now [in 1982] that, on grounds of expendiency if none other, more of the revenue should have been lavished on programmes and less taken as profit. Or, to put it another way, some of the immense revenue potential should have been sacrificed in order to present in peak time programmes more conspicuously in harmony with the public service tradition in broadcasting.[9]

The political and cultural grounds were prepared for a franchise application aimed at the intelligentsia; however, one other element must be added to this mix of cultural change and political pressure before the ITA's endorsement of LWT begins to make sense – the appointment, in 1963, of Lord Hill as the ITA's chairman.

Lord Hill was an energetic man who, after ten years as a Cabinet minister, enjoyed the exercise of power. He was recruited, in the words of the Postmaster General, Reg Bevins, to be 'a strong man' who would sort out ITV. In his memoirs Hill disclosed that when he arrived at Brompton Road the Authority 'was still licking its wounds after the severe mauling it had suffered in the inquisition and report by the Pilkington Committee. Rather than answer the attack, it was standing in a corner and whimpering.'[10]

In part the Authority's predicament was self-inflicted. The ITA's greatly respected Director General, Sir Robert Fraser, regarded the companies with the fondness of a Dutch uncle.[11] Consequently, it was difficult for his staff to persuade, cajole and threaten the companies to produce more public service programmes and to schedule them in peak-time. It was Fraser's benign and avuncular attitude which Hill was expected to change. On the other hand, the ITA's problems reflected the perennial difficulties of commercial companies acting as if they were a public service. The permanent and irresolvable tension between the need to ensure consistent profits and the desire to produce the best programmes possible was intrinsic to ITV. However, Pilkington, in many ways, failed to comprehend the ways in which profits are come by in television; the committee seemed to want a commercial broadcasting system which was, in some way, divorced from the need to make profits.

Hill came to understand some of the ITA's problems. Despite his interventionist policy it was necessary to issue the following memorandum to the network in 1966:

In general, Independent Television has a very good record. Taken as a whole our programmes embrace the serious as well as the light; informing, stimulating and entertaining most groups in the community. Minorities do not go to the wall in Independent Television. We prove this by an analysis of our total programme output.

Yet despite the validity of our rejection of the criticism that a commercial service can never be a public service, the charge sometimes made that one motive behind our service is numbers, and so profit, might be held to find some semblance of support from a scrutiny of our offering, which is limited to peak hours . . . What then are we after? Quality, of course, at all times – there will be no two views about that. But also at all times – sufficient variety . . .

The Authority asks all companies to take a fresh, hard look at the make-up of their schedules between 7 and 10.30 pm with a view to securing within these times a generally wider range of programmes.

The aim should be to whet the appetite of the more intelligent viewers by providing more variation from the standard fare.[12]

Three separate pressures built up as the ITA set about considering the future of ITV. Although Pilkington had not had much of an impact on government policy, it established and confirmed a climate of opinion in which the ITA was regarded as being too soft on its rapacious contractors. Moreover, such attitudes confirmed the BBC's status as the senior partner in the broadcasting system, and led directly to the award of a second channel to the BBC.[13] Secondly, ITV, a child of the 1950s, was struggling to keep pace with the 1960s – a decade in which an endemic restlessness within culture and politics militated against the preservation of the *status quo*. Finally, the very success of ITV was a problem; some areas of the country were complaining that as consumers they were contributing to ITV's profits, but as viewers their region was not adequately represented by the 'local' television service.

The ITA responded to these influences by establishing a Contracts Committee which explored, among other things, the future pattern for the franchise areas. The committee concluded that there was room for change; in particular, it noted the existence of sufficient advertising revenue to support a new franchise in Yorkshire. This split the Granada fiefdom, whose contract was awarded for both Lancashire and Yorkshire, and it introduced a fifth 'major' to the network. Other root and branch changes included launching seven day franchises to serve Yorkshire, Lancashire and the Midlands, and carving London up between one franchise which would operate for five and a half days, and another which would run from Friday evenings until closedown on Sunday. This replaced the untidy system in which ATV held the weekday franchise for the Midlands and the weekend franchise for London, Granada and Rediffusion held five day contracts for, respectively, the North and London, and ABC served the North and Midlands at the weekend.[14]

When the new ITV franchise round opened, the ITA made it clear that its expectations were different from those which had previously guided the process; it anticipated a genuine challenge to the BBC for quality as well as for audiences.

How to Marry the ITA

Organizations savour authority. If they are courted and flattered then their power is more likely to be used to benefit the suitor. If petitioners are arrogant, self-important and high-handed then bureaucracies turn on them with the full armoury of obfuscation, red tape, and rejection. The ITA exemplified this process. The protocols for a franchise application were almost as sophisticated as the conventions of courtship. The rules appeared to be out of the pages of an etiquette book which combined *How to Marry a Millionaire* and Machiavelli's *The Prince*.

Certain lessons had to be learned: first, the applicant had to present himself in the best possible light; he had to put together an imposing financial package, an impressive and promising creative team, and an exceptional management group. Secondly, the aspirant franchise holder had to concoct a franchise proposal which promised to fulfil the Authority's ideals for the system.

These rules and protocols on occasion militated against good sense. Some companies portrayed themselves as bizarre parodies of public service broadcasters. Applicants stated that their programmes would be more expensive and more popular than those of their rivals. Moreover, that these high quality popular programmes would not undermine the company's resolve to create dozens of minority programmes; vast quantities of shows about the arts; local news and current affairs by the bucketful; and series for the blind, deaf, dumb and epileptic. Candidates affirmed that they were forward-looking with a sense of history, and outward-looking with a profound understanding of their local roots; furthermore, that their programme-makers were young but experienced, daring but sensible, and irreverent but cautious.

By and large the Authority ignored applications which were clearly designed to try to pull the wool over their eyes. The Authority's problems occurred when the applicants sincerely believed in what they were trying to achieve and looked as if they might be able to pull it off. The London Television Consortium made one such application; it followed the rules of courtship to perfection, and the Authority was charmed by the applicants.

Lesson I – Become the Perfect Suitor

In order to become the perfect suitor a consortium needed three types of people: executives, financiers, and talent. It was possible to win a franchise without one group in place, but to wrest a franchise from the company already in possession required strength in depth. LWT's application showed how it should be done.

1 The Executives

In December 1966, the ITA divulged its plan to alter the pattern of the franchise areas, and on 28 February it invited applications for new contracts. The closing date was set at 15 April. The feverish atmosphere which prevailed over these four months was ideally suited to one of the men who epitomized both the restless energy of the 1960s and the new breed of television professional – David Frost.

The television critic, presenter, and author, Clive James, once remarked that all you have to do on television is be yourself, provided, he added, that you have a self to be. Frost created his self on television and, as a result, he fitted the contours of the small screen as if the cathode-ray had itself created him. As a performer, Frost understood how to manipulate television as well as anyone in the history of broadcasting. At one level the medium was his toy – it was a giant train set and he wanted to control the points. On another level, however, broadcasting was the source of Frost's money and of his status. The medium provided him with an extraordinary amount of influence. It was characteristic of an age when old men grew their hair long and women of a certain age wore mini skirts, that authority should no longer be the preserve of those who had spent decades learning how best to use it. In their different ways the Kennedys and the Beatles undermined the idea that a society was best run by its elders. At 28, Frost was roughly the same age as John Lennon but, unlike many of his contemporaries, Frost had no intention of following Timothy Leary's advice to the flower generation to tune in, turn on, and drop out. Frost planned to turn up, take charge and make money.

Frost was at the height of his creative powers in the mid-1960s. His apparently unstoppable rise began after Ned Sherrin chose him to act as link-man for the BBC's seminal satire show, *That Was the Week That Was*. He moved on to make three programmes a week for Rediffusion under the eponymous title – *The Frost Programme*. Some of the shows, most notably with the con-man Emile Savundra, made television history. Frost developed a singular interview style which was far removed from the calm and detached discussion programmes which, by and large, had prevailed before his arrival. At his best, he orchestrated and conducted discussions; waving his hands and his clip-board at the audience and his interviewees, he drew them into debate and confrontation. Sometimes the programmes generated more emotion and turmoil than clear thinking, but they were sufficiently well-regarded for Frost to be rewarded in 1967 with the Richard Dimbleby Award and the Royal Television Society's Silver Medal. He was startlingly ubiquitous in 1966 and 1967. He had his own one-man show at the Edinburgh Festival, he published several books, and he starred in the appropriately named *Frost Over England*, which won the Golden Rose of Montreux. Although there have been many pretenders to Frost's position over the years, it is difficult to imagine any of them repeating Frost's 1966 breakfast meeting at the Connaught Hotel in London at which the Prime Minister, Harold Wilson, was present as well as half of the political and cultural establishment.

Frost refused to fit the mould of television performers. Instead of turning his career over to a management team and agents, he took control himself. He established his own production company – Paradine Productions[15] – through which he sponsored and profited from a new wave of comedians, such as John Cleese, Ronnie Corbett, Ronnie Barker, and Graham Chapman.

He had his critics. Kitty Muggeridge (wife of Malcolm) is said to have commented acidly that Frost 'rose without trace', and, some years later, Christopher Booker, an old colleague from *That Was the Week That Was*, denounced him for reducing everyone to 'bit players in a universal dreamworld.' No matter whether he was loved or hated, no one ignored him. Whenever Frost phoned people took the call.

Frost loved television for its own sake, but he was a cultural entrepreneur whose intention was to spin his talent into gold. The most obvious way to make money in television was to own shares in an ITV company. Roy Thomson – Chairman of STV – had notoriously identified ITV as a licence to print money, and although ITV's phenomenal growth was slowing down in the mid-1960s, many companies were still making a 50 per cent return on capital. Frost wanted a piece of that action.

Owning his own television station was an extension of owning his own production company. As a proprietor of an ITV contract he would have absolute control over his own career and would make a great deal of money. Yorkshire was the obvious candidate for an application; however, at least ten other consortia were gearing up for the Yorkshire franchise and, on past evidence, the ITA was likely to award it to a group with local connections. Try as he might, Frost could not transform his London twang into a Yorkshire growl.

An audacious thought struck him at a Rediffusion staff party in January 1967, not long after the ITA had announced its intention to change the franchises. Frost was wandering around chatting to people who had been making the same programmes at Rediffusion for years, when he had a flash of inspiration. If *he* thought that Rediffusion was badly in need of an overhaul, and was dated in its approach and unadventurous in spirit, perhaps the ITA could similarly be persuaded?

He needed co-conspirators and he disclosed the idea to Clive Irving, a close friend who was working with him on *The Frost Programme*. Irving was a successful journalist; he had been a Managing Editor at the *Sunday Times* and had helped to found the award-laden *Insight* team of investigative journalists. However, he was restless and looking for a new challenge and he jumped at the chance when Frost, with the full glow of revelation still upon him, outlined his plan in a Kardomah Coffee House nearby Rediffusion's head office in the Kingsway. Irving recalls the moment vividly: 'We were sitting there gossiping about the franchises when David blurted out his idea: "Why not go for London?" I took a few minutes to recover from that notion, and then I said: "Which franchise?" David said, "whichever one we can win." So we had another cup of coffee and talked about the job that was being done by Rediffusion because we knew Rediffusion very well from the inside.' These reflections on Rediffusion's shortcomings convinced them that it could be challenged and that even if their consortium could not snatch Rediffusion's franchise, the weekend was equally attractive.[16]

Although successful, Rediffusion's management had also widely been regarded as idiosyncratic. The first General Manager, a retired Royal Navy Captain named Tom Brownrigg, had a habit of hiring ex-naval personnel; this so affected the company that the management floor at head office was called 'The Bridge'. By 1967, however, Brownrigg had given way to John McMillan, considered by his contemporaries to be capable and astute. Under his management, Rediffusion consolidated its record in children's programmes; maintained its respected current affairs show – *This Week*; promoted *The Frost Programme*; and produced a phalanx of highly popular light entertainment shows.

There seemed to be no particular reason why Rediffusion should be more vulnerable than Granada, ATV or ABC. Indeed, ATV should have been more exposed. Although it held the weekday franchise for the Midlands, it broadcast to London at the weekends and it was resolutely London-based; the main studios were at Elstree in London, and the majority of its Board of Directors, executives and programme-makers lived in the Capital. However, as Lew Grade – ATV's Deputy Chairman – was part of the fabric of ITV, it was difficult to imagine anyone taking away his franchise.

As in all the best folk tales, three separate events confirmed that Frost and Irving were setting off on the correct path. First, Frost bustled off to see Lord Hill, who plainly wanted to set this particularly energetic cat among the somnolent ITV pigeons, and he assured Frost that there was to be genuine competition for the franchises. Second, the consortium was joined by Dr Tom Margerison, the Science Editor of the *Sunday Times*, who was a neighbour and friend of Irving's. Margerison had been involved with a bid for Yorkshire but had independently come to the conclusion that Rediffusion was vulnerable. Margerison's scientific and analytical approach confirmed Frost's intuitive insight and Irving brought them together. Finally, and crucially according to Frost, a couple of days after the Kardomah meeting Peter Hall expressed an interest in enroling in the consortium. Frost decided that 'what might have seemed like a wildly impossible scenario was do-able if one of Britain's most distinguished stage directors came on board.'

In order to turn an ambitious idea into a plausible application Frost and Irving urgently needed a high-profile and respected chairman. After several fruitless suggestions Irving hit upon an idea which was to have repercussions throughout the history of LWT. 'Why don't we ask John Freeman?'

Freeman was renowned for *Face to Face*, a BBC series in which he conducted a number of, what seemed at the time, relentless interviews with leading figures from industry, philosophy, politics and popular culture. He was a genuine laird o' pairts; he had been a junior minister in the post-war Labour government; an editor of Britain's foremost left-wing political magazine; and after Labour's election in 1964 he was recruited by the Labour Prime Minister, Harold Wilson, to become British High Commissioner to India – a prime diplomatic post.

Frost flew to Delhi for the day and sought out his quarry. Freeman was both amused and intrigued by this frontal attack and expressed some interest in the project. He informed Frost that he was committed to the diplomatic service for the foreseeable future; however, he did hold out the hope that if for some reason he was to leave he would consider seriously Frost's proposal. Although this was a vague promise, Freeman had hinted that he might leave the service if he was not offered the US or the Soviet Union, and Frost felt that it was worth cementing the relationship. He offered Freeman some shares in return for a commitment from Freeman that the LWT position would be first in his mind when he left India. This indeterminate promise was subsequently to lead to all sorts of confusion. Freeman was entered in the application form as Deputy Chairman, and several of the consortium members believed that he would become Chairman in due course.

Before Frost and Irving came up with an alternative to Freeman, fate took a hand. Frost approached the banker, David Montagu, for financial advice. Montagu explained that he was involved with a Conservative MP, Aidan Crawley, in a bid for Yorkshire. Frost said: 'Well, why not merge our two groups and you can mastermind the application?'

Although Crawley did not possess a particularly strong team, he had an ace-in-the-hole. He had secured the interest of Michael Peacock, the Controller of BBC1 and widely tipped to be a future director-general. Peacock epitomized the new breed of television professionals; he was articulate, successful, and aggressive. He had risen extremely quickly within the BBC and, at the age of 37, if he had played his cards right, might have become DG in his mid-40s. However, he wanted out: 'I had a sense that I didn't want to spend the second half of my life at the BBC. So I felt that when the right opportunity came along then I would benefit in every sense by changing.'

Peacock was attracted to ITV by the possibility of a share deal and of a higher salary; however, more than that, he relished the thought of running one of Britain's largest independent broadcasting organizations and of initiating programme policy without the cumbersome BBC bureaucracy.

He was convalescing in hospital after an operation on his elbow, and this provided him with sufficient time to mull over the options: should he remain with the BBC and take the chance on becoming director-general? Or should he make a dash to run his own company immediately? ITV offered flexibility, freedom and the prospect of evangelizing commercial television on behalf of public service broadcasting. Success would reward him financially and personally.

Although Peacock had some kind of moral obligation to Crawley, like Frost, he was essentially a metropolitan creature. He was prepared to gamble for a London franchise, and he recommended that the consortia merge and that he should become Managing Director of the proposed company. Consequently, he invited Crawley and Frost to meet one another at his bedside in the hospital. Frost's entrepreneurial instincts identified immediately the importance of Peacock for a successful pitch to the ITA: 'I felt that Peacock was the big one, the grand prize,' he remembers.

Each gained something from the deal: Frost and Irving acquired a chairman who would add gravitas to their campaign and who would look good to both the ITA and to the City, and a Managing Director whose recruitment would be widely regarded as a breathtaking coup. Crawley's group procured one of British broadcasting's most famous personalities.

Now they were five: Crawley, Peacock, Frost, Irving and Margerison (only one of whom was genuinely famous). These five, advised by David Montagu, set out to recruit talent and money. They were spectacularly successful.

2 The Money

The next two months consisted of a frenzy of lunches, dinners, telephone calls, arm-twisting, entreaties, demands and inquiries. The consortium decided that as they were among the most important cultural market makers in the country they would enlist the nation's most eminent financial figures. David Frost, one of nature's recruiting agents, accepted the responsibility of assembling the requisite businessmen. Irving recounts that: 'there was this galaxy of men who were making the new Britain, and we thought that we were making a new television so we went along to them.'

The charmed circle of businessmen included two of Britain's top industrialists – Arnold Weinstock of GEC and Donald Stokes of the Leyland Motor Corporation – both of whom were busy generating Harold Wilson's white heat. Three others, Sir Christopher Chancellor – Chairman of the Bowater Paper Group – Sir Geoffrey Kitchen – Chairman of Pearl Assurance – and Duncan McNab of the London Co-operative Society, provided the security of large amounts of anonymous cash; moreover these three represented the type of established financial institution whose presence was guaranteed to delight the ITA. This group, along with David Montagu and Sir Jock Campbell, Chairman of the publishers of the *New Statesman*, became the non-Executive directors.[17] Other corporate shareholders not represented on the board were the publishers William Collins and Weidenfeld and Nicolson, two educational institutions, University College London, and Magdalen College, Oxford, and, finally Lombard Banking and the Imperial Tobacco Company Pension Fund.

This was an inspired Board with which to apply for a franchise. It united self-effacing money men with high flying industrialists, and it combined the intellectual credentials afforded by the *New Statesman* and the universities with the solid local support of the London Co-op. (How many Co-op stamps do you need for a franchise?)

The company planned to raise £15,000 in voting and £1.5 million in non-voting shares, with up to £3,075,000 in unsecured loan stock. Furthermore, thirty per cent of the share capital was earmarked for senior management and sundry artistic and creative contributors to the consortium (such as John Freeman). Frost was to own five per cent of the voting shares and £75,000 of the non-voting stock. The loan capital was provided by seven corporate shareholders, five of whom were on the board.

Why would such important industrialists become involved with the London Television Consortium? A modern Machiavellian may reduce their motives to those of money and profit. This would be facile. Although television companies earned a good return on revenue, in absolute terms the profit was insignificant compared to that generated by electronics, pension funds or car manufacturing. The weekend franchise was likely, at most, to make a couple of million pounds profit in its first few years compared to the tens of millions earned by GEC or Thorn.

Glamour and status were – and on occasion remain – more important than money. Television was dazzling and exhilarating, and it exercised a fascination for businessmen who, like everyone else, was open to the allure of the stars. Furthermore, television was a public service and, as such, conferred status on those involved at Board level. The road to a knighthood is paved with such good investments. One member of the

Board confirms this judgement: 'some of us joined because City men, like everyone else, can be very naive and very human, and we wanted to be in this rather exciting, glamorous world of television.' Furthermore, the Board were buying into television at a relatively cheap rate: 'If the company had been successful' a Board member pointed out, 'then everyone would have made relatively easy money, but even when it wasn't a success it did not constitute a serious loss for most of them.'

Other than easy money and status, several had personal or political reasons for becoming involved. Arnold Weinstock, for example, recollects: 'My interest at that time was as a manufacturer of televisions to get better programmes. I thought the programmes were not very good and something needed to be done to improve them.' Lord Campbell persuaded the Board of the *New Statesman* to join in order to introduce 'public service broadcasting into the commercial sector.'

The ITA could not help but be impressed with this Board of Directors; however, most of franchise applicants had imposing boards, the real challenge was that of recruiting an impressive and balanced range of talent. The consortium found the perfect solution; they created a dream team by importing star programme-makers from the BBC and uniting them with senior ITV executives.

3 The Talent

Most of the big names in television were approached by some consortium or other during the period leading up to the 1967 franchise applications. At media parties around the country the usual gossip and backbiting was accompanied by a choreography of hints and insinuations, nods and winks, handshakes and small, but knowing, signals. The smell of the hunt – a mixture of greed and creative excitement – was in the air.

There was one important difference between this and other franchise trails: the BBC's lofty disdain seemed somewhat hollow. There was a barely concealed dissatisfaction among key BBC personnel and many were recruited by the new consortia. This break with tradition occurred for a number of reasons: first, most television professionals were aware that the gap in quality between ITV and BBC was exaggerated and, moreover, that ITA had made it clear that it wanted commercial television to become more like the BBC; secondly, many young professional broadcasters wished to exercise more control over their careers; thirdly, there was a plethora of talented people in the BBC, all of whom were pushing for promotion; fourthly there was a suspicion that after seven years, Greene was running out of steam; finally, there was a great deal of money to be made.

The prospect of owning shares attracted many of those who were prepared to hurdle the great divide. These shares were tokens that programme-makers would have some influence over the business dealings of the company that was producing their programmes.

Moreover, share ownership appealed to an atavistic middle-class need to possess capital. Many of the executives were from first generation middle-class families without any real solid financial foundation and, although they earned a comparatively high salary, it was not sufficient to satisfy their sense of status.

Two ideas governed the London Television Consortium's recruitment strategy. First, the ITA had complained for some time that ITV was not producing children's, arts, music, and comedy programmes of any great quality and distinction. Therefore, the LTC's application had to reflect these gaps. Secondly, the ITA had cast covetous eyes at the BBC's output in these areas, and, therefore, the BBC's standards were those at which the LTC was aiming. The simple solution was to hire the BBC's programme-makers. Frost set to work with a vengeance.

Comedy was first on the list. ITV has always found it difficult to develop long running, interesting, and entertaining situation comedies to match those of the BBC. This was especially true during the 1960s when ITV had nothing to compare with *Steptoe and Son*, *Hancock's Half Hour*, and *Till Death Us Do Part*. Consequently, the consortium recruited Frank Muir, one of Britain's most eminent comedy writers, who was also the BBC's Assistant Head of Light Entertainment (Comedy). Muir, along with his partner, Denis Norden, had written some of BBC radio's most celebrated comedies. This partnership was, according to Asa Briggs in his history of the BBC, as worthy of celebration as that between Gilbert and Sullivan. When Norden wanted to try his hand at film scripts, Muir decided to accept an offer from the BBC to run its comedy output. Muir had no intention, however, of being a manager at the BBC for the rest of his life. The Consortium's proposal that he establish his own innovative comedy department, as well as its offer of large amounts of cash and shares, was sufficient to sway him.[18]

With Muir on board, children's programmes were next. Frost rang Doreen Stephens, Head of the Family Programmes Department at the BBC, who had encouraged the development of two of the BBC's most innovative and best-loved children's programmes – *Jackanory* and *Play School*. Stephens resisted: 'Look David', she said, 'if this phone call is about joining your consortium: I've only got six years to go before retirement and I'm not interested.' Frost, in his inimitable manner, invited her out for an expensive lunch at which he outlined the names of the people who would be working for the new station. These names were sufficient to win her support.

Finally, the Consortium needed someone to run their arts and music department. Frost approached Humphrey Burton, the Head of the BBC's Music Department and responsible for much of its output. Burton was different from the other BBC people. Muir and Stephens had come late to the BBC and, although both were proud of their connection with the Corporation, they were not steeped in its folklore nor did they regard joining ITV as some kind of betrayal. Burton, on the other hand, had been brought up in the BBC. He was heir to several BBC empires. As the protégé of Hugh Wheldon – who presented *Monitor*, the BBC's seminal arts programme, and who was head of the BBC's arts department – Burton would have moved rapidly up the BBC hierarchy. He joined the Consortium for two reasons: first, the share deal and the increase in salary were simply too good to pass up; secondly, he left the Corporation because he 'felt that the BBC was set it its ways and was rather smug. So the idea of starting something new, of doing one's own thing on a smaller scale was attractive.' 'I wanted to be a Trojan Horse inside ITV bringing culture to the masses', Burton recalls.

Clive Irving's relationship with the *Sunday Times* 'Insight' team was a useful asset, and he took on the task of running the current affairs programmes. The ideal programme team was secured. However, the Consortium needed also to convince the ITA that it was not an effete group who would be swamped in the hurly burly of ITV. Consequently, Frost secured secret pledges from Rediffusion's Director of Programmes, Cyril Bennett, and Guy Paine, its Director of Sales, that they would join the company if it won the franchise. These were experienced, respected and, supposedly, tough commercial television men whom the ITA knew and respected, and who would calm any fears concerning the inexperience of the BBC team. Bennett had, in fact, been part of the team from the beginning. He was at the first lunch at which Margerison met Frost, and the latter had involved him in the secret planning sessions during which the consortium developed its programmes strategy.

Recruiting Bennett and Paine was a mixed blessing. There was an obvious conflict of interest between Bennett's position with Rediffusion and that with the Consortium. Indeed, it was somewhat unethical for Bennett to take part in programme planning for the LTC when still developing shows and series for Rediffusion. Consequently, the Consortium dithered over the London franchise in which they were primarily interested. The talent which they had recruited clearly led them in the direction of the five day franchise, which would allow more room for children's series, experimental and popular arts and drama, and for comedy. However, the ITA would certainly have looked askance at Bennett and Paine leaving the interview room at Brompton road with Rediffusion and being announced ten minutes later as Executives with Rediffusion's competitor. After much shuttling back and forth, the Consortium settled on the safer bet and applied for the weekend franchise.

Peacock resigned his position just before the ITA interviews in May – to the great consternation and pain of Hugh Greene. The others decided to sweat it out until the franchise had been won.[19]

Lesson 2 – Making the Perfect Proposal

In order successfully to woo the ITA the proposal document had to be attractive and, at the same time, seem realistic. Clive Irving was deputed to write it. The basic ideas and themes were hammered out at sessions in the various homes of the senior consortium members.[20] After much discussion and argument the proposal was completed and it was presented to the ITA on 11 April 1967 – three months after Frost first conceived the project.

The key to the application was the following statement:

> These programme makers have been united by a common belief that the quality of mass entertainment can be improved while retaining commercial viability.

This was followed by a financial commitment:

> [I]t is a basic tenet of this application that a higher proportion of the company's revenue will be spent on programmes than has normally been the case.

Finally, the introduction to the document made a promise which came back to haunt the company time and again:

> The applicants make no claims in this document which they feel they cannot fulfil.

There were many, many claims in the application. Some of the ideas outlined in the proposal, particularly those relating to minority programmes, were ahead of their time. The central theme was that:

> [N]o audience is exclusively either mass or minority. The audience is a constantly changing formation of groups with differing interests and tastes and each has a right to be served by the public air. We believe that these interests and tastes aspire to new experiences and that they should find such experiences through television. This means that we are concerned not only with the sheer numbers of the audience, but why people watch and who watches. We believe that the commercial viability is strengthened by evidence of an active, perceptive and participating audience.

The application continued:

> Independent Television has the capacity to be as complete a public service as the BBC, by being able to deploy the output of a variety of companies, each with its own character, to make a comprehensive and balanced whole.

Much of this echoed the Pilkington Committee's appeal for quality popular entertainment and fitted with the ITA's approach to commercial television; the application was sweet and harmonious music to the ears of the ITA.

The proposal pointed out that the company's output would be co-ordinated by four programme units – Entertainment; Children's, Educational and Religious; Drama, Music and Arts; and, finally, Public Affairs. The very word 'unit', as opposed to 'department', conjured up images of a high-tech, modular, modern way of producing programmes.

Specific programme promises in the proposal included David Frost (exclusive to ITV for the first time) in his own show on Friday, Saturday and Sunday, and *Seven Days* – a current affairs show scheduled to run for forty minutes on a Sunday afternoon and intended to 'relate one event to another, bring out special points overlooked under the pressure of the normal bulletins, and develop the future consequences of the week.' Although Saturday afternoons were to continue to be dominated by a 'comprehensive and imaginative sports service', Sunday afternoon was to be given over to Music and the Arts.

The application argued that the franchise holders in the revamped system should concentrate and specialise in order to achieve a balanced and coherent output. To no one's surprise the company suggested that if it had its arm twisted it would take on the burden of comedy, the arts, science programmes (step up Dr Tom Margerison) and children's programmes.

These programme commitments were accompanied by a guarantee to spend £2.2 million on new technical equipment and a further £2.6 million on building a 'Television Centre' in central London. The application also contained detailed floor plans for the three studios which would be housed in the new centre. These facilities were to open by Spring 1969. With such a detailed, thorough, optimistic proposal, how could the ITA refuse?

Yes

The ITA would have done well to take heed of Jonathan Swift's dictum that 'the reasons why so few marriages are happy, is, because young ladies spend their time in making nets, not in making cages.' Sexist, but very appropriate as far as the franchise process is concerned. The ITA should have guarded itself against idealistic promises and great hopes, however much in line with ITA thinking. It was surely improbable that the other ITV companies had, for twelve years, been mismanaged by people who had wilfully and malevolently refused to broadcast arts and current affairs programmes at prime-time on a Sunday. The sneaking suspicion that it might be difficult to show such programmes at the weekend filtered through to the staff, but the Authority were buoyed up by the consortium's idealism and confidence.

The consortium had the magnificent good fortune to follow John

Spencer Wills into the interview room. After Wills' belligerence the members of the Authority were simply yearning to be informed that commercial television should be a public service; that high quality programmes could be made without sacrificing audiences; and that the ITA's strategy for the future of ITV was correct. They were ready to be bowled over by Peacock's literate, cultured and exhilarating performance, and by Frost's tigerish enthusiasm. Wills and the LTC came to represent a skein of opposing values: Wills was a businessman, Peacock and Frost were programme-makers; Rediffusion was the home of the quiz show, the LTC promised everything from Leonard Bernstein to experimental comedy; Wills resented the ITA, Frost and Peacock welcomed its involvement; Wills symbolized the past, Frost and Peacock the future. Similar points could be made about ATV, ABC and Granada; however, the socialism and the populism of the Bernsteins was entirely in keeping with the 1960s, Lew Grade's rumbustious, infectious, entrepreneurial drive balanced up his obvious defects, and ABC's team of Howard Thomas and Brian Tesler was regarded as having the safest hands in the network. Wills had no protection other than running a professional and successful business. It was not enough to save Rediffusion. Hill looked on with benevolent pleasure as the young Turks – Frost and Peacock – sold themselves to the Authority. He was subsequently to remark that LWT 'had to have its chance whatever the repercussions.' On 12 June, 1967, the ITA awarded the contract for weekends in London to the LTC.[21]

Don't Look Back

The dream team celebrated. 'It was a wonderful and exhilarating feeling to have won', Frost recalls, 'but then it hit me. "Bloody hell", I thought, "we've really got to do it now." ' Others felt a similar mixture of visceral excitement, fear, and sense of purpose. First, though, they had to explain to their colleagues and friends at Rediffusion and the BBC. The BBC felt betrayed when it discovered the defections of Muir, Stephens and Burton; it excommunicated the three that remained at the BBC. Frank Muir – who offered some of his younger colleagues the chance to join him – was accused of acting as a recruiting agent within the BBC and he was sent home five months before his contract was due to end. Muir, with typical urbane equanimity, called it a remission for good conduct. Bennett and Paine were thrown out of Rediffusion on the morning after the new franchise was announced.

This team of cultural visionaries took up temporary residence in Arnold Weinstock's GEC offices in Stanhope Gate, just off Park Lane, and named themselves Thames Television. Eventually, they moved to offices behind the Royal Academy in Old Burlington Street, by which time they had adopted the name London Weekend Television.[22]

The company continued to expand. Derek Granger, a respected drama producer at Granada, came to relieve Burton of the drama output. The company also struck out in new directions in the area of drama by working with a group of drama producers called Kestrel Productions. The prime movers of the group were two BBC producers – Tony Garnett and Kenith Trodd – and a BBC director James McTaggart. When they were asked to join the company, Trodd recalls, 'we took a snooty, leftist attitude. We said that we would only join as a collective.' LWT rose to the bait and installed resident revolutionaries. Joy Whitby, a highly creative producer of children's programmes and a close colleague of Doreen Stephens, was recruited from the BBC. On 16 August Peacock signed up Jimmy Hill, the manager of Coventry City, to run LWT's, and therefore most of the network's, sports output. Hill was an experienced negotiator: as a player he had led the players' union in its fight to break the maximum wage rule, and he was recognized as an innovative and sophisticated analyst of the game.

Tito Burns, one of London's best known agents, who became famous for representing Bob Dylan in the Denmark Street scene of the documentary, *Don't Look Back*, joined the company in March 1968. Cyril Bennett recruited Burns to put together packages for the dance, star, jugglers and variety shows. As a flashy, joking, boisterous figure he provided a useful counterweight to the BBC people.

Frost and Peacock trumpeted their team's qualities to the press. Frost explained: 'we hope to give [the public] what they will grow to want. We have a duty to lead public taste to a higher ground.' Peacock went for ITV's jugular: 'The present weekend programmes are bland, featureless, and tasteless', he declared. Moreover, he continued: 'You won't have to be a moron to get something out of London Weekend Television.'

The programme-makers had to invent ideas which lived up to Peacock's rhetoric. At the beginning, the dream team were crammed together in one large office, a phase that is remembered with fondness by all of the participants. Everything seemed possible; they could re-invent television comedy, add sparkle to arts programmes, educate the nation, spice up and, at the same time, add analytical depth to current affairs. Everyone was in high good humour; everyone was happy to be working together. Although anxious, the programme executives believed in what they were trying to achieve.

The office was a confused, bustling, noisy, effervescent, chaotic centre for programme ideas. Programme-makers felt liberated from the constraints and conventions that had previously governed their output. Muir, for example, commissioned a Russian writer, Alexei Kapler, to write a one-hour comedy, and he announced that he intended to create some situation comedies which would last for an astonishing 45 minutes (most ITV comedies could barely limp along for 28 minutes).

Muir also persuaded Nyree Dawn Porter – one of Britain's best known dramatic actresses who was starring as Irene in the BBC's phenomenally successful drama series *The Forsyte Saga* – to sign up to make a situation comedy. He picked up a comedy-play from Johnny Speight, the writer of *Till Death Us Do Part*, entitled *If There Weren't Blacks You Would Have to Invent Them*. This had been turned down by the BBC and LWT's decision to produce it was further evidence of the company's desire to take chances. Muir also announced that he would star in a comedy review called *We Have Ways of Making You Laugh*.

Doreen Stephen's unit, not to be outdone by this torrent of ideas, developed a children's drama to be shot on film (which was unusual) and made on location (which was extraordinary). Other ideas were spun: for example, a financial advice programme, provisionally called *Money Go Round*; *Degree or Diploma* – an adult education programme which would advise people about which courses to apply for; *Discovering London* – a 26-part series tracing the history of the capital; and a kind of intellectual *Ready, Steady Go* called *The Roundhouse*. This latter took place at the Roundhouse theatre in Camden Town, which was transformed into an electronic Hyde Park Corner. Audiences milled around speakers and stopping to listen and argue with the most interesting.

Jimmy Hill, full of enthusiasm, pinched the Gillette Cup cricket competition from the BBC and he promised livelier and more interesting coverage of cricket and football. Along with John Bromley, who had been with *World of Sport* from the beginning and had remained with the new team, Hill developed new ideas for the presentation of sport. First, they recruited BBC radio's Brian Moore – widely regarded as the best football commentator in the business – to present their football programme. Secondly, they brought in Michael Parkinson, also from the BBC, to front a new programme designed to explore the political and sociological aspects of sport.

Burton signed up major international stars to appear in a series of specials on a Saturday night: Leonard Bernstein was to conduct the New York Philharmonic Orchestra at the Festival Hall; Yehudi Menuhin was to perform in Stravinsky's *The Soldier's Tale*; operas by Britten and John Gay were to be produced. This heavyweight material was balanced by a one-off programme with Robert Morley, and a dance programme with Gillian Lynne.

Irving was likewise determined to be different. He felt that current affairs was 'dull men in the studio saying dull things.' He was going out into the streets to find the action; he was going to create an electronic *Insight*. By adopting the term 'public affairs', as opposed to 'current affairs' he pointed away from the traditions of *This Week* and *World In Action*. He intended to pioneer new techniques for the presentation of public affairs; graphics and pictures were to replace talking heads.

The quality press nicknamed the new company, BBC3 (the name of a BBC satire programme). The *Sunday Telegraph* summed up the relationship between the BBC and BBC3 when it exclaimed that LWT was: 'A bright nephew chasing Auntie.' The old stagers in the ITV network adopted the epithet, and gave it a malicious spin; as far as many ITV men were concerned the precious BBC values espoused by BBC3 would crumble under the impact of competition.

By May 1968, one year after being awarded the contract and four months before they were due to go on air, Peacock promised a television revolution; it was to spend more per programme hour than any ITV company had yet done. Even before the public had a chance to sample these programmes a number of pressure points developed which were subsequently to undermine the programme dream team, and set the executives and the board at one another's throats. The dreams were never to become a reality.

2

THE MORNING AFTER

Like many a marriage, LWT's honeymoon period ended with the realization that they had to live with the foibles, caprices, arrogance and personality defects of their partners. As soon as the euphoria of winning the contract had died down, several of the people within LWT rapidly became convinced that the excitement of the chase had disguised fundamental incompatibilities in the team.

Peacock, as Managing Director, carried most of the burden for turning this new company into an efficient and sophisticated television service. It was his responsibility to ensure a collective understanding of the aims and objectives of the company. He was the link between the Board of Directors, the broadcasting trade unions and the programme-makers. It was his duty to guard against financial complacency among the Board and the unions and to make sure that his programme-makers were not profligate.

Each of these different groups spun away from Peacock's control. Peacock's problems were exacerbated by a protracted battle for control of the station. His relationship with Frost degenerated. Frost's age, celebrity, and financial independence were essential to the task of forging the winning franchise application; however, they led also to a great deal of resentment both within and outside of the consortium. The very factors which helped to win the franchise accelerated the unravelling of LWT's first management team.

Frost was proud of pulling off his stroke of entrepreneurial genius. However, he did not control LWT as he had imagined he might when he launched the idea at the Kardomah. The ITA would not allow individuals who were performers with a company to sit on the Board of Directors. Moreover, there was an entire layer of management between Frost and decisions on programmes. He had to go through Peacock, Bennett and the programme committee if he wanted anything to be made. As far as the programme executives were concerned Frost was 'talent', not management. Frost saw the situation somewhat differently. He was an observer at Board meetings – where he had an influence over management policy – and he fought Peacock and Bennett for the right to sit on the programme committee. There was a clear clash of interests in this arrangement. Frost was theoretically in the position of recommending that LWT buy programmes made by his own production company. As it was, Frost irritated Bennett and infuriated Peacock. This situation was an inevitable outcome of the ITA awarding a franchise to a company with a performer as its prime mover.

Peacock was stunned by the amount that Frost was earning for his three shows a week; the fees amounted to ten times the figure Peacock was being paid. Frost was, in fact, only making roughly the same as was provided by his joint BBC and Rediffusion contracts; however, coming on top of the other struggles, it appeared as yet another contradiction between Frost the shareholder and Frost the performer. Justified or not, Frost's fees added to the grinding dislike building up between the BBC people and the Frost supporters. The relationship between the two leading figures in the LTC, which was never close, became openly antagonistic.

Peacock's exchanges with his Board were plagued with misunderstanding and problems. His model for his dealings with his non-Executive directors was drawn from his experience of the way that Hugh Greene seemed to dominate the Board of Governors of the BBC. Reflecting on this period, Peacock accepts that his problems stemmed from the fact that he had 'no experience of dealing with Boards of Directors – not in any sensible sense, not in any direct sense.' Peacock is adamant, however, that many of his problems stemmed from Aidan Crawley's Chairmanship: 'I think Aidan did not forgive me for the way I spoke to him and treated him.' Reflecting on the arguments that they had during the first two years, Peacock comments: 'He and I were at a distance and I should have sensed how dangerous that was. He wasn't at all good as a Chairman – I'm afraid that has to be said. Given the problems we had, above all I needed a good Chairman. It is sad that John [Freeman] did not take over as Chairman of the company when I was there.' Unlike the Governors, however, LWT's Board was full of important businessmen who resented the notion that they should leave the television professionals to run the company. Some of the Board, with images of Louis B. Mayer and of Lou Grade floating before their eyes, thought that they were going in to the television business. Peacock, whose natural aggression became entangled with his idea that the only people able to understand television were those who had made programmes, made it clear to the Board that they would not be a major influence on his decisions, particularly with regards to programmes 'Perhaps we were a bit cocky,' Peacock recalls. One member of the

Board recalls: 'Michael Peacock was an arrogant young man of immense abilities, but he made it clear that he was not going to be influenced by the Board as far as programmes were concerned.' Some other Board members either simply did not like Peacock or did not believe him capable of running the company; one member noted that 'Michael Peacock was offensive from an early stage', and another stated: 'it became clear that the executives had no idea about money, no control, no idea about numbers. Furthermore, Peacock was very hostile to the rest of the management.'

Peacock's problems might have been alleviated if the Board had not contained quite so many high-powered men. Frost had gathered a Board guaranteed to impress the ITA, but not really able to settle for the long haul of running a small television company. Those for whom LWT was a toy wanted to play with it; several others were desperate to see it making good programmes, and wanted to be reassured that these would be forthcoming; and those who were involved for the money began to worry at the high costs of starting the business.

If Peacock's chairman had been stronger, and if key senior executives – such as Margerison and Irving – had been more supportive, the breaches between Peacock and the Board might have been healed. Peacock needed to be taken to one side and told to be calm, and the Board needed to be alternately smoothed, reassured and faced down. As it was, Crawley was too nice a man to control the directors or to convince Peacock to tone down his aggression. Crawley's difficulty in running the Board and his executives resulted in a power vacuum which several Board members, used to exercising authority, attempted to fill. Various factions broke out in which Board members joined up with senior executives to attack Peacock. Those who were not part of the factions were part of the problem. LWT became an embarrassment and Michael Peacock became the target for the Board's irritation and a symbol of LWT's failure. It was difficult for the Board to disentangle Peacock's performance from LWT's structural problems.

Apart from trouble with the Board, Peacock ran into difficulties with some of the chairmen and managing directors of the other network contractors. His outspoken comments about ITV's dreary and un-adventurous programmes, and his abrasive attitudes in network committee meetings, undermined the goodwill of some ITV grandees, such as the Bernsteins. However, Peacock's programme policies had the support of Granada and, to a certain extent, Yorkshire – where Peacock's old colleague, Donald Baverstock, was Director of Programmes. Lew Grade was still annoyed at losing his London franchise and was not pre-disposed to help LWT; particularly when the young whelp would not allow him to stage his favourite show – the Royal Command Performance.

Other structural problems built up. For example, Charles Hill, to whom Peacock looked for support, resigned as Chairman of the ITA when Harold Wilson offered him the Chairmanship of the BBC. This meant that the changes in the ITV network, which Hill had personally promised to Peacock, and which might have been delivered had Hill remained, did not come about.

ITV relied on networking. None of the companies had the resources to produce a full service on its own, and the largest four companies (which increased to five with the inclusion of Yorkshire) were required by their franchise contracts to produce or develop a full range of programmes which became the core of the network schedule. They did not make a profit from the sale of their programmes to the other companies; however, on the basis of an arrangement approved by the ITA, they recouped their direct costs and a proportion of their indirect, overhead, costs. The other companies contributed to this expenditure on the basis of their share of the network's total Net Advertising Revenue – their NAR share. These companies paid by the hour for the number of programme hours they took from the major companies; the regional companies guaranteed to take a minumum number of hours – at that time 30 hours a week – which, in turn, the majors guaranteed to supply.

Each of the five 'majors' offered programmes to one another for the network schedule. In 1968, two committees organized this market in programmes: the Network Programme Committee – on which sat the managing directors or chief executives, and the Major Programme Controllers Group – which consisted of the programme controllers of the five largest companies. Programmes accepted by the committees were guaranteed a network slot – these were known as Category 'A' programmes. A second group – 'B' programmes – did not receive a confirmed network agreement and it was left to individual companies to conduct a trade in such series. Although companies exchanged network programmes, it was left to individual stations to choose when, and if, to broadcast them. If a station did not think that a series would play well at prime time in their region, then they could play it whenever they liked.

The exchanges in Category 'A' programmes were conducted not in cash but in 'points'. Each of the big five possessed a certain number of points based on their share of overall advertising revenue earned by ITV. For example, if ITV earned £100 million, which was translated into, say, 100 million points (although the match between revenue and points was not that simple), and if LWT earned 10 per cent of the revenue it would be awarded 10 million points. It was up to LWT to turn these points into programmes. Each type of programme was awarded different amounts of points; drama, which was the most expensive form of television, was awarded many more points than, say, a talking heads programme. Programme exchanges ideally carried on until each of the 'majors' had used up their points.

The system was fraught with difficulties, particularly in 1968. When the new franchises were coming into operation LWT's, and Yorkshire's

NAR share was an unknown quantity. The schedules for Autumn 1968, therefore, were exchanged on the basis of a purely hypothetical share. Consequently, the negotiations were a shambles; each of the majors offered programmes for every available slot regardless of their ability to pay for them or of the resources needed to produce them. Moreover, LWT assumed that the expertise of its programme team would allow it to have a disproportionate access to network slots; the other companies rapidly disabused Peacock of this notion.

Peacock is adamant that his problems with the network would have been averted if Lord Hill had remained as Chairman of the ITA. Peacock recalls that:

> Hill insisted that the companies should exchange programmes on a basis that reflected the costs of production on a competitive basis. LWT, ill-advisedly with hindsight, was always on the opposite side of the argument with the other companies, which made us look as if we were claiming to be the best, which I'm sure irritated the others. But, we really had been told by Hill that this was the way that the majors would be exchanging programmes within the context of the network schedule. As soon as Hill went that all changed and within six months a very different system of programme exchange was agreed which grossly affected the economics of our station: it threw us into loss, it was that important. We had built our whole production planning on the assumption that we would be recouping X% of our costs and with the change in networking it turned out to be less than X%.

Peacock had assumed that some kind of costing system would be worked out which would reflect above and below the line costs; in other words which would take into account the costs of the studio as much as the price of hiring the stars.

It took time to learn the recondite rules of the network, and Peacock simply did not have the opportunity to play himself in slowly. Moreover, he was used to running his own channel, and controlling all of its output, and he was suddenly thrust into a situation where, in effect, he controlled only one-fifth of his peak-time output. He had to take programmes from the other companies, even if he did not wish so to do. Moreover, Peacock was up against people who knew this system intimately.[1] The system required patience and guile to negotiate, and Peacock possessed neither quality in sufficient measure in his early days as a network negotiator.

Apart from these problems with the Board, the executives, and with the network, the unions were not happy. The employees at Rediffusion were hardly delighted when LWT contributed to the demise of their company. However, there were no redundancies in ITV; every non-management employee had to be re-employed somewhere in ITV before any new staff could be recruited. Consequently, rather than starting afresh, LWT picked up most of its staff from Rediffusion and from ABC. The broadcasting unions had also insisted that redundancy payments should be made by the outgoing company to every worker – including those who would simply be walking out of the door one day as employees of Rediffusion and returning the next as employees of LWT. Fortunately for LWT, Rediffusion picked up the bill for these payments. LWT had problems, however, negotiating agreements with staff who were accustomed to having their weekends to themselves. Setting up new working practices for the weekend franchise led to all sorts of ill will. Moreover, LWT's Chief Engineer, recruited from the BBC, found it difficult to reach common ground with the senior Rediffusion technical staff. These conflicts added to the general sense that the sands were shifting under Peacock's feet.

A cohesive company spirit was difficult to forge. The programme staff had moved to the top ten floors of a monstrous twenty story office block in Wembley. These offices were a mile from Rediffusion's studios – which LWT had rented while awaiting the completion of their own facilities – and many miles from the Chairman and the Managing Director who remained at Old Burlington Street. These three centres of the company's activities may not have mattered much in other circumstances; however, they contributed to LWT's unstable corporate culture when things started to go wrong.

Another looming, ominous problem was that the growth in ITV's revenue was slithering to a halt. The licence to print money was looking distinctly frayed.

Finally, all of these difficulties were exacerbated by the growing threat of a national strike. The Association of Cinematographic and Television Technicians had been greatly infuriated by the uncertainties produced by the change in the franchises, and this spilled over into the new wage round in 1968. The ACTT threatened a national strike in August 1968 if new pay and conditions agreements were not met.

It was against this background of frenzied creative excitement and menacing structural and personal problems that LWT began broadcasting. At 7 o'clock on Friday, 2 August 1968, the LWT logo proudly came up on the screen and Frank Muir began to introduce *We Have Ways of Making You Laugh*. 15 seconds later the screens went black. The unions had carried out their threat. The laughing stopped.

3

NIGHTMARE TOWERS

Ideas cannot be too much prized in and for themselves,
cannot be too much lived with but to
transform them abruptly into the world of politics
and practice, violently to revolutionise
this world to their bidding, that is quite another thing.
Matthew Arnold: Essays in Criticism

On Monday, 8 September 1969, Michael Peacock returned from holiday hopeful that the Autumn schedule – due to begin the following week – would rescue the ailing station. He barely had time to greet his secretary before he was called to a meeting with Aidan Crawley at which he was invited to resign. The experiment was over. The dream team fragmented into antagonistic groups whispering in corners, whining in memoranda, and worrying about the future. By 19 September, all of the ex-BBC programme-makers, and several who identified with them, had departed. Their ideals and hopes had crashed to earth trailing wreckage to be picked over endlessly and mischievously by the newspapers and the other ITV companies.

It remains difficult for many of the protagonists to put this painful first year on air into perspective. The antagonism between the board and the broadcasters is as firmly entrenched now as it was during the critical weeks in September 1969 when the passionate and extraordinary drama was played out. The broadcasters persist in regarding the Board as philistines who failed to understand the creative objectives of the channel, and who panicked at the first sign of financial difficulty; the board continue to regard the broadcasters almost as rowdy children who were incapable of deferring their creative gratification until the company was on a secure financial footing.

Both factions wanted good creative programmes that were well regarded by the audiences to whom they were directed; however, during the weeks of crisis which led to the mass defection the sound judgement of a number of fair-minded people simply disappeared. (As in any crisis, the turmoil was exacerbated by a number of people who were, for their own purposes, gleefully setting fire to any oil that was being poured on troubled waters.)

Dunkirk Revisited

LWT was designed to be the cultural flagship of the renovated and invigorated ITV and to lead the assault on the BBC's intellectual dominance. By the end of LWT's first month on the air, with ratings plummeting at the weekend,[1] it was clear that an appropriate military analogy would refer to defeat rather than to victory. Peacock argued that LWT's difficulties stemmed from working with old, unreliable and unsuitable equipment at Wembley studios, producing new programmes, and rescheduling those which had not been broadcast because of the ACTT strike. LWT had, Peacock believed, met its Dunkirk.

The metaphor of Dunkirk is striking and appropriate. The retreat of the British Army from Dunkirk was the final stage of a military disaster – namely, the German conquest of France. The withdrawal occurred as the result of a disastrously idealistic foreign policy; logistical ineptitude; a well-equipped enemy which played by different rules; and, finally, allies who distrusted and resented one another. LWT's Dunkirk was the result of an idealistic programming policy; organizational confusion; an enemy – the BBC – who attacked Saturday night with all of the resources at its disposal; and a bickering and divided management. The comparison is inaccurate in one decisive respect: the hundreds of small boats which rushed to the aid of the British Expeditionary Force, and which turned tragedy into, almost, glorious triumph, have no equivalent in LWT's story: there was to be no rescue.

The events which led up to and which followed LWT's crisis appeared to outside observers as an organizational burlesque; amid general chaos people seemed to be running in one door and out of another, hiding behind potted plants and listening at keyholes. Although aspects of the proceedings were farcical, LWT's predicament was a nightmare for those involved. Careers, reputations and ambitions were at stake, and even Frank Muir's laughter was tinged with anger. Two separate crises provided the background against which this bitter farce was set: first, the public's lukewarm response to the new ITV turned into a ratings disaster for LWT and, secondly, LWT's financial security was jeopardized by the government's stubborn refusal to recognize the decline in ITV's advertising revenue. LWT's response to these crises was played out before a jeering, booing and catcalling press which savoured its slaughter of the television innocents.

It is not uncommon for new channels to take time to establish themselves, particularly if they are innovative. British viewers dislike broadcasters who adopt a hectoring or pompous tone, and channels founded self-consciously on a grand idea inevitably have been met with indifference or hostility. The public has been unwilling to adapt quickly to new television services – as witnessed by the difficult birth of ITV. However, this reluctance is compounded if – rightly or not – viewers suspect that broadcasters are talking down to them. Three examples stand out: first, BBC2 – also under Michael Peacock's direction – was, for its first year, subject to critical animosity and a lack of public interest; secondly, Channel 4, which was enjoined by the government 'to cater for tastes and interests not otherwise catered for by ITV', was met with public indifference and then subject to a campaign of vilification in the press; finally, TVam, the IBA's breakfast television station – also created by David Frost – which was dedicated to its 'mission to explain' spectacularly failed to reach a public which preferred the BBC's homely alternative.

If they are to respond to cultural innovation British viewers would rather be courted and offered blandishments than subjected to a lecture. The British are deeply distrustful of 'intellectuals' bearing gifts. This attitude was reflected in viewers' response to LWT. Other broadcasters, the press and the general public felt that Peacock, Frost and co were more interested in producing programmes for their friends in Hampstead and Chelsea than in the tastes and concerns of the ordinary viewer.

The collapse in the ratings was accompanied by problems with the government levy on advertising revenue, and with the lack of growth in income from advertising. The levy was first introduced in 1964 when the Conservative government – embarrassed at the high return on capital achieved by the ITV companies for what was a government created monopoly – decided to impose an additional charge on the contractors. Apart from the usual corporation tax, the government extracted an extra proportion of advertising revenue as payment for the monopoly.[2] The levy was, however, a blunt instrument. It did not take into account levels of profitability and resulted in STV, for example, paying £750,000 in levy in a year in which it made a trading loss. When revenue was buoyant the companies could live with the levy; however the additional charge compounded the effects of a financial downturn in 1969–70.

The massive expansion in ITV's revenue to almost £90 million between 1956 and 1968 bred a false sense of security in the government and in the industry. There seemed no reason for the gravy train to stop rolling. At the end of 1968, however, a number of factors coalesced to initiate a decline in confidence among advertisers and a consequent slump in ITV's fortunes.[3] The economy in general was lurching from one predicament to another. In November 1967 the government had devalued sterling from $2.80 to $2.40 to the pound. Also in that month, the government was forced to approach the International Monetary Fund for a loan, the price of which was a severe deflationary package aimed at cutting home consumption. Further problems throughout 1968 were met at the end of the year with rises in taxes on petrol and alcohol and an increase in the general purchase tax. This economic gloom hit advertisers who reduced or, at best maintained, their expenditure on ITV's airtime. Moreover, by 1968 ITV was available to almost every home in the country and the Network was unable to attract advertisers by offering new audiences.

ITV's problems were enhanced by competition from the BBC. The network reached its highest audience share – between 72 and 80 per cent – in 1957. The BBC fought back after this point and ITV's share slowly declined until the launch of BBC2 in 1964, after which BBC1 was turned into a mass-audience channel – particularly at the weekend. ITV's dominance was no longer assured. This loss of audience share was compounded by the introduction of the new contractors and by the strike in August of 1968, after which viewers' loyalty was badly shaken and they began to sample BBC programmes to which they might not otherwise have paid much attention.

ITV was faced by a government which failed to grasp the extent of its short-term difficulties. The Chancellor of the Exchequer – Roy Jenkins – increased the levy on advertising revenue in the 1969 budget. Jenkins believed that the companies should sort out their overmanning and excessive expenditure and squeezed another £3 million out of ITV just at the point when the network was heading into a tailspin.[4] LWT suffered greatly from the levy and from heavy start-up costs, but the company managed to turn in a profit for 1968–9 only to see it drip away into the levy.

Apart from these general difficulties LWT suffered a specific problem not shared by its network partners; it had a competitor for advertising revenue in its region – Thames Television. Although colleagues in the network, their respective sales forces contended for a share of London's advertising cake. Advertisers had to be convinced that the weekday or weekend was the most appropriate time to reach their target audience and, consequently, salesman criticized the programmes of their network partner. By 1969 Thames, much to LWT's chagrin, was raking in over 60 per cent of London's television advertising revenue.

This absolute and comparative deterioration was magnified by a change in the way that the ITV companies reported their advertising revenue. In February 1969 the companies announced that their revenue figures would be published on a monthly, rather than on a quarterly, basis. Armed with this new information, and the figures for ITV's annual revenue, the advertising agencies were able to target stations which had a low share of network revenue relative to their coverage of the population. Such stations were desperate to have guaranteed revenue to offset the problems of selling a low share and weak programmes, and this allowed the agencies to force concessions, special deals and discounted airtime. London Weekend Television was top of the list.

The public's reluctance to watch LWT, and the company's financial problems, were greatly exaggerated for one simple reason: LWT was one of the local stations for the Fleet Street newspapers. The difference between parochial London issues and national concerns is often blurred in the London press. Take, for example, the mysterious case of revolutionary politics at the London School of Economics. When the student riots erupted in the 1960s the LSE became a byword for radicalism. The LSE was, however, little different from several other universities; its notoriety was the result of its proximity to Fleet Street. Whenever an editor wanted a revolting students story, the reporters would literally pop round the corner. Full scale riots or sit-ins may have occurred in other universities but these seldom attained the column inches of an LSE story. Similarly, throughout 1968 and 1969 many ITV companies were in deep trouble. Harlech and Yorkshire reneged on most of their franchise promises and STV at one point in early 1970 could not pay the bills. However, the story that caught the imagination of the London press was that of a London television company.

A well-documented decline in audience, fears concerning advertising revenue, press hostility, and network belligerence provided the drop scene before which LWT's Dunkirk was acted out. The figure at the heart of the drama was Michael Peacock. It was his motives, his attitudes, his reactions, his values, and his relationship to LWT's Board of Directors and to the other ITV companies which were the focus of the confrontation.

The Peacock Parallax

Although LWT possessed sound financial credentials and enthusiastic programme makers, the downpayment on the franchise was Michael Peacock. Hill and Fraser looked to Peacock to provide the moral and ideological lead to the other ITV companies. There is a revealing anecdote from the period: at a lunch for senior ITV executives, sometime in the Autumn of 1967, Sir Robert Fraser was walking towards the dining room when he noticed Michael Peacock ahead of him. Fraser turned to his companions and proclaimed rather grandly: 'There goes the man who will save ITV.' Fraser bestowed his blessing on Peacock in order to endorse LWT's vision of commercial television, and to broadcast his view that Peacock was the only real visionary in the ITV companies.

Fraser's confident prophecy was founded on Peacock's BBC career. Peacock took a degree at the London School of Economics and then joined the BBC in 1952. He was marked out as a high flyer: he became a producer on the seminal current affairs programme, *Panorama*, at 25, editor of the programme at 29, and the youngest editor of BBC news at 32. After gaining some experience of administration he was summoned by Hugh Greene to launch BBC2 – of which he was Chief of Programmes between 1963 and 1965. After a disastrous introduction and difficult early days, BBC2 was settling into something approaching normality when Greene promoted Peacock to Controller of BBC1: he was still only 36.

Peacock was associated with a number of young men cultivated by a remarkable woman named Grace Wyndham Goldie who, in the mid-1950s, from the relatively lowly position of Assistant Head of Television Talks, stamped her mark on the Corporation. She trained and stimulated a coterie of producers whom she believed would dominate the BBC. Goldie had the reputation of having a heart as tough as a Free Presbyterian minister's tongue. She was known as a woman of iron whim whose opinion of their talent reduced some producers and researchers to tears (or worse). She exacted a high price for her endorsement, but those who survived the storm acceded to power and authority in the BBC as if predestined.

The star shocktroops were Peacock, Donald Baverstock – who went on to become Controller of BBC1 – and Alasdair Milne – who rose to the top as Director General. These three were encouraged by Goldie and subsequently by Hugh Carleton Greene who, as Director of News and Current Affairs, encouraged them to challenge the shibboleths of BBC news and features. At the forefront of these developments was *Tonight* – a series edited by Baverstock and produced by Milne which took a fresh, quirky, and popular look at the world. It encouraged its journalists to break free of the BBC tradition of effacing their own distinctive voices, and it made stars of, among others, Alan Whicker, Trevor Philpott and Fyfe Robertson. As well as transforming the practices of BBC features, Peacock, Baverstock and a third producer, Ian Atkins, wrote a report for Greene which attacked the holy of holies – the style and content of BBC news.

In her memoirs Goldie noted that Peacock's

abilities were obvious . . . His years in America at school and college had had a great effect upon him; he learned to be tough, but with good manners; he despised Oxford and what he felt to be the dilettante attitudes of Oxford men and revealed in action a clear mind, a respect for facts, and a remarkable ability to express himself . . . he knew that he had ability . . . He was much less personally creative than, for instance, Donald Baverstock, who was soon to come from the BBC's Overseas Service to be trained in television and who was attached to the Current Affairs Unit. But both were unusually talented. They went step by step upwards within the BBC's television service. And the complicated relationship between them, based on liking but streaked with rivalry, had a major effect upon television output within the BBC . . .

These very different men had one thing in common. They were all of unmistakable quality. It was impossible to believe that any of them could behave meanly or with emotional or intellectual dishonesty.[5]

Others saw it rather differently. In his book – *The Last Days of the BBC* – Michael Leapman notes that Goldie's boys 'won a well deserved reputation for arrogance and cliquishness. Some thought them quite off their heads. They trod on the toes of people in other departments deliberately and with apparent relish.' All three had a turbulent period at the BBC: Baverstock and Milne resigned in 1965, Milne returned a few years later and rose to the Director Generalship before summarily being dismissed in 1987. Moreover, Baverstock, like Peacock, parted company from commercial television when he left Yorkshire in 1973.

Regardless of whether Peacock was personally combative or abrasive, the real key with which to unlock his motives was his dedication to an ideal of professionalism. In the report for Greene which was mentioned above, Peacock reflected on the BBC's failure initially to compete with ITV: 'What we were confronted with was the constant repetition of professional failure.' Peacock helped to form the ethos of the professional broadcaster. To be called 'professional' became the highest accolade in the BBC, as Tom Burns demonstrates in his sharp analysis of two generations of BBC executives – *The BBC: Public Institution and Private World*.

The concept of the 'professional' was not entirely clear. The classic model of the profession includes skills based on theoretical knowledge; an extensive period of education; the theme of public service and altruism; a code of ethics; self-regulation; and the testing of the competence of members before admission to the profession.[6] By these criteria, broadcasting was at best a quasi-profession; however, Peacock, and many of his generation, used the term to distance themselves from the dilettantism which had characterised the BBC and, indeed, much of the higher reaches of British administration.

The belief that good chaps, with reasonable degrees in PPE, could run anything has even yet fully to be eradicated from British life. However, eliminating the dilettante began in earnest in the late 1950s when the managerial revolution was aclaimed by James Burnham in the book of that name. The 'revolution' was the result – so argued Burnham, and others such as Peter Drucker and Anthony Crosland – of the way in which power had passed from the owners of capital, the multitude of shareholders who possessed shares in joint stock companies, to the controllers of capital – those who managed such companies. The divorce of ownership from control ensured, so the theory ran, a new managerial elite which would satisfy the interests of consumers and workers as much as those of the shareholder. The elite managers would be as comfortable in public as in private enterprise and would carry their public service values into both realms. The BBC professionals were part of this new elite.

The antithesis of the professional was the amateur; this latter group included the Board of Governors of the BBC. The Governors were expected by professional broadcasters to protect the BBC from outsiders, and not to meddle with executive decisions.

Peacock's actions and attitudes were framed by the broad change in perceptions as to how institutions should be run. These attitudes were confirmed by his tutelage under Hugh Greene who was the focus for and living embodiment of the new BBC. Greene's perceived dominance of the Board of Governors, and his single minded determination to force the BBC to go in his direction, was Peacock's model for dealing with his employers and his staff. Peacock's relatively undisturbed progress, his professional arrogance, and his organizational model left him ill-prepared for failure.

That Sinking Feeling

Station House – a 20 storey Wembley office block which towered over a railway goods yard and the river Brent, and in which the programme executives lived and worked and had their being – was a brutal and numbingly ugly structure. It was reminiscent of one of Stalin's palaces of culture which he insisted on donating to the grateful working people of Eastern Europe. LWT's palace of culture was welcomed by the London audience with the same degree of enthusiasm with which the grateful working people of Eastern Europe saluted the Red Army. Even the very fabric of this building seemed to conspire against the company; static electricity built up in the offices and produced electric shocks whenever anyone touched anything or anyone else. It was from his eyrie in this building that Cyril Bennett surveyed the emerging nightmare that became LWT. The other senior executives and the Chairman remained at Old Burlington Street where they became increasingly isolated from the programme-makers.

LWT had a few critical successes in the first year – among them Speight's *If There Weren't Any Blacks You Would Have to Invent Them*. Apart from causing palpitations with *The Franchise Trail*, Kestrel came up with a number of major critical successes. In particular, Colin Welland's first important piece of writing *Banglestein's Boys* captured the spirit of the 1960s most famous play *Cathy Comes Home*, and Denis Potter's *Moonlight on the Highway* continued his intellectual development. Kestrel also supervised Godard's one and only foray into British television. *British Sounds* was a classic piece of Godard agit-prop which was full of bleak images, interviews with factory workers, and a mother catechizing her child in the works of revolutionary politics. It bemused viewers. Ken Trodd recalls that Godard smiled but once in the whole of his time in the UK. He phoned Trodd and informed him that he wanted his payment in cash, and that he did not want to set foot in London; the furthest he would come would be Heathrow. Trodd duly turned up with the cash; Godard's smile flashed briefly when he looked approvingly at the bag which contained the money; he got back on the plane and returned to Paris.

As well as these critical successes, LWT had several popular successes such as the highly acclaimed classroom comedy, *Please Sir!*, some of the early Frost shows, and the populist comedy, *On the Buses*. Despite these programmes, LWT's first year was, by and large, disastrous.

The reasons for this failure are not hard to discern. LWT's need for publicity meant that it had to announce its programmes and its schedules well before its opening night. This enabled the BBC to prepare for the challenge. Against Brecht, Britten, some uninspired situation comedies and uninteresting variety programmes, the BBC broadcast a number of attractive, popular programmes. The evening typically began with a chat show which starred an archetypical 1960s figure, Simon Dee. This was followed by Britain's most popular police series, *Dixon of Dock Green*; a variety show hosted by the popular Irish singer Val Doonican; and the football programme, *Match of the Day*.

Apart from the problems with the quality of the programmes, LWT had to deal with the ACTT strike which had begun on opening night and lasted two weeks. A reasonably full network service was provided by the combined efforts of the ITV management who used ATV's transmission centre to maintain the service; but LWT could not meet the BBC's attack with any real confidence. The flagship shows, including the Frost programmes and the Frank Muir review, were live and subject to the strike. In order to broadcast one of the Frost programmes most of the senior executives were pressed into service as camera-men, continuity girls, sound engineers and technicians. Peacock directed the show. (During the programme someone guiltily sidled up to Frank Muir and whispered in his ear 'It's all right, I'm Equity'.)

After the strike was over, and LWT's ratings remained in the doldrums, pressure built up within the network aimed at forcing Peacock and Bennett to redesign their schedule. On 9 September, Lew Grade chaired a Network Programme meeting at which the network's concerns were made clear to Peacock. Granada remained roughly faithful to LWT, but ATV, and other companies, belligerently refused to schedule LWT's programmes in peak-time. In October most were showing the Friday Frost at 11 pm or later and Southern, Westward and ATV refused to have the Saturday Frost or the Sunday play at all.

In mid-October, Bennett relaunched Saturday night. *Frost on Saturday* was moved from 6.45 pm to 10.55 pm and in its place appeared a variety show entitled *Saturday Stars*. This latter was followed by a feature film.

The *Saturday Special* – the cultural flagship of LWT – was brought forward to 10 o'clock. In November the specials were cut to one a month and eventually moved to Sunday. An ironic and fundamentally depressing moment occurred when Lew Grade's ATV produced some of the specials in the period allotted to the other ITV companies. ATV came up with a series entitled *Opening Night* which was intended to capture, in the words of the press release, 'the arrival of VIPs, the animated crowds, the dresses, hairstyles and jewels; all talking points which the viewers can share.' Very Brechtian.

The only success, apart from situation comedies, was the coverage of sport – in particular, football. Hill, John Bromley – Hill's bluff and inventive deputy, who had been with the original *World of Sport* team – Brian Moore, and the director Bob Gordam forged a new, aggressive and exhilarating way of covering the national sport. More cameras, more angles, more everything; overlain with the authority of Moore's commentary and the insight of Hill's analysis. The BBC acknowledged Gardam's contribution to the coverage of television when one of the camera pits at Wembley was designated 'Gardam's pit'. Moreover, *World of Sport*, which had been originated by Brian Tesler at ABC and taken over by LWT who could not afford to relinquish the Saturday hours to an independent sports unit (as the other four wanted), was moderately flourishing. Even in this successful enclave, disaster struck. Hill had made a major breakthrough by acquiring the rights to the final of the Gillette Cup – a one day cricket competition. The BBC and the cricket establishment generally looked down on ITV, and Hill was delighted by his coup. The final turned out to be one of the most exciting in years and, just when the last over was about to be bowled and the audience was on the edge of its seats, ITV cut to the advertisements. The programme was over. A howl of execration went up around the country, and the County set sneered at the failure of commercial 'chaps' properly to broadcast England's sacred sport. LWT was never to show another cricket match.

Sport also suffered some casualties during Bennett's rush for ratings. Michael Parkinson's programme – *Sports Arena* – was moved from Friday evening to Sunday afternoon at 2.30 pm – just before the *Big Match* – and Parkinson, who felt that most of his audience would be returning from the pub when the show was on, refused to present the first Sunday edition. Bennett could tolerate no further nonsense; he exiled Parkinson to LWT's equivalent of Siberia – Clive Irving's department – from where Parkinson soon departed the station.

Apart from the general problems with attracting a consistent audience for the weekend, LWT also suffered several costly and well-publicised muddles over programmes. Nemone Lethbridge's *The Franchise Trail* – a satire about the ITA – was scheduled for LWT's first weekend. The characters included a chairman of the ITA named Lord Everest and a trendy young media executive named Wesley Dagenham (Frost's father was a methodist minister) who wandered through the entire satire with a cast on his broken leg (Peacock had an operation on his arm during the real franchise trail). The satire was produced by Kestrel productions who, as we have seen, thought of themselves as iconoclasts; they held distinctly radical and left-wing positions and proclaimed loudly that they wanted to challenge ITV – the capitalist monster – from within. Peacock felt that while such attitudes were capable of prompting insightful and challenging drama, they were not exactly appropriate during a strike. It was carrying freedom to the bounds of recklessness, so Peacock thought, to lampoon LWT, the other companies, and the ITA during a bitter dispute with ACTT. He had no intention of asking Bennett to shelve the play entirely, and it was rescheduled for the following week. When it was cancelled again – much to Lethbridge's loud consternation – LWT's reputation as a brave and radical broadcaster was severely dented. Kestrel added fuel to the flames by pirating a copy of the play which, unusually for the time, was produced on video tape. The critic Milton Shulman, on seeing the play, became its champion. Eventually *The Franchise Trail* crept on to the air after the strike concluded.

A similar mess developed in late November when LWT tried to broadcast a play based on a fictional account of Harold Wilson's life as seen through his wife's eyes. *Mrs Wilson's Diary* – a fortnightly column which appeared in the satirical magazine *Private Eye* – had been successfully transformed into a theatre production and, consequently, a television script. The adaptation contained some rather cruel jokes about the drink habits of George Brown – a former Labour foreign secretary who had just resigned from the Cabinet – and the ITA insisted that some cuts be made. Peacock and Bennett, standing on a point of principle, withdrew the programme. (Some time later, it was broadcast without fuss.)

These two conflicts could have been seen as the price of innovation, but the same could not be said of the axing of a series entitled *The Inquisitors*. This costly series was to be the equivalent of ABC's long-running and successful series – *The Avengers*. The programmes – about two psychological investigators – were, according to contemporary reports, terrible. In December, the series was scrapped before one foot had been aired.

LWT's first tranche of innovative programmes – some good, some bad – was never given a chance. The old pros taught the new boys a few lessons about playing without shinguards, and by January 1969, the Palladium and the Tiller Girls were back on Sunday nights. It was almost as if LWT had never been born.

Deeper and Deeper

In January 1969, the board began to exert pressure on Peacock to drop Bennett and either take over himself or find someone who could increase the ratings. Bennett's commercial instincts – fuelled by his worries at the precariousness of his position and the influence of the other ITV controllers – told him to restore the previous ITV mix of variety packages, feature films and situation comedies.

Bennett's new schedule was thoroughly populist and it entirely depressed the BBC3 group.[7] Saturday evening opened at 6.15 pm with *The Leslie Crowther Show*, and was followed at 7.00 pm by an American series. *Corbett Follies* was transmitted at 8.00 pm and was succeeded by a feature film at 8.30 pm. Saturday night closed with a topical satire programme from Granada which was produced by a future LWT stalwart – Nick Elliott. Even this populist schedule did not work. Bennett had to postpone the Crowther show – which he believed was uninspired – and, consequently, in the middle of February he had to rearrange the schedules once more.

By this point Station House was seething with discontent. Little cliques formed; criticism, carping and discontent were rife; trust was at a premium. Humphrey Burton expressed the discontent of the senior creative staff. In February he wrote to Bennett (and copied the memo to Peacock) complaining that the new schedule underestimated the need for, and possibilities of, intelligent programmes. 'Something has gone crucially wrong with our company', Burton protested. 'Part of it is teething problems – shaking out a budgetary system and so on. But the central failure is to do with the mix on the screens. It is insufficiently different from what happened before; it is not broadly enough based in subject matter, it relies too heavily on show biz and narrative drama, and it doesn't take into account the changing nature of the weekend, the increasing number of young adults who are potential viewers etc.' Burton inquired, somewhat plaintively: 'we didn't join forces only to make money, now did we?'

Burton specifically mentioned the need for 'a regular intelligent programme . . . in order to keep faith with that lovely white-coloured proposal we sent to the ITA.' Furthermore, he told Bennett that he hated the variety programmes which were hosted by 'barely adequate' smoothies who did not 'represent our kind of thinking, our outlook on life.' He concluded: 'There is precious little excitement in our schedule, virtually no sense of occasion, and no feeling of LWT (except Jimmy Hill's appearances) since Frank Muir's show came off.'

Bennett's terse and tense reply to Burton's memo summed up the divisions in the company:

> There is plenty of evidence that until we have secured high ratings with those shows intended to secure high ratings, we cannot spend time, energy or manpower on shows that push-back the television frontiers . . . Before we keep faith with proposals put to the ITA, I would like to think that we are keeping faith with the viewers, who are our first customers and to our advertisers to whom we have also made promises and have obligations.

Bennett poured scorn on Burton's rather grandiose, BBC-like notion that LWT had an 'outlook on life'. Fulfilling lofty ideals, Bennett argued, had to take second place to producing some decent entertaining programmes: 'First let us make the programmes sufficiently better than they were before', he asserted, 'then we might, just might, be able to make them different.'

Bennett felt that he was hamstrung in his attempt to rescue the station by self-indulgent and snobbish prima donnas. This may have been an ungenerous interpretation of the motives of the BBC3 executives; however, the fact remains that there was a large gulf between Bennett's deep knowledge of commercial television, and the ideals of those without that experience. Michael Peacock points out: 'I blush to say but I don't think that we knew as much about ITV as we should have done. We tended to be – parochial is the wrong word – narrow in our view. We tended to think that the BBC way of doing things was probably better than the ITV way of doing things.' Huw Wheldon, one of the BBC's most respected executives, once memorably summed up the BBC's philosophy of broadcasting: programme-makers, he declared, should not produce what the public says that it wants, nor what the broadcaster thinks that the public should have, rather, programme-makers should make what it is in them to give. Bennett simply refused to accept this assertion which was, in Bennett's opinion, a charter for self-indulgence. Bennett agreed with Burton on one point, and one alone: Clive Irving's Public Affairs Unit – which Burton described as 'too ponderous' – simply had to go.

Irving knew that the long-knives were poised to strike. At the end of December 1968 he had complained that LWT had no interest in making serious current affairs programmes. Most of Irving's staff had a feeling 'of having stepped into a timeless backwater,' he said. Irving's paranoid instincts were, in fact, correct; everyone was out to get him. His problem stemmed partly from his close working relationship with David Frost – who was public enemy number one for the rest of the senior staff. Irving was a proxy target.

Apart from these personal differences, there was a deep-seated dissimilarity between Irving and Peacock. Peacock and Bennett had been editors of, respectively, *Panorama* and *This Week*, and both felt that Irving had not adjusted to the ways in which television current affairs should operate. 'Peacock came from a BBC tradition,' Irving recalls, 'and he hated anything that wasn't tightly controlled; live shows caused him enormous pain. He and I were very different animals.'

Irving's case was not helped when his team were thrown in jail on their first location shoot. They had decided to investigate race relations in Brixton and set up a hidden camera to film some drug producers; unfortunately, the police monitored their behaviour and arrested them for passing drugs.

Peacock and Bennett were determined that the public affairs unit had to go and, in April, they announced that the contracts of several of the staff had not been renewed and that the unit was to be closed. Irving remained as an executive director with special responsibility for the Frost programmes. Peacock and Bennett had no intention of reneging on LWT's responsibility to produce current affairs programmes; unfortunately, when they announced the closure of the unit they omitted to produce evidence that other programmes were being planned. The quality newspapers crucified them.

Peacock feels that closing the unit 'was one of those things if you had to live your life again you would certainly do differently.' 'It was a crazy situation. I decided that we were going to close the unit down and start again. I should have cleared my lines at Brompton Road and with the Board members before announcing this, and I certainly should have paid more attention to what we had said in the flaming application because we gave the impression that we were running away from our undertakings. The problem, in fact, was a flawed prospectus.' It would have been difficult sustaining this argument in 1968; LWT's critics argued that it was the prospectus which won the company the franchise. Peacock believed, however, that the franchise was won because the ITA trusted the Consortium's programme-makers, and not on the basis of what he regarded as vague programme ideas.

The furore intensified when someone leaked LWT's franchise proposal and the press contrasted the grand promises and the actual programmes. Bennett, increasingly under pressure and irritated by constant carping from within and censure from without, responded with a statement which has become famous in the history of ITV: 'the first duty of a commercial station', he declared at a press conference on 3 July, 'is to survive.' Michael Peacock supported this assertion in an interview in August: 'As a commercial company, we have shareholders and *have* to survive. You can't get into a loss situation and just go deeper and deeper into loss.'

Although Bennett's assertion concerning the responsibilities of a commercial television company is a truism, it indicated to a sceptical world that LWT had deserted its ideals for mercenary and grubby materialism. Some critics believed that LWT should either commit suicide or be put out of its misery by the ITA. In the Evening Standard, under the screaming headline 'The Scandal of London Weekend Television' the television critic, Milton Shulman, worked himself into a lather of indignation. He fulminated against commercial television ('the rotten apple that has corrupted the standards of broadcasting'); BBC1 ('engaged in a Gadarene rush to the destruction of the most significant and mature values the medium has to offer'); the British political system ('apathy is the woodworm in the edifice of democracy'); and, finally, LWT 'which is distinguished only by the fact that its films are older that

that its comedy and variety shows are worse than ATV's.' He concluded, charitably enough, the LWT's 'first duty is suicide.' In *The Listener* Peter Black accused 'the glittering band' of running out of nerve and of not facing up to the network or to the shareholders.

At the beginning of August, the *Sunday Times* set its *Insight* team on the company. The resulting debunking of LWT pointed out that although the other new companies had not delivered on their franchise promises, 'all of Yorkshire's delinquencies – and, indeed, most of Harlech's – pale into insignificance beside those of Frost and co at London Weekend.'

This was the last straw for most of the members of the Board: 'Peacock had to go. He had no supporter on the Board', one remembers. He continued, 'It wasn't a question of what the programme-makers were spending; it was a question of their attitude to that expenditure. They were being quite well paid and what constituted misery for the investors caused them no pain whatsoever. However, this need not have caused problems if the programmes had been better.' Another director reported that what upset him was that 'these people were supposed to be good programme-makers but the programmes were lousy.' Another noted that the programmes 'deservedly got very bad ratings because they were very bad programmes.' According to yet another, Peacock irritated the Board by apparently not listening to a word which anyone else said. 'He pointedly stared into space. It was like having a dialogue with someone who was deaf.' Another pointed out that as the Board did not know much about television they looked to Peacock for advice, and they were disturbed when it was not forthcoming. One board member is quite explicit: 'Michael was very aggressive and he was extremely articulate. He knew what he wanted and he was motivated by programme quality; however, he was not responsive to any of the disciplines of running a company employing a lot of people.'

One story illustrates the sad nature of the conflict. A standard television practice was to offer free theatre tickets to senior programme-executives, on the grounds that they had to attend the theatre to maintain their contacts with actors, directors and playwrights. Each executive had two tickets, on the assumption that they would be accompanied by a companion. Arnold Weinstock raised the allocation at a Board meeting, at which he made it clear that he objected greatly to this, in his view, profligate practice. Instead of patiently explaining the practice, and attempting to justify the second ticket, Peacock seemed to snap at Weinstock, and to state simply that it was a management problem. Peacock did not, so his Directors thought, respond properly to a man who was, after all, one of the most successful businessmen in Europe. Weinstock raised the issue to signal his worries that the financial system was out of control and, on being snubbed, turned irrevocably against Peacock. A powerful enemy had been made.

The story of the spare ticket illustrates the clash of cultures between Peacock, who was used to the protection of accountants, lawyers, personnel officers etc. at the BBC, and a Board used to cash flow projections, regular financial reports and, perhaps importantly, respectful managers.

Peacock had also become embroiled in an acrimonious dispute with Crawley, Montagu and Frost. Jimmy Hill had informed Peacock that the above three were partners in a closed circuit television company specialising in sport. They had asked Bob Gardam – LWT's top football director – to direct a first division football match for them. Peacock was troubled by the fact that LWT was the nominated contractor for sport in the network, and that it was going against the spirit of the agreement to sanction a competitor to ITV – no matter how small. Moreover, this was a stick with which to beat Frost and Peacock drew Crawley's attention to the conflict of interest. When ignored, Peacock became abusive and, in his own words, engaged in 'a dangerously ill-tempered argument' with Crawley.

Peacock and Frost clashed again over the details of Frost's move to the States. Frost was negotiating with Westinghouse, a US production company, to make a series of chat shows and Peacock – in Frost's eyes – was being deliberately obstructive. Frost felt that he was on the verge of a major career move; Peacock, on the other hand, could not see why Frost's live shows for LWT should be jeopardized. Peacock pointed out to Frost's agent, Richard Armitage, that Frost may be in the middle of the Atlantic when his cue began to start the programme; moreover, Peacock believed that Frost's primary commitment should be to his LWT contract. Frost turned for support to the Board of Directors, and the acrimonious dispute over contracts which followed sealed the enmity between the two men.

As well as the non-executive directors, and both of LWT's co-founders, Peacock also alienated his fellow executive directors. Clive Irving wrote to a member of the Board expressing the 'recurrent despair which Michael's immediate colleagues have felt at not being able to establish any lasting personal communication with him. This accounts for the fitful and impulsive personal behaviour in which he had indulged, and also for the fact that help has not been given because it has not been sought, or has been rebuffed.' The letter continued: 'on the point of commercial grasp, this has been an idealogical [sic] adjustment which Michael's true character has not allowed him to make. He has moved some way since the beginning, but he cannot always conceal his basic antipathy for the process of selling and the meretricious performance which this sometimes calls for. Indeed, his lack of sympathy for this side of the job has left some prominent self-inflicted wounds on the company.'

The Board was determined to be rid of Peacock and some executive directors – who had been slighted or ignored by Peacock – did not stand against them. The Board had options; there were others willing to run the company.

Two extremely ambitious figures had joined LWT some time after the launch – Stella Richman and Vic Gardiner. Stella Richman was a small, chic woman who owned one of London's most prestigious restaurant clubs – *The White Elephant* – at which she entertained on a lavish scale. She had made her career as a drama producer with ATV and Rediffusion and, in the late Autumn of 1968, she produced a series of six plays for LWT. Peacock liked and admired her energy and professionalism and, in January 1969, he offered her the position of Managing Director of London Weekend International – a subsidiary designed to make programmes to sell in the United States and the Commonwealth. She was the first woman to hold a senior executive position in ITV – another first for Peacock.

Stella Richman became a mysterious figure in the various conspiracies in the company. One of LWT's programme-makers recalls that 'Stella was a bit like Becky Sharpe in *Vanity Fair*. She had amazing front, and she knew how to manipulate men.' Others felt that Richman added style to the bleak wastelands of LWT, and that her long experience in ITV was exactly what the company required. She was available and, as events proved, ready to join the new LWT.

The other new figure was Vic Gardiner who had succeeded the first Chief Engineer – Bill Fletcher. Fletcher exercised little control over the production process; the man really in charge was an ex-ATV operational manager named Bernard Marsden. In addition to every other battle that was being waged within the station, that of Marsden and Fletcher was extremely debilitating; it undermined the smooth and efficient organization of the studios. Peacock realized that drastic action was necessary and he fired Marsden and invited Gardiner – a former Rediffusion employee – to restructure the production division. Gardiner, with Peacock's support, subsumed Engineering into the production division – which led to Fletcher's resignation – and re-introduced Rediffusion's operational system – much to the relief of the ex-Rediffusion production staff. Gardiner's reorganisation helped to create an efficient production team which, in ten months, managed to turn an antediluvian complex into one which was capable of colour production. Gardiner was available and willing to join the new executive team.

The pressure was building inexorably, but Peacock thought it possible that success was still within his grasp. Reflecting on his first year, Peacock felt that the most important lesson to be learned was that an ITV company can only produce one-third of the programmes which appear in its schedules: 'by definition our chances of leaving any sort of radical imprint on our transmission period are fairly small. We can only inject ingredients into a larger pattern.' 'Within months, if not weeks of the contracts,' he added, 'we were talking to the other companies about their plans and ours, and we found that some of our plans could not be carried out.' Peacock summed up the first year in *The Times* of 8 August as 'Patchy, but promising'.

The Ten Days of Crisis

Exhausted by the tensions and persecutions of the year, Peacock and Bennett were looking forward to a holiday. Bennett took off to the North West of Scotland with his family at the end of the first week of September, secure in the knowledge that Peacock was due to return from his holiday on Monday morning. He arrived at his holiday destination, and was settling down, when the phone rang informing him that Peacock had been sacked. Although aware that this was a possibility – he had spoken to Arnold Weinstock some time before about ways in which he could protect himself from the fall-out – he was stunned. He loaded his kids into the car and began the long, tedious trip back into the centre of the storm.

Inside Station House a revolution was fermenting. Most of the senior programme executives were raging at the board's high-handed attempt to commandeer 'their' company. The ITA had given the franchise to them, they reasoned, not to the grey men who sat on the board of directors. Moreover, although few were close to Michael Peacock they thought that he deserved another chance with the Autumn schedule. They were unlikely revolutionaries. Frank Muir was one of the most gracious and pleasant men who ever wrote a gag; Doreen Stephens was a calm, sensible woman who was a pillar of the Liberal Party; and Joy Whitby was an implausible tricoteuse. However, rebels they were; and, along with almost every other senior executive, they refused to accept Peacock's resignation.

A campaign swung into action. The programme executive maintained their clamour until Crawley invited several of the senior staff to an early evening meeting at his home. He rationalized the Board's reasons for dismissing Peacock; he explained that Peacock and the Board had reached an impasse; that the decline in revenue and ratings required a change; and that the Board had no faith in Peacock's managerial talent. This meeting might just conceivably have convinced the programme-makers if Crawley had not taken the opportunity to announce that the Board had appointed Dr Tom Margerison – who had no record as a programme-maker – as Managing Director. This selection confirmed the programme executives' view that the Board understood nothing about television. One recalls, 'We all fell about laughing when Tom was introduced to us as the new MD. Tom was an excellent fellow in many ways; a first class staff officer to have inside a company – apart from a few gimcrack ideas – but television wasn't his game.' Others pointed out that Margerison had been Deputy Managing Director and was therefore no less guilty – if guilt was to be apportioned – than Bennett or Peacock. Moreover, the production staff pointed out that although Margerison's much vaunted cost control system was highly logical it was also considered impracticable. Margerison's appointment was greeted with widespread dismay and was ultimately the reason for the fragmentation of the programme team.

At the Crawley meeting the programme executives claimed that, despite the early problems, the company was beginning to turn around. The Autumn schedule was, most of the senior executives believed, the best the company could have offered under the circumstances. They indicated that the board had been seriously misled about the mood of the company and they argued that those who had suffered under Peacock's reign were spreading disinformation.

They pointed out that the Chairman was ensconced in his office in Old Burlington Street – half a city away from the offices and production studios at Wembley – and that no soundings had been taken among senior staff who were closer to the company's disposition. Also they expressed their contempt for the way that the Board had treated Cyril Bennett. It was common knowledge in the industry that Bennett was to be sacked and, indeed, at least two BBC and two ITV executives had been solicited as potential successors. Peacock was later to recall that Crawley and Montagu had been pressing him to sack Bennett from January onwards, and he speculates that one reason why he was asked to resign was his tenacious refusal to bow to this pressure.

The executives departed from Crawley's home in a foul temper and set to work reversing the decision. They approached the ITA for guidance and support. However, Sir Robert Fraser, although shocked and saddened by the departure of a man on whom he had pinned so many hopes, remained true to his principles and refused to interfere in an internal management problem. Cyril Bennett arrived back from Scotland on the following day and began to inform the rest of the staff of Peacock's resignation. Joy Whitby, from the children's department, remembers the day in great detail: 'My memory is of screams – sudden screams – and then little rings of people in corridors. We were told to go into this room and our Heads were asking whether we would support Peacock on a show of hands. Some hands shot up saying that they would and then others said that they wouldn't.'

The ACTT, in its best unionese, asked for 'clarification on reports that there is a change in the Senior Management of the Company and the repercussions arising therefrom.' When the story broke, a staff-meeting was held at the Wembley studios at which the following resolution was passed:

This Meeting urges the Board to reaffirm its confidence in the current

management Team, thus silencing rumours of change which inevitably
endanger the morale of the Company and requests that:

1 No irrevocable decisions be made concerning the present Management of the Company at the moment, without prior consultation with
a committee, representative of the Staff as a whole.

2 Any changes in the structure of the Management in no way
prejudice the basic aims and policies of a programme-making
Television company either in respect of its public duty or its
responsibility to its staff and Executives.

The rebels regrouped after Bennett's arrival – although Bennett showed
no sign of joining them – and composed a letter to the members of the
board. This they delivered by hand before the Board meeting scheduled
to take place that night. In this letter the mutineers warned 'the board
that if a decision is taken today without . . . consultation the signatories
to this note will ask for immediate release from their contract.' The
programme-makers asked the board to take into account the fact that
'the people who make the programmes believe that there is a constant
and growing improvement in their production'; that 'morale in the
studios and offices is rising. Waste has been checked and teams have
been streamlined'; and that the press attacks on the company were par
for the course.

The Tuesday meeting at Old Burlington Street was fraught with
tension and fury. The Board had been lulled into believing that Peacock
was fundamentally unpopular with everyone in the company. The surge
of support for Peacock caught the Board completely unprepared. They
had not reckoned with the militant reaction of their employees, who
adopted the pattern of industrial relations typical of the late 1960s. A
mere three months before LWT's crisis Barbara Castle, Labour's
Employment Secretary, had been ignominiously defeated in her attempt
to introduce compulsory ballots before striking, and to outlaw wildcat
strikes. This was the age of employee sit ins and work ins; and of
vociferous middle class struggles, such as that against the siting of a
major London airport at Stanstead.

If the employees were adopting the styles and strategies of the age so,
initially, did the Board. After Tuesday's heated Board meeting they
caved in and announced that: 'A Committee of the board, in conjunction
with the Managing Director and Deputy Managing Director, has been
set up to consider the future management of the company and to report
to the next board meeting, which will be held on September 18th.' Such
was the embarrassment of the board that several hid their faces from the
waiting press cameras as they left the meeting.

The sub-committee – which comprised David Montagu, Lord
Campbell and Aiden Crawley – had meetings with all and sundry within
the company and they, in Campbell's words, 'explained till we were blue

in the face the reasons why Peacock had to go.' On the 15 and 16 September the committee met separately with the ACTT, the middle management, and the engineering, production and programme divisions. The one person they did not speak to was Michael Peacock.

Reflecting on the crisis, in an *aide-memoire* prepared for the ITA, the programme executives outlined the sub-text of their submission to the committee: 'We do not question the integrity of our Board; what we do doubt is its competence to run a television company. Apart from the Executive Directors, there is nobody with any knowledge of television or show business . . . Television remains a public utility, the air is publicly shared, ITV is licensed by Parliament for the benefit of the populace as a whole, as well as of the entrepreneurs whose capital is at risk. *It must be run by professionals.*'[8]

In their evidence to the committee the programme executives made it clear that as far as they were concerned the Board were blundering amateurs. There were three key points of difference between themselves and the Board. First:

> The business of running a television company is a multiple process the success of which depends upon a very delicate and sure balancing act between programme-making, networking, rating performance, finance, development, commercial salesmanship, union restraints and the available resources of people, studios and machinery.

The second and third points elaborated on this theme:

> The man who has that multiple function should, in our view, be a television man of great character and experience and of high managerial competence, but one also who above else commands the respect of his working colleagues. It is our contention that Michael Peacock is that man. It has also been become obvious to us that any failure in the company's recent performance is more justly attributable to the fact that an inexperienced Board has quite failed to recognize that for a Managing Director to carry weight in all these difficult areas requires close and massive support from colleagues of great experience and stature. To our mind none of the Executive Directors of the Company comes into that category.'

A paragraph which was omitted from the final presentation to the committee illustrates the personal reason behind the executives' fury. 'It was a mistake', the note ran, 'to propose an alternative Managing Director [Tom Margerison] whose intellect and character are not in question but who demonstrably lacks the human gift of being able to persuade many different kinds of people to accept managerial decisions.'

The professionals felt that their world could be understood only by another initiate. Margerison, as a journalist, did not fit this description: even if they had liked him they would have found it impossible to work with him. Margerison's unpopularity with programme executives (and with the production executives) merely confirmed to the Board, however, that they were correct in appointing him. The Board reasoned that Peacock's popularity stemmed from his being too lax with financial systems and that LWT needed someone who would become unpopular as the result of imposing stricter budgets on the programme-makers.

Margerison's appointment was championed by Clive Irving and by Frost. Irving, who was primarily a journalist and therefore also excluded from the guild of programme-makers, warned the board not to listen to the scandal mongers. He suggested that they appoint Margerison as a commercial manager who would leave the programmes to the producers. Irving informed the Board that the programme-makers' concerns were based on a lack of understanding of the real reasons for Peacock's failure and on a phantom impression of Tom Margerison.

The Board had come to a similar conclusion about the relationship between the MD and the Controller of Programmes. In a response to the programme-makers the directors argued that the roles of Controller of Programmes and of Managing Director were being confused in the discussion about Peacock: the MD, the board asserted, was an administrator who should not be closely involved in programme decisions – the preserve of the programme controller. The programme executives maintained that they were well aware of the administrative duties and responsibilities of an MD; however, the Board, they alleged, did not appreciate the need for an MD to have a creative vision and to motivate his or her programme-makers. Although the executives rejected 'the vainglorious notion that making television is unique', they asserted that, '[I]n the end, it is the influence of the top man which makes the Company. Television is not quite the same as other commodities. While no one denies that to fulfil our function as broadcasters we need to have a profitable operation, we are still engaged in work which comes into the realm of public interest.'

The programme-makers wished the Board to understand that Peacock was a man of great integrity and had their full support. The real truth was that as professionals they were unwilling to be dominated by the Board and they did not want a non-professional in charge. The fight was about control, rather than about personal relationships. Peacock was a fellow television professional under attack from outsiders. Humphrey Burton summed up the real reason for the conflict: 'WE thought "You can't sack him because you haven't asked us whether you could sack him, and without us, you wouldn't have the franchise in the first place." ' Another rebel agreed that they felt that 'Michael had hung himself. However, there was the issue of loyalty. We felt that we had gone in there as a team, and we felt that they had got us in under false pretences and that Tom Margerison was the last straw.' Joy Whitby recalls fondly that a feeling of comradeship had built up over the period during which they were under pressure and therefore that they thought that 'it was unbelievable that a group of financial men could break the leader of our team.'

Despite reports that Peacock was to be offered another chance, there was never any real possibility that he would be saved. The Board believed that he had alienated and embittered too many people. Moreover, he had not helped his cause when, unable to face real failure for the first time in his life, he had, on occasion, become abusive and aggressive. Some of the Board thought he was on the verge of a breakdown. Peacock confirms his mood at the time: 'I was shattered. There were two moves, one to get rid of me and the other was to replace me with two people who did not really know enough about the job to have a reasonable chance of succeeding.' Furthermore, Frost and Irving were determined that Peacock should go, and they lobbied hard in order to achieve this end. Finally, Bennett, who might have rescued the situation by offering his own resignation, was preoccupied with his own financial and personal troubles – in particular, the fatal illness of a member of his family.

Although this story has often been portrayed as money versus culture, the chief executioner was not a typical businessman such as Weinstock (who did play his part behind the scenes). The man who pulled the trigger was Lord (Jock) Campbell of Eskan, a lifelong socialist who had brought the *New Statesman* into LWT. Lord Campbell was deeply embarrassed by the lack of decent programmes produced by his station, and he simply did not believe that Peacock had the managerial and administrative skills to transform the company's fortunes. He did not believe him capable of great leadership. This latter point was important in that Aidan Crawley was widely regarded as too much of a gentleman to be an effective commander in the cut-throat world of commercial broadcasting. Peacock felt that Crawley's inability to impose his authority on the Board had undermined his own position almost from the start. Campbell stiffened the Board's resolve and, on 18 September, ten days after the crisis began, the board announced its decision:

The Board of London Weekend Television Limited, after the fullest consideration, has decided to terminate the contract of Mr Michael Peacock as Managing Director. He has resigned from the Board. Dr Tom Margerison becomes Chief Executive of the company and Mr Guy Paine Assistant Chief Executive. Mr Cyril Bennett, a Director of the Company, is Controller of the Programmes. Miss Stella Richman, Managing Director of London Weekend International, and Mr Vic Gardiner, Controller of Production, have been invited to join the Board as Executive Directors.[9]

Lord Campbell has agreed to serve as Deputy Chairman of the

Company. There has never been any dispute between the Board and Management about the programme objectives of London Weekend Television Limited. The Board is confident that the new management will fulfil these objectives and that the Company will discharge its responsibilities to the public the staff and its shareholders.

We regret the decision of the six members of the programme staff who have asked to be released from their contracts and respect the sincerity of their convictions. They have undertaken to complete the projects on which they are working and to ensure a smooth hand-over.

The rebellion had failed. Burton was in Italy where he was a judge on the Prix Italia television awards jury and was called to the phone and asked to return to London. He dashed back on the first flight and rushed to Station House where he was met by an irate Derek Granger and the rest of the dissenters (Jimmy Hill and John Bromley, neither of whom had slightest intention of throwing their career away for an abstract point of principle, and neither of whom were involved with the original franchise team, held their own counsel.) At the decisive meeting in Wembley, Burton disclosed that he was wavering and uncertain. 'I have a new wife and small babies', he groaned, 'I simply cannot afford to resign on a point of issue.' Granger snapped back 'Oh, don't be silly. There is no problem, you will always get work in your field.' Granger continued, 'If we cannot be masters of our own destiny – if the board can ride roughshod over us – it is best to leave.' Burton was persuaded that his resignation was the only honourable course. However, his point was valid. Not everyone had the equal opportunities for new employment. Frank Muir, for example, was a professional script writer who had been making a perfectly decent living prior to his BBC career; Doreen Stephens was within a couple of years of formal retirement; Joy Whitby was one of the most experienced and respected producers of children's programmes in the business; Derek Granger, likewise, was in great demand as a drama producer and had reason to feel confident about his future prospects. Bennett, however, would have been tagged with failure for the rest of his life. He had to go along with the Board while planning his escape (it was made clear to him that he could not remain with the company for too long).

After this intense and difficult meeting the six declared their intention to resign:

In spite of the opportunities given for consultation, we remain unconvinced of the need for a change in the management of London Weekend Television and deeply regret the decision announced by the Chairman on Thursday, 18th September, which we do not believe is to the ultimate benefit of television. We believe that the influence, leadership and integrity of Michael Peacock as Managing Director will be vindicated by the success of our programmes on the television

screen in the coming year. Whilst some of the original signatories of
the letter asking for consultation have understandably made their
decision to stay on and accept the new management, the following
have decided to accept the Company's offer to allow them to resign
from their contracts under the same terms and conditions that were to
obtain were the Company to terminate the contracts:

Humphrey Burton	(Head of Drama, Arts and Music)
Derek Granger	(Head of Plays)
Terry Hughes	(Executive Producer, Features)
Frank Muir	(Head of Entertainment)
Doreen Stephens	(Head of Children's, Religious and Adult Education)
Joy Whitby	(Executive Producer, Children's Programmes)

Tony Garnett, James McTaggart and Kenith Trodd of Kestrel
Productions also wish to be associated with this statement, although
their contractual situation is different. They will make individual
arrangements with the management to enable them to complete their
professional commitments and to keep faith with the members of
London Weekend Television with whom they have had the pleasure
and honour to work and create good programmes. They are deeply
grateful for the sympathetic resolution of the Joint Consultative
Committee (representing all staff and Union personnel) asking them
to stay on. It is with very great regret that they have, after the most
careful consideration, made their decision. They are also grateful for
the friendship and stimulating guidance of Cyril Bennett, the
Controller of Programmes, with whom they have worked happily
since the Company was formed. In view of John Bromley's absence in
Athens, he and Jimmy Hill have decided to reserve their positions for
the time being.

Each of the new executives had previously worked for Rediffusion – the
ghost of which had returned to mock BBC3. The new team had acted as
an unofficial opposition during Peacock's period, but they were by no
means a coherent coalition. They were suspicious of one another and
they were united only in regarding themselves as hard-bitten commercial
people who would rescue a company ruined by pretension.

The last, sorry remnants of the original team retreated. Cyril Bennett
left at Christmas to join a film company. With Bennett and Frank Muir
gone, Tito Burns decided that he could not face going through the
process of rebuilding. To Burns belongs the best gag of the whole sorry
episode. When leaving his office one day during the crisis, he turned to
his secretary and declared: 'If the Managing Director calls, tell him to
leave his name and I will get back to him.' Burns was the ninth

programme executive to leave. However, as there was no one else who could leave, the company seemed at last to be capable of restoring some of its pride.

Heroes and Villains?

In order to succeed, an institution founded on a grand idea needs momentum; it requires hope and anticipation. When it meets failure and obstructions, the institution's servants must be rallied with promises and a vision of the future. Without this vision they turn in on themselves. LWT's grinding failure with programme after programme created the conditions for the acrid and hateful dispute of 1969. As the sociologist, David Martin, points out in his analysis of religion, 'the greater the hope the more violent the schism'.

With the perfect vision of hindsight it is easy to see that the instincts that brought the team together to bid for the franchise were correct – ITV was moving increasingly towards public service. However, the financial crisis of the late 1960s and early 1970s militated against rapid change. As Matthew Arnold affirmed in the epigraph to this chapter, ideas are to be valued for their own sake; however, to change the world and to bid it dance to the tune of the idea is quite another thing, particularly when cash is at stake.

Peacock tried too much too soon. Moreover, the programme team which he had acquired was more suited to a five or seven day franchise, than to that of the weekend. There was precious little room for experimentation, for persevering with a show that might succeed after building an audience, or for investigating scheduling options. The shortness and peculiarity of the weekend franchise has taken by surprise almost every senior executive who has worked at LWT. However, by the time of his sacking Peacock was beginning to come to grips with the brutal realities of commercial television during an advertising slump. Similarly, his programme-makers were groping towards an understanding of how to retain their ideals and, at the same time, confront the demands of a commercial network. If the team had managed to survive until the government reduced the broadcasting levy, then they might have inherited the secure financial situation which allowed LWT to become a trusted, secure and successful broadcasting company in the 1970s. Peacock, under different financial and structural circumstances, might have succeeded.

The Board's decision to sack Peacock was not taken lightly. It emerged from a deep disillusionment – justified or not – with Peacock's executive skills. The Board, as was demonstrated in the last chapter, wanted to be part of a company that produced programmes of which they would be proud. The problem, as one of the directors clearly identified, was not only that the station was in a financial mess but that they hated the programmes. The Board was deprived of kudos and of cash and wanted a plan for the future which would outline how both could be attained. If Crawley had been tougher both with Peacock and the Board, and if Peacock had been able to present a strategy in which the Board believed, and to make the Directors believe that he trusted or, at least, listened to their judgements and concerns, then the Gotter-dammerung might have been prevented.

The failure of LWT to become BBC3 must be seen in the context of the amount of energy and insight and time that it took to turn LWT into a successful company. However, before the calm waters of the 1970s were reached, another storm had to be navigated.

A WILD KIND OF JUSTICE

Revenge is a wild kind of justice.
Francis Bacon, On Revenge

On 3 October 1969, a few weeks after Peacock's resignation, David Frost presented a *Frost on Friday* which, as well as being the first live colour programme to be broadcast on ITV, also introduced the British public to an Australian newspaper proprietor, Rupert Murdoch, who had acquired Britain's largest-selling Sunday newspaper, the *News of the World*, and was poised to buy an ailing national daily newspaper called the *Sun*. Murdoch had been extremely reluctant to appear on the programme. Not only was he uncomfortable as a television performer, he was under fire for publishing the salacious diaries of Christine Keeler who, six years before, had precipitated the downfall and disgrace of John Profumo, a Conservative Minister of War. Apart from Tory MPs, who were extremely concerned about the enduring political damage caused by the Profumo debacle, Murdoch was under attack from, among many others, England's premier Roman Catholic cleric, Cardinal Heenan. The Cardinal accused Murdoch of refusing to take into account the many charitable works by which Profumo had purchased his redemption. Despite the hostile response to his ownership of the *News of the World*, Murdoch had been convinced by his public relations people, and by Frost himself, who had assured him that the programme would be balanced, that he would be able to explain himself to the British public.

Frost's signature tune faded out and the host said, 'Good evening and welcome!' After that it was downhill for Murdoch, who found himself at the centre of a censorious whirlwind. The audience were encouraged by Frost to denounce Murdoch's morals, his values, and his lack of responsibility. Frost had also interviewed Cardinal Heenan who, in a filmed insert, expressed his sorrow that Profumo was yet again being undermined by the brutal behaviour of the press. Frost was tormentor-in-chief; he orchestrated the attack and encouraged the condemnation and censure. As the programme progressed, Frost became more

argumentative and abusive. He accused the *News of the World* of running
'pathetic' stories and he demanded of Murdoch, 'I wish you could give
us one reason why this thing is worth taking the risks of damaging a
man, damaging a man's work.' He rounded on Murdoch's press officer
who enthusiastically applauded Murdoch's rebuttal of Frost, 'Your PR
man's going mad again. Your PR man is the only person who's
applauded – you must give him a rise. We've got to leave it there. Thank
you very much indeed.'

The combatants were in vastly different humour at the end of the
programme. Murdoch was seething with fury, whereas Frost thought
that the programme had been lively, contentious, and raucous – the
embodiment of the controlled chaos from which he had spun his
reputation. Frost grinned in Murdoch's direction and sent over a young
man to invite him for a drink in the hospitality room. A choleric
Murdoch dismissed the messenger and stormed out of the studio. As he
reached the front door Murdoch turned to his entourage and, pointing at
the studio complex, he vowed revenge. 'I'm going to buy this place', he
declared. And he did.

Dr No and the Studio of Doom

Murdoch's intervention in LWT's affairs was made possible by the
disintegration of the unsteady alliance between the Board, Margerison
and the new programme team but it was, in its own way, symptomatic of
the end of the short age of innocence in the mid-1960s. One by one the
building bricks of 'the new age' collapsed: by the middle of 1970
Labour's technological revolution had ground to an ignominious halt;[1]
the glory of the housing boom was tarnished by the damp, rot and
deprivation of the new housing estates – which became gulags for the
poor; the Beatles broke up; and the decade petered out in a mood of
confusion and cynicism.

Television reflected these cultural and economic changes. After the
explosive and innovative programmes of the Greene era at the BBC, and
the potential of LWT's first incarnation, television became increasingly
cautious. Greene retired as DG in March 1969 – pushed, it was said, by
Charles Hill – and he was succeeded by the sensible but unadventurous
Charles Curran. Commercial television, under tremendous financial
pressure, drew in its horns to await better days, and LWT, the flagship
of change, sank like a cultural Titanic beneath waves of old movies,
variety packages and uninspired drama.

This was the inauspicious background to Tom Margerison's time as
Chief Executive. Apart from the general economic gloom, and ITV's
specific problems with levy, Margerison inherited some particular
complications: he had no Director of Programmes, and no Head of
Drama, Arts, Children's Programmes, Light Entertainment or Public

Affairs. Margerison was undaunted by the scale of his task; he believed that his varied career had prepared him to guide LWT through the crisis. After taking a doctorate in solid state physics at the University of Sheffield in the late 1940s, Margerison turned to script writing for feature films and then entered publishing. His most conspicuous success as a publisher was the co-creation of the popular science magazine *The New Scientist*. After a five-year stint as this magazine's science editor, during which time he worked as a science reporter on the BBC's *Tonight* programme, Margerison became science correspondent of the *Sunday Times* and subsequently Deputy Editor of the *Sunday Times Magazine*. In addition to this latter position he served as a director of Thomson Technical Developments – the new technologies wing of the Thomson organization.

Margerison's scientific education inclined him to the view that the world could be reduced to propositions, measurements and causal relations. LWT's failure was, in his mind, the consequence of malfunctioning financial and organizational systems. These problems, so he thought, could be resolved by stripping the components down to individual relationships, formulating flow diagrams to indicate how decisions, personnel and resources should be distributed within the company, and integrating this system in a methodical fashion.

Like many men and women capable of the relentless application of logic, Margerison found it difficult to appreciate that others did not share his views. Some colleagues felt that he was unable to discern suitable contexts for the use of formal or mathematical logic. The principles of scientific management and of systems analysis may have been appropriate for mass production; however, some staff felt that these rules were inappropriate to television. Even the engineers, carpenters and scene shifters – whom Margerison may have looked to as allies against the creative staff – considered television to be an artistic as much as an industrial process; the medium's indeterminate, 'soft', creative features could not be reduced to components and relations.

Margerison believed that in order to turn the company around he had to be tough where the Board had perceived Peacock to be weak, rational where Peacock had been seen as intuitive, and frugal where Peacock had been regarded as wasteful. Consequently, he exhorted the staff and attempted to impose his leadership on the company. The workforce was, by and large, unconvinced by his leadership qualities. Margerison's actions which, in other circumstances may have been regarded as necessary to transform a failing company, were considered by many to be arrogant and insensitive.

Margerison's appointment triggered powerful and tangled emotions in the company. For some colleagues he came to symbolize LWT's failure. Feelings ran extremely high in the company, so much so that criticisms of Margerison became extremely personal. One senior executive recalls that he had an almost visceral response to Margerison. 'I hated everything about him, from the dandruff on his collar to the fact that he tied his shoes with string.' Fair or not, just or not, similar feelings – although expressed less pungently – were widespread in LWT. Another executive indignantly recollected that 'Everything had to be done according to the slide-rule and not according to the combined wisdom of those who actually had spent decades making programmes. He was the sort of guy who would say – "how many hours of television do you think that you can make in a day?" – and the guys who knew about these things would tell him, and he would then say, "Well I'm surprised to hear you say that because I've worked out with my slide rule that if you have X men working Y hours they will produce Z hours of television." And we said, "but it's just not like that." He simply ignored us.' Yet another executive recalled the disdain with which Margerison was regarded: 'Margerison worked out that we needed four and a half video tape recorders for the amount of programmes that were being produced. Everyone was wandering around muttering to each other: "Anybody found half a tape recorder?" '

Although Margerison's background as an editor and manager demonstrates that he was better versed in dealing with practical problems than the above picture would suggest, this reputation did not enhance LWT's bargaining power in the network committees. Indeed, he more than reconfirmed LWT's reputation for arrogance. At one meeting at which were present the men who had nurtured commercial television and who had an intimate knowledge of its character, Margerison reportedly whipped his slide-rule from his inside pocket in order to refute Lew Grade. The assorted network grandees were speechless.

Margerison was considered to be an awkward and difficult negotiator by the unions, and he was dubbed Dr No by the ACTT; the unions were, however, unimpressed: one senior ACTT official reflected 20 years later that Margerison lacked a pressing sense of the rubble to which the unions could reduce LWT.

Margerison's difficult financial inheritance, and his own personality, left him exposed to Murdoch's attack. The Board progressively and inexorably turned away from Margerison as bit by bit the company fell apart, and one by one many programmes failed.

Come Together

Rebellions or *putsches* unravel the ties of influence, power and charisma that bind organisations together. Once the principle of authority is overturned, it needs to be righted. This delicate task paradoxically is undertaken by those who undermined the old order. To be successful, the new team needs an inspiring leader, a plausible apologist, an efficient bureaucracy, and receptive followers. Without these elements organisations descend into chaos. Furthermore, turmoil can only be quenched if a taste for intrigue, developed in the coup, is eradicated. In LWT's case, conspiracy was elevated to an organizational first principle.

After the coup, Margerison's first task was to appoint a new Controller of Programmes. He scoured the BBC for a replacement for Cyril Bennett. The position was offered to Aubrey Singer, the BBC's Head of Features, who turned it down. Other BBC executives whom Margerison approached such as Bill Cotton, the Head of Variety, offered him scant encouragement. LWT's rancorous failure was a sufficiently clear warning to those who may have considered crossing the divide.

Guy Paine, who had become Assistant Chief Executive in the October reshuffle, had his own candidate for job. He had absolutely no desire to work with another ex-BBC executive and he wanted someone who would deliver a solid commercial schedule which his beleaguered department could sell. Paine was unused to failure. As Rediffusion's Director of Sales he had enjoyed the luxury of simply allocating time to competitive buyers. This background had ill-equipped him for the rough and tumble of selling the weekend franchise in a declining market. LWT had to squeeze sales from buyers aware of the company's weakness and unimpressed by its performance. The sales department was in deep trouble; the advertising agencies regarded LWT as a soft touch and advertising time was discounted in order to increase the volume of sales.

Paine was aware that his reputation was at stake and he pressed Margerison to appoint someone schooled in the realities of commercial television.[2] In particular, he recommended Stella Richman.[3]

Margerison, who had been disappointed at the reluctance of BBC programme-makers to join the company, and aware of the problems of breaking someone new into the company, settled, reluctantly, on Richman. It was, from the first day, an unhappy compromise and an uneasy relationship. Neither liked or had respect for the talents of the other. Clive Irving recalls, 'Stella was very much her own woman, and she was Margerison's greatest enemy – they had no way of communicating at all.' Instead of presenting a unified face to the world LWT's executives were enmired in suspicion; jealous of their own prerogatives; disinclined to co-operate, and unwilling to negotiate.

Secrecy became endemic in the company. Stella Richman, for example, had a war room to which only two or three people were allowed keys. One wall of this room was covered with a huge planning board on which her programme strategy was planned; all of the windows were covered by locking curtains. Margerison did not possess a key.

It was clear to all quite quickly that Margerison, Stella Richman and Paine were struggling for dominance. The station had become Balkanized; pockets of authority and power were dispersed throughout the company and no-one was capable of uniting the various factions.

Stella Richman was caught between resignation and undermining Margerison. Within a few months of starting, she asked to be released from her contract. David Montagu, horrified by the renewed spiral of disarray and confusion, managed to persuade her to remain with the station. However, it was clearly only a matter of time before it would become necessary to overhaul the senior management.

As well as conducting this internecine struggle with Margerison, Stella Richman had to put together a new programme team and to develop some new and interesting programmes. The new team included Francis Coleman, who had been a producer in Stephens' department, as executive producer of education, religious and children's programmes, Humphrey Burton who had returned as a freelance producer of arts programmes, Verity Lambert, a BBC drama producer who was to go on to a glittering career elsewhere, and Rex Firkin, who continued as an executive producer in drama. The most significant appointment was that of Barry Took as Head of Light Entertainment.

Took was, in a sense, a doppleganger for Frank Muir. Like Frank Muir he had been a member of a famous script writing duo (in Took's case with Marty Feldman); moreover, he had worked at the BBC's comedy department before joining LWT. When the LWT debacle was taking place in 1969 and early 1970, Took had been in the US, where he had worked on one of the cult shows of the late 1960s – *Rowan and Martin's Laugh-In*. Consequently, when everyone else was treating LWT as a television version of a plague ship, Took regarded Richman's offer as an opportunity. The deal was clinched when he was offered, in his words, 'a LARGE sum of money to join.' (He was later to recall, 'I think that I wouldn't have joined had I known how horrid the situation was to become.')

Richman had to face a unique problem. As a woman, as with women throughout the executive level, she had to prove herself twice over. Top management in Britain was dominated by men, and ITV was a bastion of what people were learning to call sexism. Stella Richman's activities were subject to close scrutiny; if she broke into tears – which she did on many occasions – she was regarded as weak and a typical woman; however, if she was tough and resolute she was ridiculed as hard and over-ambitious.

Unfortunately for her, one of her early actions as Controller of Programmes allowed many of her colleagues to shake their heads, click their teeth together and mutter: 'Just like a woman.' Richman was sitting at home watching *World of Sport* which, as ever, was taken up with horse racing. Bored by the repetition of starters' prices, betting, and analysis of form she called the transmission controller and instructed him to replace the racing with a feature film. This request was met with blank incomprehension. *World of Sport* was a network programme and any changes in its composition and timing had to be negotiated at network level. Richman's decision would have blown a hole in that agreement. Moreover, punters from Ayr to Epsom would have exploded with rage at the decision, and LWT would have been held up to ridicule in every newspaper in the country. After some frantic debate the controller of transmissions returned Richman's call and spelled out the implications of the decision. She withdrew the request. This story passed from bar to bar and from station to station, and it strengthened the conviction of LWT's staff that the company could not afford to have a controller of programmes who was learning on the job.

Making the Break

Tom Margerison and Stella Richman agreed on one thing at least: they had to disentangle themselves from the network which, they believed, was undermining the station's recovery. Margerison recalls:

> We had terrible problems because the network would schedule against us . . . One always worries whether perhaps one's reactions are paranoid, but ATV, in particular, scheduled against us. For example, they had a ghastly programme called *Humperdinck*, or somesuch, and it was an absolute killer, it got very little audience at all . . . and this thing was pushed into the middle of Saturday evening. What was really happening was that the other companies had seven nights a week, and we only had Friday night, Saturday and Sunday. For the others it did not matter that the weekend was unprofitable – they put their jewels into winning the weekdays. We, on the other hand, were killed if we did not have anything good on Sunday; and, from the beginning, right through Stella's reign, we really did not have anything much of our own and everything was being scheduled against us.

Margerison's suspicions were not misplaced. Over lunch at the end of May 1970, Sir Robert Fraser, the ITA's Director General, had been invited by Lew Grade's ATV to speculate on the ways in which LWT and ATV might enter into some form of association. Fraser indicated that the ITA could not look favourably on such a merger and that if LWT did eventually collapse the only rational amalgamation would be with Thames; however, Fraser continued, as the ITA had a long-standing policy that the London market should not be dominated by one ITV company, even this solution was untenable. Lew Grade was, in fact, reacting to rumours that Thames and LWT had been discussing various forms of co-operation from August 1969 onwards. Thames had decided to bide its time and wait to see how LWT would fare before precipitating a conflict with the ITA over a merger.

Throughout the spring and summer of 1970 rumours and gossip concerning the take-over of LWT by one or other of the majors, or by a combination of all of the ITV companies, circulated around the network. Adrift in this sea of machinations, Margerison attempted to anchor his station by developing a programme strategy which was independent of the network and which focused principally on the London market.

Before Stella Richman and Margerison agreed on this policy, they had yet another major, and very public, disagreement. On 1 April 1970, the government reduced the levy on advertising revenue. Although this released money for new programmes, Margerison and his Controller of Programmes could not agree on how much the new programme budget should be. In March, Margerison had informed Stella Richman that she would have to trim £10,000 a week from her budget. In May, subsequent to the government's announcement about the levy, Richman responded with a plan to spend an extra £29,000 a week on programmes. Margerison attacked Richman at the Board meeting which followed Richman's bid for more money; he argued forcibly that the company could, at most, afford to spend around £9,500 a week. Stella Richman was furious at this public attack on her policy and she resigned. Once more Lord Campbell and David Montagu were pressed into service to persuade her to stay. Montagu was, by this point, tired of the whole affair; in a letter to a friend, he uttered the heartfelt description of LWT's predicament as 'this wretched business'.

Richman and Margerison papered over their disagreements and, in June, they announced their new strategy. Instead of pressing the network for more category 'A' slots, and facing the inevitable battle which seemed to accompany such offers, Margerison and Richman decided to invest heavily in 'B' programmes which were primarily intended for local consumption. This, Margerison reasoned, would provide LWT with more room to manoeuvre and would allow them to target more precisely the London market. Moreover, in the long term, Margerison hoped that his strategy would provide him with some leverage over the other majors who, worried that network arrangements would be jeopardized, might accommodate LWT's needs.

This grand strategy – a combination of the slide-rule and the war-room – was outlined in middle of June 1970. Margerison revealed that LWT would focus its energies on new situation comedies and drama. 'We are not satisfied with all the programmes being made', said Margerison in a gibe at the network, '[we] feel that someone should take the lead in strengthening weekend ITV schedules.' LWT announced that its schedules were to run for a full year – from September 1970 until Autumn 1971 – rather than the usual seasonal approach adopted by the network. LWT could not, however, develop a consistently successful schedule. The strain of bad programmes was sustained throughout the year. In July *Bodyguard*, which was the sequel to one of LWT's few successes *The Gold Robbers*, was scrapped after one programme had been made. A series of dramas entitled *Big Brother* ran into problems in the following month; the second programme in the series had to be shown at the press preview because the first was, apparently, terrible. The press pilloried the station for yet another failure.

Barry Took inherited a dispirited and rudderless department. Before he had time to break in his desk blotter, he was asked by Stella Richman to fill in a gap left by yet another drama series which had not materialised. He commissioned six different writers to work simultaneously on an idea about computer dating (an appropriate theme for a series which seemed to have been put together by malfunctioning IBM software). Most of the scripts for *The Dating Game* were ready in two weeks and, to say the least, were patchy. Their quality was overlooked in the struggle to fill the holes in the schedule.[4]

A further two comedy series whose scripts were inherited by Took were thrown into the breach. Took's gimmick this time was to broadcast them without laughtracks. He recalls: 'I wanted to throw the critics off my tracks by playing to their hatred of canned laughter.' The television critics, who had the malicious instincts and relentless determination of Hyenas, savaged the programmes – as they continued to savage the majority of LWT's productions.

The general problems were enhanced by the behaviour of one of the station's star performers. Simon Dee, a former pirate DJ and a successful BBC chat show host, had seemed an ideal replacement for (and perhaps competitor to) Frost while the latter was off the air. Dee was consquently recruited to front a network chat show on Sunday nights. The show was commissioned before Took arrived and, in his words, 'was pretty dull'. The show's failure was exacerbated by Dee's apparently eccentric behaviour. For example, Dee wanted to interview the Archbishop of Canterbury. Although Took considered this a reasonable request, he was less than happy with Dee's insistence that the Archbishop appear on the regular Sunday night show. Took argued that it was entirely inappropriate to interview the Archbishop sandwiched between 'a trumpet player who looks as if he is on drugs and a pair of half-dressed young women.' Dee was insistent and Took was forced to invent a Sunday afternoon Simon Dee Special during which the eponymous interviewer and the Archbishop discussed the pressing issues of the day. Honour was saved and antagonism averted.

Dee came up with another request. He wanted to interview Orson Welles ('terrific', thought Took), in Rome ('damn', thought Took). With as much patience as he could muster, Took pointed out that in order to do the interview in Rome they would have to take 'the producer and his assistant, the cameraman and his assistant, the sound man and his assistant, the lighting man and his assistant, and a researcher.' Took suggested that instead of LWT flying *en masse* to Rome it would be cheaper to offer Welles a first-class ticket to the UK; provide him with a chauffeured Rolls Royce for the duration of his visit; book him into the

Dorchester; and wine and dine him in London's most expensive restaurants. Nothing more was heard of Welles.

By the third week in March 1970 Dee's producer Bryan Izzard departed and Dee promptly became embroiled in an argument with his successor. Dee had personally invited the singer Matt Monroe to appear on the show without consulting the producer who had booked the jazz singer Cleo Lane. After a furious discussion Dee stormed out claiming that he had a cold and stomach ache, and that he might not be able to perform on the following Sunday. Took immediately contacted a BBC1 DJ – Pete Murray – and explained that Dee was too ill to perform and invited Murray to appear in his place. Murray was delighted to accept the invitation, whereupon Took's ailing star was fortunate to be blessed with a remarkable recovery. By June Took decided that 'it was best for all concerned to cancel the show.' Another major programme initiative had slowly, ignominiously and publicly ground to a halt.

Some programmes did emerge with credit from Margerison's and Stella Richman's year in charge. The coverage of the 1970 World Cup in Mexico elevated the *Big Match* team to new heights of public and professional acclaim. LWT brought the techniques pioneered over the previous two years in the coverage of London games to a surprised public. Moreover, it married this technical prowess to a flash, funny and furious discussion between a panel of three raconteurs – Pat Crerand, Malcolm Allison, and Derek Dougan – who were accompanied by Bob McNab, a nice, ordinary professional footballer who acted as a straight man for the others. Jimmy Hill and Brian Moore anchored the shows and the whole package was widely considered as an innovative and refreshing approach to televized soccer.

Although the drama department suffered greatly from the withdrawal of the talented Kestrel team, and from Derek Granger's departure, it eventually came up with one of the 1970s cult series – *Budgie* – which starred Adam Faith as a cockney wide boy. Moreover, another series, created by the actresses Jean Marsh and Eileen Atkins and the producers John Hawkesworth and John Whitney (later to become Director General of the IBA) told the story of an aristocratic Edwardian family and their servants. *Upstairs, Downstairs* became London Weekend's most enduring success. Unfortunately for Richman, before these series were broadcast she had resigned from the company.

Stella Richman also kept faith with LWT's commitment to the Arts when she continued to support Humphrey Burton's series *Aquarius* despite lack of enthusiasm or support from the rest of the network.

Despite all of this effort, energy, skulduggery and tears LWT remained stubbornly in the doldrums. LWT remained the most publicized sick man of ITV.[5] The trade paper *The Stage and Television Today* summed up the opinions of the public, the critics and the rest of the network: 'LWT's performance in programming is dismal' it proclaimed at the beginning of 1971. It argued that the station's dramas were 'badly chosen, weakly edited and poorly cast'. Something simply had to give.

Here Comes the Sun King

In September 1970, the press finally broke the story that Rupert Murdoch was bidding for Arnold Weinstock's GEC holding of 7½ per cent of LWT's voting stock. Murdoch had been moving in on LWT for some time before this. Weinstock, along with other holders of voting shares, had been approached early in the summer by Murdoch's legal adviser, Lord Goodman, who indicated that Rupert Murdoch was interested in buying shares in LWT. Weinstock was receptive to Murdoch's bid because, as he recalls, 'our industrial purposes had long since been fulfilled: the BBC programmes, at least, had improved greatly. Furthermore, I really did not want to become involved again in all of the rows – it was too embarrassing and it wasn't our business. I agreed to Murdoch's bid provided he undertook to do something to change the station.' Weinstock is adamant that he did not, as was widely reported at the time, simply wash his hands of LWT: 'We could have walked away but it wouldn't have been responsible. I thought that provided we got a guarantee that Murdoch would turn the company around then it would be constructive to sell.'

This bid for Weinstock's shares was stage two of Murdoch's plan. Murdoch had been stalking his prey ever since the interview with Frost in the previous October. In May 1970, Murdoch met Margerison and Crawley at an awards ceremony organised by the *Sun*. Murdoch beguiled and charmed them. Before the night was over, he dropped some hints that he was interested in buying into an ITV company. Margerison swallowed the bait. On the following morning he telephoned Murdoch and pointed out that the commitment of many of LWT's shareholders was fragile and that Murdoch would probably be able to buy into the company. Although this was akin to hiring a poltergeist as a housekeeper, Margerison was convinced that he and Murdoch would make a good team. 'I wanted to bring him in', Margerison recalls, 'because the board was lacking in anyone of any strength and because the non-executive directors were not really taking much of an interest. I thought that I wanted someone who knew about media organizations and who would act as my ally.'

Murdoch was extremely active over the following few months and, by the time he had lunch with the ITA's Director General Sir Robert Fraser on 13 July 1970, he was able to claim that around 63 per cent of LWT's shares had been offered to him. Although Fraser was cautious, he did not warn off Murdoch.

Four months later, Murdoch bought Weinstock's shares.[6] He joined the Board in November 1970 – in the same month that Crawley announced a loss of £67,000. (The company actually made a profit of £2.92 million but it paid a levy of £2.99 million.) Within a month of this bad news Murdoch initiated the third stage of his plan. He played on the financial insecurities of some members of the board and on the desire of others for strong leadership and he pushed for full operational control of the company. On 18 December, Murdoch piled problem upon difficulty as he analysed LWT's predicament; he pointed out that LWT had used up all of its share capital; that the loan stock of just over £3,000,000 was being devoured at an alarming rate; that the company had overdrafts of around £2.5 million; and that, although the National Coal Board Nominees were underwriting the costs of the new offices and studios, it was inevitable that the move would involve the company in extra expense. Murdoch argued forcibly that the station was starved of cash for new programmes and that he would willingly inject £500,000 for such programmes in return for new shares for a seat on LWT's executive committee. Crawley was unconvinced. He wanted the Board to explore other financial options which would have prevented the concentration of power in Murdoch's hands. However, other voices prevailed and, at a Board meeting on 21 December, Crawley accepted David Montague's proposal of a new share issue in which holders of non-voting 'A' shares would be entitled to apply for one new share at £1 for every three held. This produced an extra 555,000 new shares, the majority of which were purchased by Murdoch. It had taken over a year, but Murdoch had fulfilled the promise which he made to himself when he stood outside the Wembley studios in October 1969.

A great deal of backroom negotiations with ITA were required before Murdoch was allowed to acquire such a large stake in the company. Margerison, convinced that Murdoch would support him in his struggles with some of his senior executives, approached the ITA and informed them that Murdoch had his full support and moreover, that without Murdoch's financial intervention LWT might not survive. Murdoch played his hand very carefully in order to ensure that he would emerge with control of the station. The ITA's Chairman, Lord Aylestone, recalls, 'I saw no reason why Murdoch was not suitable – other newspapers were already represented on the board – and once having made the decision to accept Murdoch's earlier purchase of the shares there was no reason not to accept his further investment.'

The deal was sealed and formally approved on 31 December. Subsequent events demonstrated that despite the length and intensity of the negotiations the arrangement was beset by mutual incomprehension. Murdoch assumed that he was being offered the chance to sort out the station which, in his eyes, meant control over the programme division. Murdoch's previous experience on television, as owner of loosely regulated Australian channels, Sydney's Channel 10 and Perth's Channel

7, led him to believe that the ITA would not interfere if LWT was financially secure. Margerison, however, believed that he had secured a promise from Murdoch that he would not interfere other than to support his decisions. Crawley and Aylestone for their part assumed that Murdoch understood that under the terms of the Television Act he was debarred from a close involvement with the programme division. Section 12 of the Act stated:

> if at any time there are newspaper shareholdings in the programme contractor, and it appears to the authority that the existence of those shareholdings has led or is leading to results which are contrary to the public interest, the authority may, with the consent of the Postmaster General, by notice in writing to the programme contractor . . . suspend for such period as may be so specified the authority's obligation to transmit the programmes supplied by the programme contractor.

Section 11 of the Act was also germane to Murdoch's position in LWT. It declared that:

> the appointment of the manager, editor, or other chief executive of such body or organization [programme company] [should be] approved by the authority.

The seeds of the confrontation between Murdoch and the Authority which came to a head in late February were planted in the mistaken assumptions lurking behind the negotiations.

Taking Over

Any assessment of Murdoch's involvement with LWT will inevitably be clouded by the subsequent controversy about his newspapers and his television companies. Relating the story of his time at LWT is a like telling the story of Napoleon's career as a Corporal; Murdoch's myth had far outstripped this period of his life. One aspect of the myth has him as Apollyon, the beast who was one of the Lords of Bunyan's debauched city Vanity-Fair. His detractors hold him responsible for the dissipation of Britain's moral and aesthetic values. Others regard him as a business leviathan with a multi-billion dollar empire which was developed by a combination of dazzling entrepreneurial speculation and brutal business practices. These myths crowd around Murdoch's name and obscure the fact that in 1970 he was simply one of a long line of colonial newspaper proprietors such Lord Thomson, who owned the *Times*, and Lord Beaverbrook, who dominated British newspapers between the wars. Lord Campbell makes this connection, 'Rupert was very attractive, very charming, very disarming and totally ruthless . . . I'm bound to say I found him even more magically attractive than the Beaver who could charm the birds out of the trees.' It is not difficult therefore to see why the ITA and Margerison were content to sanction and, indeed, welcome Murdoch's interest.

The Board were delighted that Murdoch wanted to sort out a station which had become, in the words of David Montagu, 'more like St Trinians every day.' Montagu sums up the board's view of Murdoch: 'Murdoch was the best thing that happened to LWT at that stage; he spent a lot of time at the company, cut a lot of fat and eradicated many of the bad practices which had plagued the company.' Lord Campbell asserts adamantly that 'Murdoch salvaged the company.'

Murdoch exploded into LWT. He, and his entourage, toured the building looking, in John Bromley's words, 'like the Mafia'. Aidan Crawley recalls that 'Rupert went round into every single department, and my telephone was red-hot with calls from department heads, saying "What's this man doing here?" '

Margerison initially was unruffled by Murdoch's direct involvement – particularly when Murdoch helped him to secure the departure of Stella Richman. Miss Richman had not helped her cause when, on the anniversary of her appointment as programme controller, she had presented the Board with a dismal diagnosis, and even more gloomy prognosis, of the company's difficulties. Margerison forced her resignation on 28 January, the week following this depressing report. Another of Margerison's rivals, Guy Paine, had fallen the day before. Murdoch agreed with Margerison that Paine had failed to provide the company with an innovative and committed sales force. Moreover, Murdoch wanted to bring in one of his own people to run sales; consequently, on 27 January Paine departed and Bert Hardy, the director of advertising at the *News of the World*, became LWT's acting Director of Sales.

Margerison thought that his plan was working. He was in sole charge of the company for the first time since taking over in 1969. Murdoch had other ideas. Stories began to filter to Margerison that Murdoch was demanding changes in the schedule. Eric Flackfield, who has 'nothing but good things to say about Murdoch', was in charge of LWT's schedules. When Murdoch arrived at the station Flackfield was called into his office. Murdoch asked, 'Do you know a programme called *Mannix*?' 'Yes', responded Flackfield, 'we tried it out and it doesn't work very well.' Murdoch pressed, 'What do we show at 7.30 on a Friday?' On hearing that it was another US series – *Hawaii Five O* – Murdoch instructed Flackfield to pull it and replace it with *Mannix*. Moreover, Murdoch notified Flackfield that any future schedules had to be cleared through him and that he would take charge of the selection of the feature films for the next quarter.

Murdoch also took a keen interest in production. He informed Barry Took that *On the Buses*, LWT's most popular show, should be on every week. Took, somewhat bemused, attempted to familiarize Murdoch with the realities of British studio production and of network negotiations (as well as the more human problem of the star, Reg Varney's heart attacks.)

Another revealing story of the gap between Murdoch and the programme-makers involved the creation of a pop show. Murdoch cancelled Barry Took's pop shows *Stewpot* and *What Are You Doing After the Show?* and instructed the light entertainment department to produce a new 'pop' programme. The producers disappeared and spent sleepless nights designing an updated *Ready, Steady, Go* complete with graphics running along the bottom of the screen and cameras moving around among the audience. They rushed off to Murdoch with this great plan, only to be crushed by Murdoch who snarled 'I want a popular programme, not a pop show.'

Murdoch ordered Charlie Squires, producer of the award-winning documentary *Derby Day*, to drop his plans to make six new documentaries. Squires, whom John Freeman described as a 'cockney heavyweight, raconteur, gentleman and social historian', exited in disgust. Barry Took decided that Stella Richman's departure and the disintegration of programme standards was too much to bear and he, too, resigned.

There was little programme-makers could do about Murdoch's interventions. It very quickly became clear that although Murdoch was a non-executive director with no formal power or authority he had become, *de facto*, Managing Director and Controller of Programmes. The new draft programme schedule, devised essentially by Murdoch, pushed LWT's solitary arts programme *Aquarius* back to 11.15 pm; *Survival*, Anglia's nature documentary, was replaced by quiz shows, one of which was presented by Hughie Greene, an old Rediffusion stalwart. Compared to LWT's new schedule, Rediffusion's output was a paragon of public service. Brian Young, who had taken over from Sir Robert Fraser as Director General at the ITA, declined to accept the changes. Murdoch was told to reinstate *Survival*, to reschedule the quiz shows and to maintain *Aquarius* at a reasonable hour.

Margerison had attempted by every means at his disposal to prevent the Murdoch juggernaut rolling over his carefully thought out plans for running the station. When Murdoch turned up at the first programme executives' meeting at the beginning of 1971, Margerison decided that benevolence was the better part of valour, and he explained to Murdoch that although his keenness to keep in touch with programme matters was commendable, as a non-executive director he had no right to appear at programme meetings. Murdoch stopped attending these meetings. However, he marginalized Margerison by inviting the heads of the programme division out for dinner every Sunday at which they would discuss the previous week's programmes and plan the new schedule.

A seething Margerison confronted Murdoch in his office and initiated a loud, public, acrimonious argument which sealed Margerison's fate. The following day, 17 February, Crawley – at Murdoch's instigation – invited some of the other directors to lunch. Murdoch outlined his disagreement with Margerison and his opinion that the latter should be sacked. The Board had long since lost confidence in Margerison and, without even the formalities of a Board meeting, Crawley invited Margerison into his office and, for the second time in seventeen months, asked for the resignation of his chief executive.

Margerison, stunned by the suddenness of Murdoch's coup, steamed around to the IBA's building on Brompton Road. He informed the ITA that as he could no longer fulfil his promise to shield the programme staff from Murdoch's intervention he had resigned. The ITA scurried off to their solicitors to establish the nature and limits of their right to intervene and, perhaps, revoke LWT's contract.

Clive Irving, Margerison's old neighbour and supporter, wrote to *The Times* on 25 February asking for a 'thorough and formal inquiry into the transfer of power in the company.' Murdoch, believing that Irving was a front man for Frost, called the letter writer 'His Master's Voice'. A few days later Murdoch announced that LWT would not be able to afford to pay Frost's salary and that the latter would either have to accept a substantial reduction for the next series of Frost programmes or he could take his talents elsewhere. Before Murdoch's wild justice could take effect, the ITA intervened.

On 25 February the Authority sent a letter to LWT which argued that the sacking of Margerison and the establishment of an executive committee, over which Murdoch would preside, was in contravention of the Television Act. The station was given six weeks to sort out its affairs and to choose a new Managing Director and Programme Controller. Murdoch's revolution was over before it had much chance to take effect.

Models and Morals

Murdoch's close involvement with LWT began with a desire for revenge and concluded with an acrimonious dispute with the ITA. He retired from the executive committee – although not from the Board – leaving behind rough notes and dead bodies. He flattened the ground, cleared out the dead wood, and prepared the company for rebuilding.

The confrontation between Murdoch and the ITA had become one of the enduring myths about British television. Some critics, most notably the Annan Committee on Broadcasting, accused the ITA of spineless misjudgement. However, such a verdict does not take into account the simple fact that if the London Weekend contractor had been sacked in circumstances which indicated that it was not a viable franchise, then a massive structural change in the whole network would have become necessary. Moreover, the persistent problem of ensuring that a seven-day London contractor did not dominate the regions remained uppermost in the ITA's list of concerns. The ITA had to ensure that LWT remained financially viable – which meant that they could not entirely alienate Murdoch, who was the largest shareholder – and protect the public service aspects of ITV.

The ITA could have turned a blind eye to Murdoch. It did not do so, however; instead it opted for a classic and, in the circumstances, sensible bureaucratic compromise: the authority invoked the Television Act, thus making Murdoch aware that this was more than a clash of personalities, and then allowed the company sufficient time to cast around for a solution which would save face and allow the ITA to confirm the contract.

The freedom of the mass, popular press in Britain, as someone remarked, degenerated into the freeom of the proprietor to print those opinions to which the advertisers do not take exception. The British model of commercial broadcasting attempted to protect television from this debilitating process. Although some Chairmen of ITV companies behaved as if they were Hollywood moguls their influence was, by and large, watered down by determined Chief Executives or Directors of Programmes who knew that they had the backing of the Authority. It was this model which Murdoch could not grasp or did not accept. He believed that, as he had taken a major risk by investing in a company in which no one else was interested, he should be able to run that company as he saw fit. The events of a March 1971 constituted a clash between Australian and British models of broadcasting. In the short term, Murdoch had simply no way of taking on the combined weight of the Television Act, British broadcasting culture, the ITA and both ends of the British political establishment. It was time to look elsewhere for someone who could reconcile the competing parties.

TWO STEPS FORWARD

We must see power – and leadership
– as not things but as relationships
James MacGregor Burns: Leadership

'What happens to people is often nothing
but the luck of the game.'
I don't believe that,' said Darcourt.
'What we call luck is the inner man externalised.'
Robertson Davies: What's Bred In The Bone

On 26 February – the day after the ITA's decision threw Murdoch into a paroxysm of rage and the company into administrative paralysis – David Frost flew back from the United States. As soon as his feet hit the tarmac Frost advanced on the telephone with the relish of a man with a mission. He believed that the only person who was capable of satisfying the requirements of the ITA, of placating Murdoch, and of providing sorely needed leadership for the ailing company was his first choice as Chairman – John Freeman.

Frost had maintained intermittent contact with Freeman after their first meeting in 1967, and he was convinced that the latter, who had retired from the diplomatic service a month earlier, would warm to an offer from LWT. Before he approached Freeman, Frost set out to ensure that he could deliver the position of Chief Executive and that the Authority wanted to find an escape route for LWT. Frost set up a meeting with Brian Young and Lord Aylestone at which he established that the ITA was predisposed to save LWT then, armed with this information, Frost telephoned the three men whose support was essential if Freeman's appointment was to be secured – Rupert Murdoch, David Montagu and Lord Campbell. Montagu was sceptical. 'I thought, "Oh my God, not another ex-politician who could not run a whelk stall with a pre-paid supply of whelks." '[1] Lord Campbell, on the other hand, knew Freeman very well and he immediately saw the sense in Frost's recommendation. Lord Campbell recalls, 'I thought that John Freeman had the same qualities as Murdoch – he wanted to do what he did as well as it could be done, which is what we needed.' Murdoch, who was in Australia launching a new newspaper and brooding over the ITA's injustice when Frost's call came through, saw the logic in the proposal. He had learned one hard lesson from his dealings with the impeccable Establishment figure of Brian Young – namely, that a diplomat who was ex-Guardsman and who had been educated at a public school, was the most likely person to convince the ITA that LWT was in safe hands.[2] Murdoch had one proviso: Aiden Crawley had to resign as Chairman. Crawley remembers 'Rupert complained that I had allowed him to be crucified. To which I replied, "Rupert, it wasn't me who was infringing the rule of the contract. I warned you over and over again." Murdoch insisted that I was no longer to be Chairman because I had not defended him. I told him he was being absolutely rotten; however, he insisted that if he was to maintain his investment then there would have to be another Chairman.'

Crawley had been under pressure to resign for some time. At the turn of the year, Montagu and Campbell had approached several successful businessmen in the hope of attracting someone who would sort out the company's problems. Murdoch's implacable opposition to Crawley, and the understanding among the various protagonists that Freeman would not accept the position of Chief Executive unless also offered the Chairmanship brought the matter to a head. Lord Campbell proposed that Crawley accept the nominal role of President of the company (at the same salary) when he stepped aside in favour of Freeman. Crawley, realising that he had no support and tired of the incessant struggle, accepted.

After this flurry of informal activity Frost phoned Freeman and informed him that the job was his for the asking. Freeman was uncertain about Frost's ability to deliver the post and was equally unsure that he wanted to take on the tangles and confusion of LWT. Frost returned to the States and Lord Campbell formally took on the responsibility of offering Freeman the job. On the Wednesday following Frost's weekend on the telephone, Lord Campbell phoned Freeman and said, 'We are in an awful mess, would you be prepared to take over?' Freeman, although by this time inclined to take on the job, wanted to establish that he would have the support of all the shareholders – particularly the one lurking on the other side of the world. Consequently, Freeman insisted that Murdoch, as the principal shareholder, would have to issue the invitation. Murdoch called Freeman and indicated his wholehearted support for the offer. Freeman replied, 'Will you give me a free hand?' Murdoch answered, 'Yes'. Freeman pressed home the point, 'You do realize that a free hand applies to you as well as to everybody else – I really do want a free hand.' The tone of Murdoch's assent was sufficiently genuine to convince Freeman and, on the following day, Lord Campbell was able to inform Lord Aylestone that Freeman and Murdoch had reached an agreement, and that he had invited both, along with David Montagu, to lunch on Sunday.

Over lunch the four analyzed LWT's problems, explored the likely responses from the ITA to the changes in the company which all four agreed would be necessary, and discussed their plans for the future. A

bond of strong mutual respect was forged between Murdoch and
Freeman which convinced the four men that the company could, and
would, be rescued. On the following morning, the ITA was informed
that Freeman had been appointed as Chairman and Chief Executive and,
on Tuesday, 9 March – the news of the appointment was announced to
almost universal acclaim.

An Honourable Gentleman

Freeman was a major coup for LWT. He was widely known and greatly
respected in television, politics, and the civil and diplomatic services. He
was an immensely complex character. A tall, severe-looking man, whose
grey hair, strongly tinged with red, was swept back from his face, he
exuded a sense of purpose. Although no one questioned his character, he
was perceived by some observers to be cerebral, dry and humourless and
by others to be awkward and difficult. However, few, if any, of these
characteristics were to the fore in his time at LWT. His staff at the
station were, by and large, proud that Freeman was associated with the
company. After years of chaos, Freeman's dignified and gracious
treatment of everyone in the company came as a great relief. There is a
zeal, a pride, in committing oneself to the guidance of a charismatic
leader whose prestige is widely recognised. Freeman not only became a
focus for company pride, he won over LWT's staff by moving
immediately from Old Burlington Street to Station House. For the first
time, LWT's Chief Executive actually experienced the world as lived by
the majority of his staff.

In his thirteen years at LWT Freeman was like a cross between one of
the strict but profoundly humane characters with which the film
director, Frank Capra, exemplified Roosevelt's New Deal,[3] and a figure
from one of C.P. Snow's *Strangers and Brothers* novels. Like Lewis
Elliot, Snow's principal protagonist, Freeman's leadership qualities were
forged by an Oxbridge education, wartime experiences, the great
economic crisis of the 1930s and the subsequent failure of the post-war
socialist experiments. Snow's heroes revelled in command: they loved
the arts of management and they had the strength of will to carry
through their ideas. However, all too often their administrative drive
degenerated into the black arts of manipulation, and their vision into a
stubborn disregard for alternative views. Freeman, as was typical of his
generation and class, was capable of exemplifying these virtues and
faults; he had to tread the fine line between leadership and domination
and he did so to the satisfaction of most of his staff.

Freeman, like many of his contemporaries, had moved comfortably in
the worlds of politics, the BBC, journalism and public service. His career
was marked by sudden changes and radical departures. He was educated
at Westminster School which, although not as prestigious as Eton nor as

austere and intellectual as Winchester, produced its fair share of the politicians and administrators who dominated Britain after the Second World War. The school induced a strong sense of public responsibility, a code of courtesy, and a powerful intellectual self-confidence; all characteristics which marked Freeman's career. After Westminster he went up to Brasenose College, Oxford, where he spent more time editing and writing for the magazine *Cherwell* than he did studying. After an undistinguished third in Greats, he worked in advertising for a few years until the outbreak of war. In 1940, he joined the Coldstream Guards and, after serving with great distinction in the Western Desert and in Italy, he advanced to the rank of Major.

In 1945, like many high-minded middle class men who were uncertain about their post-war prospects, Freeman stood for Parliament. Much to his surprise the massive Labour victory in the General Election of that year swept him into the House of Commons as MP for Watford.[4] Even among the glittering group who entered the House in that year, Freeman stood out. He was appointed by Attlee in 1945 as PPS to the Secretary of State for War, and rose quickly to become, in 1947, Parliamentary Secretary for the Department of Supply. Although destined for a career in government he resigned over a matter of principle and of loyalty. Along with Aneurin Bevan – subsequently an almost mythical guardian of Labour's socialist heart, although in fact engaged in a pragmatic leadership struggle with the Chancellor Hugh Gaitskell – and Harold Wilson (later Prime Minister) Freeman had been in conflict with the Cabinet over the costs of rearmament. However, the issue which precipitated the trio's resignation, much to Freeman's embarrassment, was the question of whether patients should have to pay for their false teeth. Gaitskell's first budget, in 1951, included this charge and within the month all three dissidents had resigned from the government. However, although committed to Bevan, Freeman wrote to Gaitskell acknowledging that 'breaking up the government on such a narrow issue appeared to me the height of folly'. Freeman's letter to Gaitskell concluded with the prescient, generous, and in the circumstances, remarkable assessment that 'the mark of greatness sits upon you.'

This unhappy and difficult experience of government, and Labour's electoral defeat in 1951, convinced Freeman to seek a career elsewhere. He declined to stand in the 1955 General Election and, instead, became a professional journalist. In 1958, he was appointed Deputy Editor of the influential left-wing magazine the *New Statesman* (whose assistant editor he had been since 1952) and he embarked on his famous and pioneering television series *Face to Face*, in which his relentless probing of guests as diverse as Adam Faith and Carl Jung made him a household name.

In 1958 Freeman was voted TV personality of the year. However, uncomfortable with attempts to turn him into a full-time television personality, he decided to accept the editorship of the *New Statesman* when it was offered to him in 1961. There he remained until Harold Wilson's victory in the 1964 General Election enabled him to offer his old fellow dissident a new challenge. Wilson invited Freeman to become British High Commissioner in India; Freeman was delighted to accept this post and immediately settled into the style of the Diplomatic Service.

His success in India was rewarded in 1968 with the most prestigious and glamorous of diplomatic postings – British Ambassador to the United States. This was an interesting appointment as the newly elected President, Richard Nixon, had been deeply upset by an article in the *New Statesman* in which his defeat in the 1962 California gubernatorial election had been described as 'a victory for decency in public life'. Nixon recalled this cutting analysis sufficiently to raise it at a dinner given by Wilson at Downing Street in February 1969. Nixon recalls in his memoirs, 'That evening at Downing Street would be the first time that he (Freeman) and I would be in the same room in an intimate social setting. I decided to relieve the tension by addressing it directly. In my toast after dinner I said that American journalists had written far worse things about me than had appeared in Freeman's magazines. It was now part of the past and best forgotten. "After all," I said, "he's the new diplomat, and I'm the new statesman." ' This curious ritual was sufficiently cathartic to provide Freeman with access to Nixon and to his confederates. He became a good friend of Henry Kissinger – Nixon's National Security Advisor and a key figure in the administration – and an intimate of John Mitchell, Nixon's tough Attorney General who was jailed for his part in the Watergate cover-up. This experience was instructive. Compared to these masters of intrigue and dirty tricks, LWT's machinations looked a little juvenile. Although Edward Heath, who took the Conservative Party to power in 1970, asked Freeman to remain in Washington, he decided to turn down the offer. It was time to move on again.

One of the more pressing reasons for leaving the service was his feeling that he 'had to go out and earn a living.' He was 56 and he had no savings to speak of. Moreover, if he had remained as Ambassador until he was 60, he would have little prospect of the kind of job which would have allowed him to retire comfortably, 'It was quite fun being an Ambassador,' he remembers, 'but you don't get rich on it.' LWT offered a reasonable salary and a large block of shares. Other positions would have offered just as much but LWT attracted him because it was a radical departure from anything that he had previously undertaken – a quality high on Freeman's list of reasons for doing anything. Furthermore, LWT was clearly in a mess and Freeman relished the challenge of sorting it out; moreover, as he had been tangentially involved in establishing the company he wanted to see it flourish.

Step One

It is in the nature of good leaders that luck – or what Machiavelli called virtue – accompanies them. In Freeman's case the omens immediately proclaimed that LWT had found its luck; a few days after his appointment the station sold two comedy series, *Doctor in the House* and *Doctor at Large*, for £200,000 to the US production and distribution company, Westinghouse (which also employed Frost). Moreover, on 15 February, the government halved the levy and restored a large measure of confidence in the future profitability of the industry. Neither event had anything to do with Freeman but, as a consequence of the coincidental contiguity of these events and Freeman's arrival, an aura of good fortune surrounded the new Chairman and Chief Executive.

Freeman had to undertake two immediate and pressing tasks. He had to prepare for the crucial interview with the ITA, and to find a new programme controller. The latter turned out to be reasonably simple. Although he was initially attracted to Donald Baverstock, who had been a star producer at the BBC when Freeman had been a presenter, Freeman approached instead Cyril Bennett, the only other senior ITV figure whom Freeman knew reasonably well. Dissatisfied with the film business and unhappy with his executive producer, David Susskind, Bennett was delighted to return and to prove that the company's failure had not been his fault.[5]

Despite the widespread relief which greeted Freeman's appointment, LWT still had to go through the mechanics of virtually reapplying for its contract. The ITA had invited LWT to present its case for the confirmation of the contract at a special meeting on 22 April. The endorsement of LWT's franchise was, in all probability, a foregone conclusion. Freeman was the ITA's escape route; revoking LWT's contract would have provoked several bitter struggles within the network over the control of the London Weekend advertising revenue. Freeman obviated the need to face up to the difficult consequences of sacking LWT. However, Freeman left no room for doubt – he gave a brilliantly controlled performance when LWT met the Authority.[6] Sir Brian Young recalls that Freeman was clearly in charge of his Board, knew his facts, was clear about the direction in which he wished to take the company, was committed to a recognizable public service model of broadcasting and, in general, filled the Authority with confidence that their problem child was about to grow up. The Authority confirmed the contract.

With the ITA's mandate to carry on, Freeman began to establish his power base within the company and in the network. He had to fight two battles to establish his ground – the first against the Network in general, and Thames in particular, and the second against Murdoch.

Allies of a Kind

Skirmishes with Murdoch were inevitable; it was simply part of Murdoch's temperament and style to test the mettle and character of those with whom he had a close working relationship. Freeman, however, had a powerful weapon which allowed him to control their alliance. He was prepared to leave the company if Murdoch had interfered. Murdoch, after his experience in February 1971, knew that if Freeman left then the game was over. The ITA could not have withstood the howls of protest that would have followed Freeman's departure and, however unwillingly and at an enormous cost to the network, they would have revoked LWT's contract. Freeman's calm insouciance about his position was the most powerful safeguard LWT could have had in the months after he became Chairman and Chief Executive. Freeman's comments on his relationship with Murdoch sum up the strained, but amicable, association between these two powerful men:

> It was my job to hold Murdoch in check, because to have allowed him to continue interfering in the company would have spelt simple and rapid disaster. I had very strong views about how the company should be run, but frankly I didn't give a bugger whether I stayed or not – I merely had to do the best I could. I intended to run the company my way and to hell with anyone who wanted it done differently. I always treated Murdoch with the respect which he commands personally, because he is a very formidable and able man, but I simply did not concede that he had any right to interfere in the day-to-day running of the company. We had a rather odd relationship over quite a long period and became, I hope, friends; I certainly became, and remain, fond of him, and I think that he is a decent and much abused man. However, our relationship was based on the fact that I had to prevent him doing what he wanted to do until eventually, and quite inevitably, he decided to focus his energy elsewhere.

Freeman was certain that he had the political and personal resources with which to build his defence against Murdoch's encroachment. However, there was another battle to be fought. Thames and the other three major network suppliers had to be informed that merger was no longer on the agenda.

Thames lost no time in putting pressure on Freeman. On 23 April, one day after LWT's franchise had been confirmed, Lord Shawcross, Chairman of Thames Television, wrote a letter to Aidan Crawley in which he suggested that their two companies should initiate 'some joint action on the advertising front' and, moreover, should 'cooperate with programmes so as to maintain consistently better ratings than the BBC.' Thames was still in the hunt for LWT and was determined, at the very least, to be the dominant London partner. A few days later, Crawley invited Thames' executive directors to dine with Freeman in order to, as Crawley put it, 'come to arrangements whereby we could schedule programmes broadly on a seven day basis and combine our sales operations, so as to eliminate the mutually destructive competition in which we indulge at the moment.' Freeman was determined to stop any thought of merger in its tracks and, moreover, he was suspicious of Thames' aggressive sales policy. Bert Hardy, LWT's acting Sales Director, was convinced that Thames had been consistently undermining LWT's ratings by handing over to them a low audience share on Friday night. Thames was incensed at this charge and wrote to the *Sunday Times*, which had reported LWT's complaints, stating that the size of the audience in the early evenings on Friday was not significantly different from that of any other day. The facts did not matter very much. Hardy and his new sales team were itching for the fight with Thames and the suspicion of dirty dealing constituted excellent motivation. There is nothing like an external threat to produce internal unity.

On 30 April, Freeman wrote to Crawley: 'I believe . . . that a joint sales operation might not end by being wholly in our interest.' Freeman decided, however, that the dinner with Thames would be a useful occasion on which to air a few strongly held views. On 2 June, at Crawley's house in Belgravia, Freeman and Bennett dined with Lord Shawcross, Howard Thomas and Brian Tesler – Thames' Chairman, Managing Director and Director of Programmes respectively.

The close-knit relationships at the top of British administration are exemplified by the fact that Lord Shawcross had been a colleague of Freeman's in Attlee's government. The mixed economy of post-war Britain ensured that businesses often required men whose business acumen was sometimes secondary to their political skills and contacts. It was not uncommon, therefore, for men such as Shawcross and Freeman to meet as MPs and to meet again, over twenty years later, as chairmen of companies.

Freeman used the dinner as an opportunity for some plain speaking. He complained that Thames' sales department had been traducing LWT's sales team both to advertisers and advertising agencies. This behaviour, Freeman pointed out, was unbecoming in a network partner and it had undermined LWT's natural desire to cooperate with Thames. Freeman expressed the hope that the two sales departments would cease hostilities, and that the two companies would begin to build a new partnership based on trust. A few alternatives were canvassed to symbolise the new relationship. However, these options – such as shared Outside Broadcast units, a master-control unit, and joint manufacture, storage and transportation of scenery – were tokens of an end to the conflict more than a positive effort to build bridges.

Having set the framework for LWT's relationship with Thames, Freeman persuaded a willing ITA to readjust the financial relationship between the two stations. This took several forms: Thames' rental was increased while LWT's was lowered; Thames was prevailed upon to show fewer US programmes thus allowing LWT to schedule more low cost, high ratings US programmes without breaking the overall quota for the amount of such programmes shown in the London region. Moreover, Thames was asked to increase its commitment to peak-time current affairs and documentaries in order to lessen the burden on LWT.[7]

LWT's relationship with the rest of the network improved under Freeman. The moguls in the other companies recognised in Freeman a man who could help to lead the industry, and who would command respect from politicians. Consequently, a great deal of the heat went out of the intra-network conflict. Freeman, however, was not entirely convinced that the network structure was sensible and, in May 1972, he circulated a memo to his senior executives which posed the fundamental question: 'Is our franchise in the long run viable?' Freeman believed that LWT had to broaden its base in order to justify the overheads incurred in securing its status as a network supplier. Moreover, he remained conscious that Thames retained its dominance in advertising revenue, that it had a more consistent programme strategy, and that it cast the occasional covetous glance in LWT's direction.

Freeman came to the conclusion that LWT had two options: to persuade the ITA to allocate the whole of Friday to LWT – an extremely unlikely occurrence – or to merge with one of the regional companies. If LWT went down that latter road, the new, merged company would be a network operator for the weekend and a regional company for the rest of the week. Although the Authority had set its face against a merger between any of the big five network providers there was a precedent for Freeman's plan; the ITA had allowed Yorkshire and Tyne Tees to be controlled by one company – Trident. Freeman reasoned that a similar arrangement could be established between LWT and one of the southern regional stations. Early in 1973, Freeman began discussions with Anglia Television – which held the contract for the East of England around Norwich and Cambridge (and contained several towns of which a substantial proportion of the population worked in London). Freeman liked the Managing Director, Aubrey Buxton, and admired the company's programmes. After some preliminary discussions the two companies began tentative negotiations with the ITA. However, after a couple of months, the Authority decided that they would rather not precipitate the difficult and acrimonious arguments with which the rest of the network would have greeted this news, nor did they want to disturb the network so close to the new franchise period. Consequently, they advised LWT and Anglia not to pursue the merger.

By the time the IBA had made up its mind, Freeman had changed his. It was clear by the middle of 1973 that network advertising revenue had begun to grow again, and that LWT was becoming an effective competitor with Thames. Freeman concluded that the weekend franchise could be sustained and, although he continued to press for more time for LWT on Friday, he effectively gave up on the idea of a formal merger with another company.

By the end of his first year Freeman had effectively seen off the threat of Murdoch and of merger. This was symbolised by the move to a new office block in June, 1972. The new building looked the part. In direct contrast to Stonebridge Park, the new offices overlooked the South Bank Centre which was one of the hubs of London life. It was across the river from Fleet Street, towered above the National Festival Hall and was minutes from Parliament. The studios were equipped to the highest standard and enabled the company to develop the high gloss 'look' which marked the best of its light entertainment shows. There were five studios which ranged from a small announcer's studio to the splendour of Studio 1, with its unique feature of 250 permanently fixed seats (which became a trademark in later shows). LWT's financial problems had prompted the company to negotiate a sale and leaseback deal whereby LWT rented the Centre (at around £700,000 per annum) from the Coal Industry (Nominees) – the coal industry's pension fund. Indeed, LWT's finances were sufficiently tight to force the company to sub-let some of the upper floors in the new building.

LWT's new studios and its major programme commitments required secure and growing revenue. Luck or virtue had bequeathed to Freeman an acting Director of Sales and a Head of Sales – Bert Hardy and Ron Miller respectively – who had energy, determination, a profusion of tricks and a total commitment to turning the station round.

Step Two

The emphasis on public service broadcasting in the UK often disguises the hard commercial realities which underlie the ITV network. The defenders of public service seem to believe that programmes are fuelled by good intentions and creative endeavour rather than by money furnished by advertisers to *sell* their product. The sales departments are the engine room which drive the system.

Successful sales departments are defined as those which fill the gap between what advertisers will pay without the salesman trying too hard, and the amount that can be extracted over and above the basic sum. The conditions for selling the airtime fluctuate with changing economic conditions; on occasion, the sales department has simply to take people out to lunch and wait for the cash to roll in. At other times the sales are sluggish and the salesmen have to slog hard to maintain revenue. The best departments are those which, when revenue is buoyant, continue to search for new sources in preparation for the downturn, and which, when the decline occurs, help to mitigate the effects.

In 1971, ITV's revenue crawled out of the slough of despond and registered the biggest annual increase since 1964. This was followed in 1972 by a jump of twenty three per cent and, in the following year, revenue expanded by another twenty per cent. ITV was running at full capacity and the network had to turn down £10 million of revenue which could not be accommodated.

In January 1971, after the majority of LWT's previous sales executives had been airbrushed out of the company photographs, Miller asked his secretary at Anglia, where he was sales manager, to put in a call to Rupert Murdoch. She regarded this as a momentary fit of madness and promptly forgot about it. She was astonished when Miller returned and was furious about the oversight. Ron Miller was an East-End boy made good; he had expensive tastes in suits and drink while remaining fiercely proud of his background. He wanted to work with Murdoch because he admired the latter's bruising and iconoclastic business methods. Miller rebelled against the old boy network and the deals made between chums, and he saw in Murdoch someone who likewise despised such methods.

Miller, determined to join LWT, contacted a senior figure in Murdoch's organisation, who took him for a drink at the American Bar at the Savoy. After passing this test, Miller was contacted by Bert Hardy who, after a further meeting, offered Miller a position as Sales Manager. Miller accepted the job with one proviso: he realised that he would be taking over a demoralised and, probably, divided department and he wanted to bring in a couple of his men from Anglia who would act as allies. This was accepted and Miller, with Hardy's support, began to build his own team. (LWT's position was so precarious when Miller left, that Anglia kindly allowed him two months' grace to return if LWT's franchise had not survived.)

Hardy and Miller had a major task of reconstructing LWT's image with the advertising agencies. When LWT ran into problems in 1968, the advertising agencies had scented blood and LWT, unable to face the agencies down or to develop strategies for bringing in new business, eventually relied on two big agencies – Lintas and Masius Wynne Williams – to provide more than half of their business. LWT received a guaranteed number of ads but it lost out in what it could charge; the two agencies not only offered discounts for block booking, they also tied up the peak-times at these reduced prices. The two agencies were boasting at parties and bars around the city that they had LWT sewn up. Hardy and Miller made it clear to every one that all deals were off, and that LWT was no longer a soft-touch. A few days after Miller's appointment he was called by a senior buyer in one of the agencies. 'Good luck Ron, I am sure you will turn LWT around,' the friendly voice said, 'but you will do it without my money.' At a stroke, even before Miller had started, LWT had lost one-third of its guaranteed revenue.

Miller decided to dispense with discounts and special deals. Discounts had seen the order of the day not only in LWT but around the network. In 1968, Thames introduced the preempt rate card in which discounts and surcharges could be applied to all rates according to demand. The percentages were set at three levels – 10, 20 and 30 per cent above and below standard rates – and any spot booked up to the superfix 30 per cent could be displaced by someone offering a higher rate for the spot. In a typical campaign a 10 per cent discount would be offered on a run-of-week booking, 20 per cent for run-of-month and 30 per cent for run-of-campaign. The surcharge allowed the advertising agency to select a particular commercial break subject to pre-emption.

Miller was unhappy with the pre-empt system. He thought that by offering security of tenure he would develop new business from the smaller agencies and from new advertisers.[8] This was the opening salvo in Miller's attempt to discover and exploit new sources of revenue. These new sources were important to LWT's recovery as it was obvious that soap powder manufacturers and producers of fast moving consumer goods, such as bread or eggs, had little desire to advertise on Saturdays. The shops were, by and large, closed on Sundays, and there was little opportunity for advertisers to sell their goods.

LWT's sales team, led by Hardy and Miller, began to acquire a good reputation and, indeed, outperformed everyone else in 1971 and 1972 when the company's revenue increased by 30 per cent. Freeman's willing participation in selling the company to advertisers helped Miller enormously. As an old advertising hand himself, Freeman understood the process of glad-handing and he was always available to meet advertisers and agencies if Miller required it of him. For example, Miller invited Freeman to a reception for the new sales staff and, during drinks, Freeman's secretary informed him that an important phone call had come through. Freeman was enjoying himself and asked her to take a message. 'I can't', she said, 'It's President Nixon'. Freeman looked round at the sales staff and said, 'It's a pity there are no advertisers around.'

Miller had considerable support from LWT's production staff who recognized the importance of high-profile selling. Indeed, when Miller arrived at LWT he was offered a virtually unheard of privilege – drinks with the shop stewards. Moreover, when Miller used the studios for presentations to advertisers, the staff bent the rules and made the effort necessary to make the event a success.

Miller was rewarded for the remarkable turn-around achieved by the sales team when he was appointed as Director of Sales in February 1972. At this point Hardy handed over all executive responsibility for the sales side to Miller (although he continued to serve on the Board as Rupert Murdoch's representative).[9]

Miller's productions were all singing and all dancing. His team would try anything to worm their way into the affections of the agencies and advertisers. For example, Miller invented a competition in which Sony portable colour televisions were offered to agencies and to their clients if they could predict LWT's top ten programmes for October 1973. They hired out all girl sales teams who would distribute leaflets in shopping centres and back-up advertising campaigns. At the beginning of 1974 Miller became the first European sales director to adopt a unique computer system – Broadcast Industry Automation System (BIAS) – which automatically scheduled spots over the whole year. BIAS, which ran the system from the initial order through to final invoicing, paid for itself by eliminating product clashes, incorrect scheduling, commercial and programme clashes etc, and by enabling the sales staff to confirm spots and to make accurate sales projections. In March 1974, Miller announced that LWT had expanded its direct response facilities. This allowed viewers to telephone the company with an inquiry about a product and, although several ITV companies also used this system, LWT claimed to service more clients with bigger audiences. Miller also set up a fairly disastrous European sales operation in Frankfurt, which was so bad that it won only one contract.

Miller's major breakthrough in the search for new sources of money came in 1974 when, in the middle of a bad year in which LWT was haemorrhaging advertising revenue,[10] he hit upon a plan to convince businesses to sell themselves as well as their products. In November 1974, Miller sponsored a seminar on corporate image which was a thinly disguised sales pitch for LWT. Miller argued to the assembled advertisers and agencies that 'it is vital, when confidence in business is lower than it has been for at least ten years, that companies should be trying to instill confidence in everybody from shareholders to consumers. The only way to achieve this is through corporate advertising.' Miller recalls 'We really started to motor in 1974. All of a sudden London Weekend had changed; the sales department changed from being a team of hustlers, good nitty gritty operators, to people that actually were going to lead the way the industry was going.'

While Freeman was reorganising the company and Ron Miller and Bert Hardy were resurrecting the sales department and bringing in the cash, Cyril Bennett was setting out to prove himself all over again. It was by no means an easy task.

THERE WAS THIS NICE
JEWISH BOY . . .

*Definition of chutzpah: A boy goes into the witness box
after killing both his parents and asks the judge for clemency
on the grounds that he is an orphan.*
Cyril Bennett

One cold Wednesday night in February 1975, Cyril Bennett, somewhat plump, in an immaculately cut dinner suit, stood on the stage at the Albert Hall; his head was tilted slightly up so as to make him appear both amused and proud. Fanned out behind Bennett in a V for victory were LWT producers, stars, presenters and technicians, all of whom were clutching an award from the Society of Film and Television Arts.[1] LWT had scooped up seven prizes – more than the rest of the ITV network put together. The trade magazine *Broadcast* stated quite simply, 'Wednesday was undeniably London Weekend's evening.' Two prodigals – the station and the programme controller – had returned to acclaim and to glory.

One programme dominated the ceremony – *The Stanley Baxter Moving Picture Show*. Apart from an award to the eponymous star and for the show itself (best in Light Entertainment category), it also took prizes for design (Bill McPherson), and for make-up (Lynda Beighton). The actor, Peter Barkworth, received the Best Actor award for his portrayal of Edward VIII in the play *Crown Matrimonial*, and LWT's two specialist factual programmes – the arts show *Aquarius* and the current affairs programme, *Weekend World* – were awarded for their contributions to television. On top of this haul, LWT won numerous awards from other organizations for its long-running drama series about an Edwardian family and its servants – *Upstairs, Downstairs*.[2]

This massive success was the product of sheer hard, grinding, work allied to some brilliant appointments and an enormous portion of good luck. Luck balanced by judgement and judgement followed by luck were the characteristic elements of the early Freeman–Bennett years. Their programme strategy was simple; they would produce entertainment programmes and popular dramas, rake in large audiences and substantial revenue and, at the same time, placate an increasingly restive and interventionist IBA. This strategy successfully bedded down LWT's schedule, and steered the station out of the doldrums. However, although LWT delivered two solid public service programmes, this was, in the IBA's view, insufficient payment for the considerable regulatory tolerance which the Authority had shown to the station. Full compensation had to take the form of a public service schedule, and a renewed commitment to drama and children's programmes.

Freeman was well aware of LWT's dilemma. He outlined his strategy in a memorandum to Bennett in October 1972:

> The objective is clear: with the exception of *Aquarius*, *Weekend World*, *Treasures of Britain* and not more than one or two other special prestige offerings over the next couple of years, we want to spend money on programmes which will earn high revenue and ratings, and economise on those which will not.

A few months later, he reiterated his scheme in a letter to the other network chairmen in which he complained that the IBA was indiscriminately forcing ITV to adopt a public service framework which was indistinguishable from, and interchangeable with, the BBC. Freeman felt that ITV's public service responsibilities had to be distinguished from the much more substantial obligations imposed on the BBC.

> I believe that we should try to make the Authority appreciate that there is, and was always intended to be, a difference in purpose between the BBC and ITV. There is no point in setting up commercial competition to a government-sponsored channel unless it is to cater primarily for popular taste, leaving the BBC, with its assured income, to accept the main responsibility for minority and public service interests. This is not to deny that ITV has duties to minorities; it is to assert that in a competitive system these duties can be discharged only on the foundation of commercial success . . . It is altogether too simple to argue that because ITV is entrusted with an element of public service, it must therefore accept the doctrine that it is its duty to schedule audience-losing programmes in peak-time. I dare say none of us would object, within reason, to losing an hour of audience share to the BBC in the interests of high-quality programming if it were not for the inheritance and knock-on effects of doing so. The truth is that, while the BBC schedules as ruthlessly as it currently does, the loss of a single hour – unless it is in a protected slot – may well mean the loss of an evening and this is commercially extremely serious.

These views were not secret or for internal consumption. In a speech to advertisers and to advertising agencies in November 1971 Freeman argued: 'Perhaps the most significant lesson that LWT, and the industry generally, has to learn the hard way is that, at weekends, against the relentless build-up of entertainment programming on BBC1, minority programmes at peak-time lost not only their own time-period but the entire evening's viewing. Our specialist programmes must be strategically placed with very great care. In other words: we will make these programmes because they are essential for our prestige and because they are important in their own right; however, we will quarantine them and ensure that high-ratings programmes are not infected.'

Bennett was ideally suited to the task of developing appropriate tactics with which to flesh out this strategic overview. Television breeds and feeds on 'characters' – larger than life figures who are explosively funny or manically obsessive or instinctively creative. Cyril Bennett – who was part Archie Rice and part Baruch Spinoza – was one of television's most loved figures. Even those who did not approve of him, or who thought him slightly off his head, enjoyed his company.

Bennett was an archetypal poor but fiercely ambitious East-End Jew. He was born at the beginning of the great Depression in the mid-1920s and his drive for success was also a press for material security. At the age of thirteen he was evacuated to Norfolk where he threw his energies into editing his school magazine. After leaving school in the following year Bennett harassed the editor of the London *Evening Standard* into offering him a job. He was farmed out to another Beaverbrook paper – the *Bedfordshire Times* – and, at 19, he became the youngest correspondent in the Parliamentary lobby. However, the lure of showbiz was too much and, on the strength of an interview with Frank Sinatra, he turned freelance. In 1956, the day after Rediffusion began its current affairs magazine programme *This Week*, Bennett contacted the programme's editor and submitted an item on entertainment tax which was carried the following week. Bennett was in, and he was hooked.

Bennett worked tirelessly and constantly and rose rapidly up Rediffusion's corporate ladder. In 1961 he was appointed editor of *This Week* and, under his guidance, the programme won the SFTA's award for best current affairs programme in 1962. In 1965 Bennett became Controller of Programmes at Rediffusion and, in the face of casual anti-semitism, a trace of which could be found at senior levels within the company, he was appointed to the Board.[3]

Bennett enjoyed and revelled in his Jewishness. He possessed an endless fund of Jewish stories which were tailored to suit any situation and occasion. Periodically, an unsuspecting member of the public – particularly someone who had written a pompous letter – would find themselves skewered by Bennett. For example, in response to an apparently incessant stream of letters from a university lecturer complaining about commercial breaks during a recital by Catalan cellist, Pablo Casals, Bennett wrote:

I fear that our correspondence may now assume overtones of Talmudic disputation but I will, nevertheless, attempt further clarification. (By Talmudic, I mean that my recital of the facts is now categorised as a 'defence', and since my views appear not to accord with yours, I am held to be disqualified from having them by virtue of the fact that I am part of the 'apparatus'. So, rather like the scholar who was asked to give the history of the Jews while standing on one leg, I will seek to overcome this handicap and deal with the points you raise.)

Although Bennett's background in journalism and his almost stage Jewishness are important components to understanding his decisions as programme controller, the single most important aspect to Bennett was that, quite simply, he was infatuated by television. Every facet of the process intrigued and delighted him, and his pleasure was infectious. During his first period as controller his instinctive effervescence was damped down by the confusion and conflict of those years, and the darker, depressive elements of his personality emerged. However, in the first few years of his second term all of his positive characteristics came to the fore. Michael Grade, whom Bennett brought into television, describes him in those years as 'tough, unpredictable, whimsical, penetrating, extraordinary, charismatic, funny, intelligent, and cosmopolitan'. Humphrey Barclay, one of LWT's most successful comedy producers, recalls trudging up to hear Bennett's verdict on one of his programmes. As he walked into the office, Bennett bounded over and exclaimed, 'Humphrey Barclay, you are a miracle! You walk into this office with that smile and suddenly the day is OK.' As Barclay goes on to note 'He criticized my show, but then he could then say anything he wanted after that introduction.'

While he electrified his friends with his warmth and humour, he was also respected by ITV's tough and unsentimental professionals. John Freeman believes that 'Cyril was a sort of genius. He had an absolute refusal to see difficulties if he was on to an idea.' Brian Tesler recalls that Bennett had an extraordinary intuition about the mechanics of developing a programme schedule, and he advances the scheduling of *Akenfield* – Peter Hall's evocative miniature of life in a small English village before the first war – as a case in point. Although this film had great charm and was a delight to watch, Brian Tesler, who had by then become LWT's Deputy Chief Executive (of which more in the next chapter), assumed that it would be scheduled during an off-peak slot where it would charm a couple of million viewers. Bennett had other ideas; *Akenfield* was scheduled during peak-time up against the BBC's entertainment juggernaut and the film not only won critical plaudits – which Tesler had anticipated – but also pulled in an audience of 14 million. When Tesler confessed his doubts to Bennett, the latter chuckled and said, somewhat disingenuously: 'What was so difficult about that?'

Bennett had no theory of scheduling. His views were closer to those of the veteran Hollywood scriptwriter, William Goldman, author of *Butch Cassidy and the Sundance Kid* and *All The President's Men*, who identified 'the single most important fact . . . of the entire movie industry [as]

NOBODY KNOWS ANYTHING

Not one person in the entire motion picture field *knows* for a certainty what is going to work. Every time out it's a guess – and, if you're lucky, an educated guess.' Or, to paraphrase Winston Churchill on political skill, predicting successful television programmes necessitates foretelling what is going to happen tomorrow, next week, next month and next year, and having the ability afterwards to explain why it didn't take place.

Films are, of course, different from television; they are one-off events and have to attract an audience which knows little or nothing about the story. Television, on the other hand, has the chance to build characters and, more to the point, has a guaranteed audience. On a cold November Sunday night at 8 o'clock, twenty million or more Britons will always, always, want to watch television. Moreover, in Bennett's days most of this audience was distributed between the two main channels. The trick was to turn an audience of, say, six million, into one of, say, ten million. The talent and luck of the programme controller was judged by how often and how well he bridged this gap; each additional viewer above the expected number for the time slot was an extra notch in the belt of the programme controller. Moreover, programme controllers during the 1970s and early 1980s were expected to deliver not only audiences but prestige. Every season the station had to deliver a programme or series which would impress the IBA and the other companies, and which would unsettle the BBC. (Deep down most BBC people believe that ITV should never be allowed to outclass the Corporation.)

Some programme controllers believe that audiences can be predicted from a mixture of research and technical assessment; consequently, they will transmit such and such a comedy which stars x and y at such and such a time and expect audience n. This is bread and butter scheduling, however, and while the station is unlikely to lose its audience, it is equally unlikely to make the breakthrough which is necessary to bridge the gap. Such a policy will certainly not deliver prestigious programmes. Bennett, although a skilled technician, believed firmly that success was 90 per cent luck and 10 per cent good luck. He summed up his views in the 1976 company's annual report:

The construction of a transmission schedule of programmes that succeeds creatively, critically, commercially and with big audiences is a formidable, but worthwhile objective. Sometimes it has been achieved. Sometimes, inevitably, it has not. The means are elusive, impossible to legislate, but recognisable at once.

Although Bennett had an almost mystical belief in the mysterious ways in which programmes, producers, schedules and audiences interacted, he was by no means superstitious in other respects. Ron Miller recalls him as a great hustler: 'Sometimes when he had an agent in, he would call me up before the bloke arrived and ask me to walk in during the meeting. When I arrived, I would pretend to be surprised and ask Cyril if I could see him later. Cyril would then say, "No, no, come and meet so and so, we are thinking of doing this programme with X. How much do you think it would earn?". And I would give Cyril a figure and he would say to the agent, "See what I mean? That's why I cannot meet your price." ' Hustle and sweat were as important to Bennett as luck and judgement.

Before he could take any decision, or ride his luck, Bennett had to reassert his authority within the programme division. When he arrived at LWT, the vestiges of Murdoch's programme committee remained in place, with Vic Gardiner representing the station at programme meetings. Bennett's first task was to re-create the authority of the Controller of Programmes. This was made clear in a memo despatched to Roy Van Gelder, head of personnel department, on the day that Bennett officially re-joined LWT. Bennett made it perfectly clear that the members of Murdoch's programme committee were to have no special rights in the new regime. Although Rex Firkin retained his title of Deputy Controller of Programmes, Bennett made it clear that Firkin's responsibility extended only to drama. 'I will have the benefits of Rex Firkin's skill, experience and opinions across a range of the company's output, but only in a *consultative* capacity. Firkin will have no direct programme commitment other than drama.' Bennett continued, 'In my absence, operational decisions affecting programmes will be taken by producers and/or responsible executives. Programme *policy* decisions will be taken by the Chief Executive.' A second member of the Murdoch team, Jimmy Hill, was also appointed as Deputy Controller of Programmes. Bennett recognized that 'Hill is an energetic and ambitious man, and if we now, inter alia, mark the boundary of his territory, we will anticipate and forestall future restlessness . . . As with Firkin, he will not deputize for me in my absence.'[4] The third member of the Murdoch team, Vic Gardiner, was invited to attend Bennett's fortnightly programme committee meeting but was excluded from any formal relationship with programmes – there was to be no management by committee.

Other changes included appointing John Bromley as Head of Sport and Geoffrey Hughes as Head of Features but, as Bennett did not feel that any suitable candidate had appeared, he himself took over the variety, comedy and light entertainment output. Having restructured his department he turned to programmes and, to his delight, he discovered that he had two hit drama series in the can. Stella Richman bequeathed to Bennett two of LWT's best, most enduring, and most memorable drama series – *Budgie* and *Upstairs, Downstairs*.[5] He also inherited two children's classics in shape of *Catweazle* and *Black Beauty*. Moreover, LWT's major comedy successes from Bennett's first period with the company – *Doctor at Large*, *Please Sir!* and *On the Buses* – still had some life in them. Finally, *Aquarius*, conceived during Bennett's previous time at LWT but developed, sustained and protected by Stella Richman, was gathering plaudits and awards (although some critics complained that it was patchy and lacked any real intellectual coherence).

Bennett, with his great love of television and deep fear of a second failure, threw himself unreservedly into the task of building on this roster of programmes. He needed quality and prestige to raise the profile of the station, and he wanted programmes which would pull in large numbers. The difficulty was to balance the need for revenue with the Authority's interest in public service programmes.

The time span for developing new series and programmes is such that it was the following year before Bennett's programmes began to flow through the system. However, his first full schedule, for Autumn 1971, was a winner. As ever, LWT took a substantial propoportion of its programmes from the other network companies. However, it made a much more solid contribution to its own success. Bennett created a schedule which contained some of the old series, mixed in with some borrowed from Richman, and increased LWT's ratings, on occasion, to fifty eight per cent of the London audience.

Although the actors who played the teenagers in *Please Sir!* were in their twenties and looking slightly the worse for wear, LWT persevered with them and created the spin-off series, *The Fenn Street Gang*, in which the characters began work. This series turned out to be one of the biggest hits of the Autumn. Moreover, *Please Sir!* itself continued by changing its emphasis from the pupils to the staff. The other comedy banker, *On the Buses*, returned on Sunday night. Bennett thought that he had won a major battle when he convinced the network – admittedly with some blackmail – that *Aquarius* should be fully networked. However, Lew Grade's ATV, as ever with LWT's arts output, bucked the trend and carried the show on a Tuesday night. The network's positive response to *Aquarius* raised LWT's profile and prestige.

Bennett, Firkin, and Lambert in the Drama Department at LWT came up with some powerful drama series, such as *Helen, A Woman of Today*. Moreover, the drama department delivered several prestige projects – most notably 1973's *The Last Days of Adolf Hitler*, which starred Frank Finlay (who also took the leading role in 1976's *Bouquet of Barbed Wire*), 1974's *Akenfield* – directed by Peter Hall – and the award-winning *Crown Matrimonial*.[6] Solid performers from the period included *Within These Walls*, a series about a woman's prison called Stone Park, and *New Scotland Yard* which helped to build LWT's ratings between 1971 and 1973.

Despite LWT's gleaming new studios, the glittering prizes, and Bennett's hard work, LWT was subject to stern criticism from the Authority. The IBA began its review of the network in the Spring of 1974, and on 7 October Freeman received the Authority's preliminary report.[7] The assessment opened with plaudits: 'The Authority . . . values the commitment your company has made to current affairs, with *Weekend World*, and to the Arts, with *Aquarius*, and recognizes the debt which ITV as a whole owes to the *World of Sport* team.' Then began the criticisms. First, 'despite notable successes, the performance in drama has not always been consistent'. Secondly, LWT's drama series for children did not, in the Authority's view, discharge LWT's responsibilities to this age group. Thirdly, the Authority argued that LWT could 'deploy more specialized resources and make a greater contribution than they have . . . [to] religion and adult education.' 'We wonder', the report continued, 'whether in either area there is quite the sufficiency of steady management support that, given a stable financial base, might be expected.' Fourthly, the IBA stated categorically that the station's heavy dependence on bought-in material was unacceptable. Fifthly, the report asserted that the station should increase its commitment to local programmes. Finally, the Authority suggested that LWT explore cross-scheduling with Thames and perhaps establish a common scheduling unit.

Freeman, irritated by the headmasterly tone of the ITA's letter, and of the opinion that LWT should not be forced into making worthy but dull drama, asked for clarification. The Authority's response was pointed. It noted that alongside *Budgie* and *Helen: A Woman of Today*, LWT had also made the critical and popular failures such as *Tales of Piccadilly*, *The Adventures of Don Quick*, *The Frighteners* and *Diamond Cut Diamond*. Furthermore, the letter from Lord Aylestone said, simply but forcefully, that LWT did not have a record of producing original plays from new or well-known dramatists. The letter asked in the bluntest of terms, 'Can there be some causal relationship between the uneven achievement of LWT drama and the proportion of full-time to freelance staff employed in your drama department? Do you have anything that can, in the normal sense of the term, be described as a drama department at all?'

Freeman was angered by the IBA's comments. In a draft reply before he calmed down, Freeman wrote, 'The blunt answer to the first question is "No" and to the second "Yes".' Tesler, who had been at the station for a year by this time, and still had the benefit of an outsider's perspective, thought that the IBA was correct. The departure of middle management in the drama and children's departments had left LWT's output looking threadbare. Moreover, Tesler's long experience with the Authority suggested another strategy. It would be better, he argued to Freeman, to disarm the Authority by promising that LWT would expand its commitment to drama and children's programmes in 1975.

Freeman was unconvinced. The IBA, he argued simply did not understand how the system at LWT worked. He pointed out to the Authority that LWT had to be flexible in order to attract the cream of London's talent. Freeman thought that the most skilled and sought-after of London's producers and directors wanted to work on a contract basis – although this did not necessarily imply short-term employment as testified by the presence of John Hawkesworth (six years) and Verity Lambert (four years). Freeman held the opinion that LWT did not need a drama department in the conventional sense; indeed, he felt that in-house productions might have an unnecessarily constricting and stultifying effect on the company's output. LWT's problems stemmed, Freeman thought, from a widespread lack of writing talent.

Freeman rebutted the IBA's other points. LWT was beginning to address itself to children's programmes, and had started a new series entitled *London Bridge*. LWT relied on bought-in material, he pointed out, because it had overproduced for the network and therefore, as the result of a lack of appropriate weekend material from the rest, LWT had to shore up its schedules by using US shows. Freeman closed his response to the Authority by making soothing noises about working together with Thames in an atmosphere of good will, but without offering firm promises of anything remotely approaching a joint scheduling unit.

Freeman's arguments did not sway Brian Young. When the IBA extended LWT's contract in May 1975, many of the criticisms were repeated:

> although the company has had noticeable successes and has for the most part maintained a high standard, its record has at times been uneven. We have had discussions with the company on possible advantages and disadvantages of alternative ways of planning and organizing drama output in order to maximize the prospects of successful achievement in this most demanding area of production.
>
> In relation to religion and adult education, the company has over the last two years reorganized its administrative arrangements for these aspects of its programming, and has assured us that its efforts in this field will continue to be given full management support.

If the station's drama met with mixed responses, much of its variety output was considered to be highest quality. LWT's production staff adored top-of-the-range glossy spectaculars, and care and attention was lavished on stars such as Stanley Baxter and Tommy Steele. Baxter, Bennett's favourite performer, summed up the spirit of LWT in the mid-1970s:

> I've always had a sort of bleak contempt for the concept of 'company loyalty'. It evokes images of Japanese electronic workers cossetted from cradle to grave by Big Daddy Sanyo in return for feudal

commitment to the firm. In show-business or the arts, company loyalty seems to me not only distasteful but dangerous. Security and continuity of employment are perhaps important to the servicing departments of a television company – but surely the shows' devisers and performers must break rules, live by their wits and survive only if they succeed nine times out of ten. This preamble is by way of an apology for the verging-on-panegyric that follows. It is in spite of my reflective distrust of organisations that I announce a love of LWT that happened almost at first sight. Certainly at first sight of Cyril Bennett who contrasted so dramatically with BBC executives of the upper echelons. It wasn't that the Beeb ones were horrid or supercilious: they were often donnish and charming but they breathed a rarefied air that always left me gasping for the aroma of the market place, with the sensation I'd had a close encounter, rather than an offer, a decision, or a 'go-ahead' about anything . . . And here was dear Cyril doing Groucho Marx impressions and plotting and questioning with non-mandarin anxiety and vulnerability. He didn't hope that my joining the organization would widen the spectrum and prove mutually beneficial or ANYTHING abstract. When I said I thought I'd like to start with three half hours he said: 'Oh for Christ's sake give us four – the Beeb'll think we don't TRUST you.' From that day . . . I realized that David Bell [Baxter's friend and producer at both the BBC and LWT] was right when he said that I would find LWT friendlier than the [BBC Television] Centre – 'I think' he added 'the cosier thing came from terror. They had a rotten start – have only two-and-a-half days a week, and it's a battle for survival.'[8]

Bennett's Groucho Marx impression indicates the extent of his love for performers. However, John Freeman once remarked that Cyril Bennett's greatest contribution to television was in the arts and current affairs. In part, Freeman was referring to Bennett's career with *This Week*, and to his staunch support and encouragement of *Aquarius*. However, the primary reference alluded to Bennett's commitment to a group of talented, aggressive and determined ex-Granada producers which produced LWT's flagship network current affairs programme *Weekend World*, and its highly-regarded local affairs show, *The London Programme*.[9]

When Freeman arrived at LWT one of his first priorities was the development of a programme of which the ITA could be proud. Moreover he, and Bennett, wanted LWT to be known for a series which made an important contribution to television journalism – both were, after all, distinguished practitioners of the form. The high-quality current affairs programme which was to emerge would, Freeman argued, be scheduled outside of peak-time. He cited as support for this judgement the excellence of some of the US networks' current affairs shows. These had a major impact on the political life of the country despite their off-peak slots.

Bennett mulled over the idea of a new current affairs programme in the Autumn of 1971. It was then that he stumbled on the man whom he realized might be able to create the programme for him – John Birt.

Birt arrived at *Weekend World* through the circuitous route of the *Frost Programme*. Frost's 1970 series had been dismal and the production staff were in open rebellion. They made it clear that Frost could not retain close editorial control over the programme and spend most of his time in the US. Even Frost's closest colleagues were aware of the danger that he was becoming a jack-of-all cultures and master of none. Antony Jay, Frost's adviser on the series, wanted the new series to come under the control of a fresh, and strong, producer. When Birt's name came up, it struck a chord with Frost who had already met him when the former had travelled to New York to produce a *World In Action* programme in which Frost was featured. Frost and Birt had chatted about *Nice Time*, a sketch and chat show which starred, among others, Germaine Greer and Kenny Everett, and which Birt had coproduced. Frost felt that Birt was an ideal producer; he combined a popular and satirical background with a good track record in current affairs.

After chatting to Birt about the prospect of becoming Frost's producer, Jay passed Birt's name to Bennett. Birt negotiated a package in which he would produce some single documentaries and some of the *Aquarius* series, as well as working with Frost. At the age of 27, and already editor of one of Britain's most important programmes, Birt was set for a rapid rise in Granada. However, he gave up editing *World In Action* after a year and he moved to London while still working with Granada. At that point Granada was the site of a flowering of talented producers and researchers; consequently few programme ideas reached the screen from any one person. Birt wanted to produce more programmes and was keen to work in London. Moreover, in his tie-die shirt, clogs and shoulder-length hair, Birt, according to one of his friends, thought that LWT was 'trendier than slightly stuffy old Granada.' LWT was certainly virgin territory for a determined young producer.

John Freeman recalls the excitement which Birt engendered: 'Cyril said that he had discovered this young man at Granada whom he thought would make an excellent executive. I met John Birt, and had a look at a couple of his programmes, and I became very high on him – he was extremely good news. From that moment on, Cyril and I agreed that not only must he be brought into the company – despite the opposition from those in the company who disliked Granada and thought that John was a trouble-maker. We felt that under John LWT would have a great future in current affairs.'

The 1972 Frost series was widely considered to be one of his best. Birt and Frost took off around the world to conduct a series of powerful interviews. Most noticeably, in February 1972, the week after Bloody

Sunday – when thirteen Roman Catholics were shot dead by the Army after a civil rights march in Derry – Frost went to the city with an LWT outside broadcast unit and conducted a discussion in a community centre before going to Belfast for another debate. The programme also went to Bangladesh within days of its declaration of independence from Pakistan, and also conducted a long interview with Ian Smith, the Prime Minister of Rhodesia.[10]

During the making of the Frost series, Bennett asked Birt to take on the responsibility of LWT's new current affairs programme. Birt was, initially, unenthusiastic and needed to be persuaded by Bennett.[11]

Even after he took on the task Birt was sometimes stronger on what he disagreed with in other current affairs programmes than he was in developing new ideas for the prospective programme. Moreover, Bennett and Freeman were unhappy during the first series. *Weekend World*, as the new programme was called, had exceeded its budget, seemed fussy and inelegant, and had achieved little that seemed new or fresh. Jane Hewland, one of the original researchers, recalls the beginnings of the programme:

> The first six weeks were in a dreadful rat-infested little bunker, and I sat there absolutely petrified among all the brilliant people holding forth. Then it went wrong. John fired about a third at Christmas, in a night of the long knives, and then there was a kind of protracted warfare with other people, and another third disappeared by one means or another. Eventually, there was a handful of us working every weekend, up every night, all night. The last six weeks were terrible; it was just a fog of tears.

Out of this chaos materialized one of the most talked-about current affairs programmes of the 1970s. *Weekend World* became widely recognized as a serious, powerful programme. On 13 November 1972, Freeman received a note from Brian Young, Director General of the IBA, which congratulated LWT on starting *Weekend World* and added:

> Its success will never be measured in ratings – though to equal, in a month or two, the reach of say the *Sunday Telegraph* is no mean achievement. But the distinction which the programme's lively and serious approach to news adds to our schedule is something that the [Programme Schedule] Committee values.

Birt remembers the first year as 'a year of discovery. Through all of these disasters we emerged at the end of the series with some creditable programmes and we discovered the formula which became the embryonic *Weekend World*.' In the second series, after much thought and deliberation, Birt and the production team came up with single issue, focused, analytical programmes, presented by Peter Jay. This format established a series which was regarded for a considerable number of years as one of the company's most consistent successes.

As the result of the success of the *Frost Programme* and of *Weekend World*, Birt was promoted to be Head of Current Affairs in the Spring of 1974. His task was to develop the new series with Barry Cox – a producer and director with *World in Action* – entitled *The London Programme*.[12]

Again a curious mixture of luck and judgement mingled in the production of this show. The IBA was leaning heavily on all of the companies and, in particular, on LWT to commit more resources to local programmes. Barry Cox, meanwhile, had been working on a programme in Liverpool where he had become impressed by his researcher's intimate knowledge of the city. Cox thought it possible that a team of researchers could acquire the same understanding of London. He discussed the idea with Birt and then Birt submitted a two-and-a-half page synopsis to Bennett in which he stated that the programme would capture the 'power and money' of London. Curiously, the idea that London could be treated as a distinct subject for a current affairs programme had not struck anyone before. However, Bennett endorsed the idea of the series and of Barry Cox as producer. The programme embarked on a number of investigative reports which established it as a serious and powerful current affairs programme. Cox and two of his colleagues chronicled the crime, corruption and problems of the capital. The major coup in the early days involved the constant probing of the corruption of Metropolitan Police. These programmes earned the respect of their contemporaries and put the programme on the map. A measure of the show's success and durability is that at the time of writing this chapter in 1990 – fifteen years after the first programme, and three Controller of Programmes later – the *London Programme* is still running and has just won the Royal Television Society's Regional Programme Award for the third time in four years.[13]

Storm Clouds

Bennett's crushing work-load, and his inability to focus on the long view, had worried Freeman almost from their first month together. By October 1972 Freeman was imploring Bennett to delegate more and to take some rest. 'I doubt if anybody could carry indefinitely the load of day-to-day detail that you have been carrying', Freeman wrote to Bennett. 'Certainly no other Programme Controller attempts to do so much; nor, you may be interested does the Prime Minister or the President of the United States! This is bad for you and bad for the company.' Apart from a natural, human concern that Bennett was pushing himself too hard, Freeman felt that his programme controller was bogged down in technical details and, consequently, was not developing a strategic overview of LWT's needs and of its future. 'We must move on from our hard-won breathing space to long term prestige and security' Freeman argued. He instructed Bennett to divest himself of many of his self-imposed responsibilities and to create more time for planning. Freeman had two specific recommendations, 'I think that you would be well advised to create an organization within which you can delegate the routine work, leaving yourself time to think ahead about the strategy of programming and expenditure – not only scheduling – to take fully considered decisions comfortably ahead of deadlines and to impose standards of quality control and programme judgement which you have been forced to forego in the first year's battle for LWT's survival. I also think it would be quite nice for you if you could occasionally finish your work in time to get to bed before 3 am!' 'Secondly,' wrote Freeman, 'there seems to me to be an urgent need for a Head of Light Entertainment and/or Head of Comedy . . . through whom you could start to insist on higher standards without having to become personally involved in production details or lengthy script reading.'

Bennett generally found it difficult to delegate. In 1972, however, mindful of Freeman's concerns, the reluctant delegator discovered someone whom he thought he could train, whom he admired, found amusing, and whom, therefore, he wished to appoint as Head of Light Entertainment. Michael Grade – nephew of Lew Grade, one of Bennett's friends – was 25 when he turned up on Bennett's doorstep to sell him some variety programmes. Grade had taken over his father's talent agency while his father convalesced from a serious illness and was therefore in contact with Bennett as a client. Bennett was, however, unimpressed by Grade's pitches. He was about to show Grade the door, when the young man began to invent a programme on the spot. A delighted Bennett's attention was grabbed and held while Grade, from the germ of an idea, created a programme about impressionists which eventually saw the light of day as a long running series called *Who Do You Do?* (the show's durable format was recycled over a decade later in the form of *Copycats*).

Bennett regarded this invention as evidence that Grade possessed his uncle's energy and, to use a favourite Bennettism, chutzpah. Although Bennett wanted to hire Grade, the arrangements could not be finalized until Grade's father had recovered. A year later Grade felt that he could extricate himself from the family business. However, he was deeply reluctant to tell his father that he wanted to leave. Freeman appreciated the young man's dilemma and offered to tell Leslie Grade himself – an act which immediately provoked the younger man's admiration and devotion. Freeman flew to the South of France, where Grade's father was convalescing, and asked if it would be acceptable for LWT to approach his son. Grade senior bestowed his patriarchal blessing and the television career of one of the most powerful men in the business was under way.

Grade could do little to prevent Bennett's all consuming zeal for the minutiae of programmes. Moreover, in the short term Bennett did little to alleviate one of LWT's long-running failings – the inability to replace the crop of popular situation comedies with which the station was launched. Bennett felt this loss keenly and, in a letter to a journalist friend who asked him to explain LWT's problems, Bennett explained:

> I try – as I was instructed by my guru, Frank Muir – to select series in which the comedy arises from the interplay of the characters. I reject, out of hand, those which are based on a predicate ('I know – the Advertising Executive who inherits a sauna bath in his old aunt's will!') which are held up, if at all, by a stream of fast moving visual gags . . . Frank calls these 'how about' series. Unfortunately – and this isn't a cop-out – the writing talent is so strained that what starts off as a concept deeply rooted in character, quite often runs for the safety of 'comedy business' (known in the trade as the 'Joey-Joeys) – I have actually heard writers, looking at their mirthless work, exclaiming in desperation 'Christ, where are the Joey-Joeys?'. However, we try.[14]

Humphrey Barclay, who produced several of LWT's most interesting comedies, believes that Bennett's problem was impatience and, in a sense, fear. Barclay recalls that when they were just completing thirteen episodes on a *Doctor* series, Bennett called him and asked him to come up with another thirteen immediately. It was one of Bennett's bankers and he was determined to have a sufficient number to play with. However, he was killing it in the process. This tactic failed drastically with one of LWT's more interesting comedies *No, Honestly*, based on Charlotte Bingham's novel, *Coronet Among the Weeds*, and starring husband and wife partnership, John Alderton and Pauleen Collins. These two have been associated with LWT almost from its first day, first with Alderton in *Please Sir!*, then both together in *Upstairs, Downstairs*, when Collins achieved rapid fame as the maid, Sara.[15]

Bennett contributed to the success of the first series of *No, Honestly* by convincing Barclay that his original ideas for the programmes, which involved exploding words and tricksy camera angles, was too knowing. 'Cut all the shit', Bennett exclaimed at a meeting, 'this is a romance; just tell a simple story.' The unadorned romance worked; the series was a great success and Alderton and Collins were voted top of the readers' poll in the *TV Times*. However, realizing he was on to a winner, the miser came out in Bennett. He told Barclay to put another series into production immediately. The stars, who were tired and wanted to try out other things before returning to the characters, eventually, and unwillingly, withdrew from the series. The first decent situation comedy in four years was lost by Bennett's, perhaps understandable, but nonetheless destructive, impatience.

Bennett's previous experience at LWT, and his sense that good programmes came rarely and were the product of luck, had instilled in him an exaggerated regard for 'bankers'. He drove each successful series to the very edge of its creative credibility until eventually nothing was left in the bank. When the network went into one of its periodic nosedives, LWT had trouble recovering.

CAMELOT, NEAR CROYDON

In the blistering heat of June 1976 Brian Tesler, who had been appointed as LWT's Managing Director a few weeks before, arrived at Brompton Road for lunch with the Director General of the IBA. In the small private dining room at the top of the IBA's offices, Brian Young in his mild – but unmistakably didactic – manner inquired of Tesler, 'Don't you think that you should be spending more time on less financially rewarding programmes?' Tesler, a veteran of ITV politics, warily countered with a question of his own, 'What do you have in mind?' Young, having set up the opportunity, pressed home his point, 'In religion and local programmes you certainly do the hours, but we are not absolutely certain that they receive as much of your programme department's attention as they might. Perhaps you ought to take a close look at the problem.'

Although the tone of this understated admonition irritated Tesler he was not surprised at its content. ATV had, a few months before, sent out a warning to the rest of ITV after it had been hauled in by the IBA and informed that it had to increase its commitment to local programmes. Moreover, the IBA had let it be known in the station reviews that it expected the franchise holders to fulfil the spirit as much as the letter of their public service responsiblities.

Tesler, sitting in the back of his car as it crawled through the traffic across the Thames, reflected that the IBA's assessment of LWT's features was correct. Apart from Charlie Squires' various excursions, such as *Derby Day*, LWT's features output had been undistinguished. Bennett and Freeman had sacrificed features in order to create financial breathing space in the early 1970s, and Bennett, after his successful years, had still not progressed beyond the strategy which lay behind his rescue schedule.

Tesler arrived back at Kent House in a thoughtful mood, and he dropped in on Bennett to inform him of Young's 'advice'. Before Tesler had a chance to speak, Bennett growled, 'I've just been to lunch with Bernard Sendall [the IBA's deputy Director General]. He was moaning about our local features.' Tesler smiled: both he and Bennett had been invited to the same building, on the same day, at the same time, to lunches after which the same advice was proferred. 'We can take a hint', he thought.

Tesler, who wished to mark his ascendance within the company by encouraging an innovative and expanding programme division, had set in motion a plan for a creative conference at which he would explain his ideas to his programme-makers and listen to their plans for the future. He and Bennett decided that this gathering was the ideal location in which to discuss ways of generating a different approach to features. Neither Tesler, nor Bennett, could have anticipated, however, that they were initiating LWT's golden age of public service programmes.

Over the five years that followed the conference LWT created a minorities unit from which emerged series about (and eventually by) ethnic minorities. Moreover, the unit took the controversial step of producing a series about and for homosexuals, entitled *Gay Life*. Also, in a couple of documentary series such as *Wedding Day*, which followed six weddings from different religious traditions, LWT began to examine the rich cultural diversity of London life. The station made important breakthroughs in the arts with the much-garlanded *South Bank Show* and in the coverage of religion with *Credo*, one of the most consistently interesting and reflective current affairs series about religion yet delivered by British television.

There was a great deal more to this phenomenon than could be traced to two lunches at the IBA. In the mid-1970s the intellectual arguments about independent television were being won by those who regarded it as part of the public service framework pioneered by the BBC. The Annan Committee, which reported on 23 March 1977, had explored options for the future of broadcasting and was composed of people such as Philip Whitehead and Dipak Nandy who were predisposed to regard ITV as ripe for change. The Labour Government was pledged to act on the basis of the report and, in particular, the Committee was to have a large influence in the allocation of the fourth channel which ITV desperately wanted. Consequently, the ITV companies had to demonstrate their credentials as public service broadcasters. No one in ITV could afford the condemnation similar in scope and intensity to that delivered by the Pilkington Committee and the IBA, in particular, was determined not to be defamed a second time.

A second strand which led to this Golden Age was the appointment of Lady Plowden as Lord Aylestone's successor at the IBA. A daughter of an Admiral, Lady Plowden became Chairman of the Central Advisory Council for Education (England) and Vice-Chairman of the BBC. She was convinced that television could be and should be a force for public good. Lady Plowden and Brian Young would have a decisive impact on the renewal of the franchises and the ITV companies, aware of the views of this powerful team, became very conscious of the need for solid and interesting public affairs programmes. Another significant appointment at the IBA was that of Colin Shaw as Director of Television in March 1977. Shaw spent seven years as Secretary to the BBC, during which time he became a master of creative fudge and an acknowledged tribal elder to whom the governors and the Board of Management could turn for advice. Brian Young's recruitment of this figure, so clearly identified with the BBC, signalled his intention fully to bind ITV into the public service system.

In the mid-1970s Brian Young summed up his view that: 'Public service broadcasting and revenue from advertising *are* compatible.'

> Much of television has no great pretentions except to pass an hour or so pleasantly for the viewer in his home. And indeed, this side is essential, not merely because viewers want this from their sets very often, but also because the serious things which television can do are only possible if they are inlaid with those things which attract the viewer when he does not want to be informed or taught or enriched in any way. Television's power to do good must rest on the broad base of its providing something which is easily watched. Its main task is not a highbrow one; it aims to make what is popular good, and what is good popular.

As well as these pressures from the IBA, from Annan, and from the Labour Government, LWT's producers responded to new and insistent ideas about television for minorities which were emerging from several sources – most notably from Anthony Smith, a former BBC producer and advisor to the Annan committee. In the early 1970s, Smith wrote a series of influential articles in the *Guardian* in which he proposed that the prospective fourth channel should be set up along the lines of a publishing house, and that programme-makers, or any one else with an urge to speak out about something, should be provided with the facilities and/or the finance to do so. This caught the spirit of the mid-1970s, during which Britain seemed to be tearing itself apart: political and cultural nationalism in Scotland and Wales was in the ascendant and, in Northern Ireland, Catholics and Protestants were paying for their nationalist aspirations with their lives. In England's inner cities, racial tension, focused on neo-Nazi groupings, appeared to melt any hope of class or cultural cohesion between immigrants and their fellow workers.

Blacks – not yet politically delineated into Asians (or, more clearly, religious or ethnic sub-groupings, such as Muslim or Sikh) and Afro-Caribbeans – considered themselves an underclass: under-represented in the media and, even worse, traduced by television programmes which relied on racial stereotypes of black people as Rastas, criminals, prostitutes, shop-keepers or, occasionally hospital janitors.[1] In the 1970s, therefore, the politics of ethnic identity was a rod for the backs of broadcasters, and a conspicuous challenge which public service broadcasting had to meet.

Other cultural transformations increased the pressure on broadcasters. The post-war phase of the feminist movement had reached boiling point. The decriminalization of homosexuality, and the explosion of Gay Rights movements onto the streets and into the clubs forced an issue onto the agenda of broadcasting which previously had been, with one or two noticeable exceptions, hidden. For a short period in the mid-1970s, teenagers created a sense that they were genuinely alienated from British life – the schlock-horror of the Sex Pistols compelled broadcasters to give some thought to their programmes for young people.[2]

These intellectual, cultural and institutional forces would not have effected changes in ITV and LWT if advertising revenue – which increased from £209 million in 1975–76 to £525 million in 1980–81 – had not been booming. Furthermore, in 1974 the Government began charging the levy on profit rather than revenue, and the ITV companies' resources for programme-making, and therefore their abilities to take more risks, grew apace. Finally, the long period between the 1967 and 1980 franchise rounds produced, despite Annan's deliberations, a sense of continuity and, almost, tradition, which in its turn allowed ITV to address itself to a renewed commitment to new and innovative work.[3]

The Next Leap Forward

One of the ironies of LWT's history is that Brian Tesler, who appeared destined to lead Thames, LWT's brother-in-rivalry, instead succeeded Freeman at LWT. At the end of 1973, when Howard Thomas, Thames' Managing Director, was due to retire, it was assumed that Tesler would be his natural successor. This apparently amicable and natural hand-over shuddered to a halt, however, when John Reid, the Chairman of Thames' major shareholder, Thorn-EMI, was unhappy that Tesler was employed through his own private company rather than as a direct employee of Thames and, moreover, that Tesler's contract was being negotiated by a business adviser.

Tesler, aware that others within the Thorn-EMI group had a similar arrangement to that which he was seeking for himself, continued to press his claims. Reid made it clear that he expected Thomas to face Tesler down, and the former, unable to find a compromise, decided that Tesler could not be supported and offered the position instead to George Cooper, Thames' Director of Sales.

Tesler was hurt by Thomas's lack of support over what Tesler regarded as a matter of extraordinary irrelevance. Industry veterans of the period recall Tesler looking upset and depressed at the round of Christmas parties which followed Thomas's decision. John Freeman, astonished by what he considered an asinine miscalculation by Thames, had more than commiserations to offer. Freeman had been looking for a successor as part of his long-term plan to convince the IBA, and the City when the company went public, of LWT's stability and continuity. He discounted the two internal candidates, Cyril Bennett and Vic Gardiner. The first seemed insecure and unpredictable and the second, who had been *de facto* Managing Director for a short time in early 1971, appeared wedded to the past and, moreover, he did not have the full confidence of the programme-makers. Tesler, whom Freeman had admired for several years, was ideal.

Poaching a senior figure from a fellow ITV company was a delicate and, necessarily, secretive task. Freeman asked Robert Clark, who had been a director at ABC and had subsequently bought shares in LWT during the financial imbroglio of 1970, to determine Tesler's interest. After several phone calls, and tentative discussions, Tesler was invited to lunch at Freeman's house near Kew Gardens. The two men wandered around the gardens and discovered that despite dissimilar backgrounds they had much in common – not least a birthday, a fondness for hard-boiled American crime fiction, and a dislike of intellectual snobbery – and, as they drifted back to Freeman's house for lunch he outlined his proposal that Tesler come to LWT as Deputy Chief Executive, with the guarantee that in due course he would succeed Freeman.

Tesler was disappointed. Having missed the top job at Thames, he wanted the equivalent position at LWT. Eventually, however, as he thought about it over the days which followed, he became convinced of the good sense behind Freeman's suggestion that the company would need time to adjust to the change and that he needed to build solid relationships with the staff if he was to achieve anything.

Tesler was free to move to LWT. His contract at Thames had lapsed and, as a consequence of the struggles for succession, no one had thought to renew it. Consequently he owed neither moral nor financial loyalty to Thames. He invited Freeman to a reciprocal lunch after which, in Tesler's study, the two men struck the deal which assured the success of Freeman's plans for an orderly succession.

Although Brian Tesler was 45 years old when he joined LWT, he had been at the top in ITV for 13 years. He was 32 when he was appointed as programme controller at ABC in 1961 and, in the following year – after demonstrating his abilities in the black arts of scheduling and, more particularly, his managerial acumen – he became the first programme controller to be appointed as a director of an ITV company.[4] Six years later one of the conditions attached to the award of the contract to the company which became Thames was that Tesler should be Director of Programmes.[5]

Tesler was a model post-war grammar school boy. In 1949, the combination of driving ambition, hard work at school and a state scholarship propelled him into Oxford (via a two-year National Service detour in British Forces Broadcasting Service in Trieste where he became a DJ, a sportscaster, a writer and producer). While at Oxford his passionate interest in drama and literature dominated his social and intellectual life. As well as serving for three terms as drama editor of *Isis*, he acted in productions for the Oxford University Drama Society (OUDS), wrote and performed for student revues and cabaret, and was both actor and director in the Oxford University Experimental Theatre Club of which he became President. While at the ETC he adapted and directed plays for the Oxford Radio Society which confirmed an interest in broadcasting which first surfaced in the army.

Tesler did not adopt the self-conscious and often priggish intellectualism of the grammar school generation. He enjoyed red-nosed variety and popular radio as much as Ibsen or Strindberg. He wrote popular songs, acted and directed in student dramas, and generally set about heartily enjoying Oxford. At the end of his three years at Exeter College he was awarded a first class degree in English Language and Literature, which, in the insular and hermetic world of Oxford, furnished him with a currency which could have been converted into a career in various Establishment institutions: the City, Parliament and, of course, the BBC Talks Department.

The Oxford intellectual style which, in the words of Ernest Gellner, the most trenchant critic of Oxford thought in the 1950s, 'converted understatement into a philosophy' did not attract Tesler. Gellner, who was one part mongoose to two parts virtuoso, savagely attacked Oxford culture in his polemic *Words and Things*:

> [We] have here a sub-group consisting of people who belong to, or emulate, the upper class in manner; who differentiate themselves from the heartier rest of the upper class by a kind of heightened sensibility and precariousness, and, at the same time, from the non-U kind of intelligentsia by a lack of interest in ideas, arguments, fundamentals or reform.

This vitriol was directed at the cult of Wittgenstein around which philosophy was organised in the 1950s, but similar charges were often laid at the door of Oxford intellectual trends. Tresler could have been swallowed up by the sometimes crippling preciousness and dry-as-dustness of university life, but he decided, instead, to emigrate to a different world altogether. In September 1952 he joined the wide boys, the clowns, the Denmark Street song writers, and the variety agents in the BBC's light entertainment department – the first graduate trainee so to do.[6]

The light entertainment specialists were not at all pleased to receive the emigré. Tesler was having a hard time at his interview with the BBC's Appointment's Officer, who was clearly uninterested in him until, in response to the final question, 'Is there anything else of relevance to your application?', Tesler blurted out, 'I'm a songwriter, and some of my songs have been broadcast'. 'Broadcast?', asked the incredulous bureaucrat, looking up at the candidate for the first time. Tesler nodded. 'On the BBC?', Tesler nodded once more. The man reopened the file and Tesler explained that several of his songs – co-written with the composer Stanley Myers – had been recorded by, among others, the Ted Heath Orchestra and Terry Thomas.[7] Subsequent to this close shave, Tesler was interviewed by the BBC's Head of Light Entertainment – Ronnie Waldman – and he was offered a job.

Tesler began his ascent up the corporate ladder as the producer of *Pet's Parlour*, a show starring the singer and actress Petula Clark, on which most young light entertainment producers were blooded. He threw himself into the job and learned how to put together variety bills, negotiate with agents who would happily take off your arms at the elbow and come back for the rest as interest, find new songs, rehash old tunes and generally attract and hold an audience. The graduate became a trouper.

In 1956, however, the cosy world of the BBC light entertainment was shattered by the success of the parvenue, ITV, and by the large salaries offered by the new companies. By coincidence, Tesler's contract was due for renewal at the end of 1956 and, confident that the BBC would recognize his loyalty in remaining with the Corporation despite tempting offers from ITV, he asked for an increase in his salary from £1,700 to £1,800. The Corporation, with its customary view that working for the BBC was reward enough, refused. When Tesler was informed of the BBC's decision he was producing a show which involved Eamonn Andrews, whose agent, Teddy Sommerfield, noticed that Tesler was depressed. On discovering the reason he asked if Tesler would allow him to have a word with ATV which, under Lew Grade, was keen to take the lead in high quality light entertainment. Tesler was offered £3,500 to join Grade and, because this was below the sum asked for by Sommerfield, ATV threw in a guaranteed two weeks 'business' trip a year to New York. Tesler, flabbergasted but delighted, jumped the divide (and Sommerfield became his business advisor).

By the end of his contract with ATV – during which he became a highly regarded producer, taking charge of *Sunday Night at the London Palladium* at its height and earning the first award for Light Entertainment Production from the SFTA – Tesler had learned the rudiments of the ITV system. However, he was unhappy with working within a company and convinced that he wanted to become a freelance producer. Sommerfield set up a number of deals whereby Tesler would spend half the year working for the BBC and the other half for various ITV companies. However ABC's Howard Thomas, on hearing that Tesler was available, invited him to become Head of Features and Light Entertainment. Tesler was promoted rapidly and within two years was Director of Programmes. By the mid-1970s he had immense experience, was skilled politically, and was widely acknowledged within the industry as the most expert manipulator of schedules in British television.

Tesler's long experience of producing variety shows in which drunken Yugoslav jugglers competed for his attention with over-the-hill American crooners, and prima donnas and prima ballerinas demanded total devotion before they would perform, stood him in good stead for unravelling the mysteries of the ITV networking arrangements and for coping with the capriciousness of the ITV barons.

Over the next fourteen years, he worked the committee system, did not make enemies, built up his reputation and experience and, despite his showmanship and his intellectual ability, did not grandstand or barnstorm in the fashion of Lew Grade, Cyril Bennett and Michael Peacock. He was widely regarded as being among the brightest and best of his generation. At Thames he was a safe pair of hands throughout the various crises of the late 1960s. Thames's roster of programmes – which included gritty dramas such as *Callan*, *Special Branch*, and *Public Eye*, variety from the likes of Frankie Howerd, Max Bygraves, Benny Hill and Tommy Cooper, and major documentary series, such as the classic *World at War* – consistently beat the rest of the network.[8] Evidence of Tesler's skill is clearly seen in Thames' comparative ratings decline after Tesler's departure.

Tesler was ideally placed between Bennett and Freeman. He shared Bennett's showbiz image. He wore expensively cut suits, was invariably suntanned as if returning from an exclusive beach, and illustrated his points with tales from his days as producer of *Sunday Night at the London Palladium*. He was closer to Freeman, however, in his opinions of how best to run an organization. He delegated responsibility and expected those to whom he gave power to exercise it without constantly referring upwards.

Those few who did not like Tesler considered him unduly circumspect and a company man. Even some ITV colleagues who admired him were disappointed that he did not deploy his intellectual talents more systematically and more publicly. Those who worked closely with him, however, realized that the last word was invariably his, and that even when it wasn't, he had achieved much of what he intended. He belonged to the Cheshire cat school of management and was often at his most dangerous when grinning and apparently fading from the argument. This attribute disconcerted many people, but it was precisely the quality Freeman wanted in his successor.

Tesler was not welcomed eagerly at LWT. Bennett was far from delighted at being passed over and the senior programme staff, particularly those who had been recruited by Bennett, felt that Cyril had been slighted. Bennett had no intention of organizing an unofficial opposition to Tesler; they were friends and, despite the rivalry between Thames and LWT, often supported one another at the Network Controllers' meeting. Bennett set about establishing a working relationship with the newcomer. The other possible internal candidate, Vic Gardiner, who at one point in 1971 had virtually administered the company, recoiled into a little clique of engineering and administrative staff.

Tesler officially joined the company in May 1974 and through the next two years Freeman increased the former's responsibilities. The new man bedded down and established himself with the board, the programme-makers and the technical staff, and he succeeded to Freeman's Managing Directorship in June 1967, with the former retaining his position as Chairman of LWT (Holdings) Ltd.

Tesler inherited an awkward situation. In 1976, ITV's revenue was depressed, the BBC was rampant, and the IBA was unhappy with LWT. David Glencross, the normally mild and courteous Head of Programme Services at the IBA, was moved to a curt dismissal of the station's 1976 schedules:

> I can't say that I am happy about your Saturday evening schedules in Weeks 22–26 and I can't believe that you regard it as a very distinguished shop window for ITV in London. If we give it reluctant approval I hope that you will not assume that such a pattern would be welcome in future quarters.[9]

These difficulties led the London listings magazine *Time Out* to comment, 'perhaps the answer is for LWT to buy Brian Cowgill [the BBC's MD for Television] and put him in Cyril Bennett's shoes p.d.q.' Tesler and Bennett had been through periods of turbulence before and were not unduly worried. Instead, they were looking forward to the creative conference – or the 'three-day skull session in a country hideaway', as *Variety* memorably called it – to be held at the Selsdon Park Hotel in Croydon at the beginning of November.[10]

Round Table

Although the young Turks of the programme division worked within a few floors of one another they had little personal or professional contact. John Birt recalls, 'There was no sense of a community or fraternity of programme-makers. I spoke to the senior programme-makers in the lift or whatever, but there was no forum in which we discussed things in general. Each of us had our own department and worked directly to Cyril, so there was little real contact.'

On arriving at the conference Humphrey Barclay looked around and exclaimed to Tesler: 'I have never had lunch with anybody in this room.' This was a damning attack on LWT's solidarity. Lunch, in television, is a ritual, an entertainment and a courtesy during which plots are devised, gossip is gleefully or malevolently divulged, and secrets are revealed. Not to have lunched *any* of his fellow producers was more than an oversight, it was alarming. The lack of unity was, in essence, the product of Bennett's management style. He preferred to conduct bilateral relations with producers rather than have structured departments. Anyone with a good idea could knock on his door and they would receive a hearing. There was little by way of a hierarchy in the programme division, and few points of contact. In part, Tesler set up Selsdon in order to forge an organizational unity in the programme division.

On the first night the bar was full, and LWT's raconteurs outbid one another with outrageous stories. Selsdon combined a rough and tumble of jokes, attacks, sly criticism and boasting – typical of groups of young men in any business – with earnest and wide-ranging debates. A feeling of solidarity and belonging developed over the few days at Selsdon, and this Camelot atmosphere – part arrogance and part unity – pervaded the programme division for the next few years.

Among those present around the conference table on 4–6 November 1976, were:

Brian Tesler	Cyril Bennett
John Birt (Current Affairs)	David Coulter (CRA)*
John Bromley (Sport)	Nick Elliott (*Weekend World*)
Rex Firkin (Drama)	Russell Harty (Presenter)
Michael Grade (Entertainment)	Andy Mayer (*London Weekend Show*)
Geoffrey Hughes (CRA)	Stuart McConachie (Sport)
Tony Wharmby (Drama)	Julian Norridge (*Weekend World*)
Stuart Allen (Entertainment)	Jon Scoffield (Variety)
Derek Bailey (Arts)	Humphrey Barclay (Comedy)
Jack Williams (Entertainment)	Nicholas Barrett (Producer)
Ann Wolff (CRA)	Barry Cox (*London Programme*)

* Children, Religion and Adult Education

The conference opened with a paper from John Birt. As usual the impact made by his speech was the result of meticulous planning. In the month before the conference he had alerted Bennett and Tesler that he wished to present a paper in which he would analyse the company's problems, criticize managerial policy, and outline options for the future. Tesler and Bennett, although they disagreed fundamentally with much of Birt's paper, recognized that the presentation was an ideal way of opening up the interrelated problems of networking, competition, finances and planning which underlay the company's schedule and of which most of the programme executives were only dimly aware.

Sitting at the table, by counterparts from the other programme divisions, Birt, in true *Weekend World* style, began his exposition with a statement of the problem before outlining the context and possible solutions. 'As a Company we are apparently making less prestigious programmes that we used to make; and rather fewer people are watching our programmes now than have done in the past.' After this startling denunciation of those sitting around him (and, to a certain extent, of himself), Birt outlined the reasons for this failure:

> the BBC has shaken off some of the cobwebs and is now under more dynamic management. It does seem now to be prepared to take advantage of its size – its capacity to make something like . . . eight times the networked output of any one ITV company. And it is now exploiting both this scale and its two channels more than before to experiment at the margin; and, above all, to display its riches in the most felicitous way.

The BBC's two channels were succeeding because their programmes were marked by

> intelligence. Not intellectuality, not what intelligent producers think the public want, [but] intelligent producers making things which they themselves find interesting.

Birt believed that the audience for television had changed and that 'a significant proportion of [the BBC's] audience has gradually stepped up to meet the BBC.' The cause of this transformation was attributed by Birt to Britain's long educational traditions and imperial experiences:

> though we as a Nation . . . have had problems in recent years acting with *collective* good sense, I have long believed that *individually* we are the most sophisticated – culturally and politically – of the world's peoples.
>
> We have always been especially vigorous. More Britons have enjoyed more power for longer than have most other peoples. And most of us have been tested, and for longer, by living in industrialized societies than other people.
>
> In consequence, the average Briton, and especially the younger Briton, is more sophisticated, independently minded and confident of his intelligence, in my view, than are other nations.
>
> And, as a special consequence for us is, of course, that nowhere is this more true than here in our capital city.

This belief led Birt to the conclusion that it is 'more the public's growing taste for intelligent programming than the new aggression of the BBC which is responsible for the dramatic change in the broadcasting environment.' Consequently, LWT had to make 'more intelligent programmes'.

Birt identified several barriers to achieving this breakthrough. First, the BBC's aggressive weekend schedules left little room for experimentation by LWT; secondly the other ITV companies were hoarding their successful programmes during the week and dumping the unsuccessful ones at the weekend; thirdly, Birt noted,

> [w]hen I arrived at LWT . . . it clearly had a flavour of the moment about it. But obsessions run dry, ideas become sterile, individuals become jaded, [and] programmes become predictable.

LWT needed to be reinvigorated, and in order to achieve this, Birt added, producers from long-running series had to break away and make individual programmes in which they were genuinely interested. Furthermore, he suggested, a fortnightly programme meeting should be instituted at which the Heads of the various divisions would discuss their programmes, and future programme strategy, in a constructive and amicable atmosphere.

Even if several of the programme-makers around the table resented the messenger, and were irritated by the tone of the 'lecture', everyone agreed with the import of the message – LWT was treading water and needed to address itself to the problems posed by television in the late-1970s rather than constantly to refer back to the rescue of the company in the early 1970s.

With Brian Young's 'advice' in mind, as well as his desire to create a working environment in which the company's crop of young production talent could flourish, Tesler encouraged the conference to debate new programme ideas, to criticise themselves, and to reflect on plans for the future.

Geoffrey Hughes, Tony Wharmby and Michael Grade each took the floor to express their aspirations and to outline the reasons for their comparative lack of success in the previous year. Michael Grade, in particular, castigated himself for his failures to develop new programmes and to experiment with new ideas. He pointed out that his department had produced only three pilot programmes in the previous two and a half years. Grade's honest self-criticism was echoed by his colleagues, who loathed and were embarrassed by situation comedies such as *Yus, My Dear*.

Bennett, in a session on new programme ideas, agreed with much of the concern about LWT's lack of forward planning, and he acknowledged that he had made mistakes in keeping series alive far beyond their creative life. He had, he admitted, taken some soft options in the previous year, and he was looking forward to rectifying this in the years to come.

Tesler and Bennett encouraged a cross-fertilization of ideas. Every one discussed and analysed the difficulties facing LWT, and made suggestions as to how departments could work together. Tesler informed the conference of the decision to spend more money on religion and adult education, and this programme area, normally a backwater, became a focus of the conference. Suggestions about programmes on books, poetry, about a series on parish priests in Europe, and a 'quote-unquote' show emerged from the general discussion. Other ideas included light entertainment documentaries, drama-documentaries, *Aquarius* specials, and a children's comedy revue.

The skull-session also addressed itself to organizational questions. Two committees were discussed, and subsequently established. The first, the Facilities Standing Committee, was to explore how best studio time, cameras, VCR's etc., could be allocated to programme-makers; the second, the Creative Committee, emerged from Birt's paper. The Committee was to be a forum in which programme-makers from each department would discuss their shows, swap performers, analyse each others' work if requested, and generally create a framework for moving the company forward.

With a conference Chairman's prerogative, Tesler made the final speech at Selsdon in which he outlined his and Bennett's survey of the past and their plan for the future. He argued that LWT's quandary was not, as Birt had implied, the result of 'hardened programme arteries':

I thought that we were suffering not from age, but from relief. That having made it, having climbed out of the abyss . . . having reached the top; having ratings, prestige, awards – national and international – [LWT] had paused to breath in pure relief and to consolidate and that had been a mistake, because the time you need to develop for the future is when you're at the top and if you don't, then you are going to find yourself at the bottom with nothing whatsoever to get you up any higher again.

Tesler insisted that the weekend had been profitable before and would be again. Moreover, he did not believe that the BBC had become more adventurous and intelligent – it had simply become more cynical. BBC1 was, he contended, mainly a channel for popular entertainment, and most of the experimental or cultural programmes – which were supposed to distinguish the BBC from the commercial sector – had been relegated to BBC2.

When Tesler had finished speaking and the conference was about to break up, Cyril Bennett proposed a vote of thanks for the sound recordist who was taping the session. They were the last words many of these round the table were ever to hear him speak. Bennett returned to his small flat in Westminster from where, later that night, he died after falling from a sixth floor window.

The press pounced on the story. Relentlessly, they probed Bennett's personal problems and speculated on his professional difficulties. Selsdon, which was a reasonably good natured thrash, with the usual in-fighting and common-or-garden disagreements, was turned by the press into a sinister occasion at which Bennett was thrown to the wolves by an insecure new managing director and was savaged by ungrateful junior staff.[11] In retrospect, this seems simply another example of the press chasing dark shadows. Bennett's death was seen by most people as suicide – regardless of the Coroner's vedict to the contrary – but, even after close scrutiny of their consciences, almost everyone who was present at Selsdon believes that the conference did not differ from any other meeting of the company.

Bennett encouraged a climate of honesty in LWT. Criticism and self-criticism was given and received without rancour (as is obvious from the tape of the proceedings at Selsdon).[12] Moreover, most people around the table at Selsdon adored Bennett. Birt sums up the views of his colleagues: 'Cyril was like a father figure, you could always air criticism and he seldom took offence.'[13] Although Bennett was deeply insecure as the result of his previous expulsion from the company, there were few parallels between 1969 and 1976. Most of the people around the table owed their promotions or their breaks to Bennett, and their loyalty had yet really to be tested, let alone used up. Furthermore, Bennett knew that his new contract was sitting in the company secretary's office awaiting his signature.

Inevitably, people involved in tragedies huddle together for protection, and in order to be with people who understand and share their emotions. In the early hours of the morning following Bennett's death, Tesler and some of his senior staff met at Kent House.[14] Although he joined in the collective grief for a man whom he had known for over fifteen years – for three of those years as a colleague – Tesler had to ensure that the company was prepared for the press onslaught. He foresaw that Selsdon would be regarded as a cause of Bennett's 'suicide', and that the press was winding itself up in hysterical denunciation of everyone involved with Bennett. Tesler maintained a calm head – at the cost of his own reputation – and began the slow, difficult and painstaking task of leading the company into its grief over Bennett's death and then into living with it.

ARCHIVES AND
BRIEF CHRONICLES

[Hamlet to Polonius] 'Good my Lord, will you see the players well disposed?
Do you hear? – let them be well used, for they are
the abstracts and brief chronicles of the time.'

Grief haunted LWT in the months after Bennett's death.[1] Tesler, because he had 'ousted' Cyril, and because he had to oversee the company's practical day-to-day affairs, became a scapegoat for other people's unfocused sorrow. These feelings simmered until, a couple of months after Bennett's death, Tesler summoned the senior staff to his office for beer and sandwiches. Over the hours which followed he allowed people to air their worries and their grievances. This was the turning point in Tesler's relationship with the company. Michael Grade recalls:

> There was an underlying feeling that Brian had been insensitive with Cyril – domineering and aggressive. We were in the pit of despondency and this meeting cleared the air. Afterwards we realised that Brian had held LWT together, even though it was a terrible time for him. I realized later that in a sense he had saved the company and made it work. He got the money, the investment in programmes and planned for expansion. Just what we needed at the right time.

One of Tesler's most important decisions was his choice of the next Director of Programmes. Press speculation suggested that Freeman and Tesler would approach the BBC's Brian Cowgill or Bill Cotton. In the meantime, however, Tesler took over Bennett's responsibilities himself. He gathered a creative committee which was intended to integrate the creative heads of department (and provide them with a decent lunch budget), to encourage the cross-fertilization of their programme thinking, to involve them in the overall planning and scheduling process and to see whether any of them was ready to succeed Bennett. The committee became a testing ground – an audition, as John Bromley called it – on which Tesler set out the practical problems of scheduling and commissioning and assessed the ways in which these were analysed and resolved. Two men impressed Tesler: John Bromley for his long experience and sound judgement, and Michael Grade for his instinct and feel. Grade's enthusiasm won the day. Tesler recalls the reasons for Grade's appointment:

> Michael had never produced a programme in his life, which for some people may have been a disadvantage, but for him was an advantage because he was not restricted to one technique or one method. He was interested in everything. He had fascinating views about drama, sport, and current affairs. His creative interests ranged more widely across the spectrum than anyone else in the committee. He was also interested in scheduling – in the effect of juxtaposing programmes, taking advantage of what was on the opposition. Finally, he was very bright and very energetic and these seemed to me to be pretty good qualifications.

Both Tesler and Bennett saw something of themselves in Grade; not least, all three shared the Jewish showbiz heritage. Grade was, in many ways, Bennett's double. Both had been journalists, both had chutzpah, and both valued instinct above analysis.[2] Grade had the added benefit of possessing much of Bennett's charisma with little of the latter's dark side.

It was still a huge risk to appoint Grade. He lacked experience, did not have a good track record in his own programme area, and, apart from running his father's agency, had little managerial experience. Grade recalls:

> It took me a long time to adjust to television, to develop the analytical skills about what was wrong with the shows. I could walk into a theatre and tell you what was wrong with a show within two minutes and it was a shock to me that I could not really call on that in television. It took me a long time to develop those skills, and I wasn't very successful as Head of Light Entertainment.

Tesler's own experience of becoming a programme controller at 32, encouraged him to take a calculated gamble on the 33 year old Grade and, in February 1977, Grade's promotion was announced. After intensive tutorials from Tesler, Grade formally took up the post at the beginning of April.[3]

Risky Business

Grade was fortunate to inherit a number of good programmes, and even more lucky to be bequeathed programme heads who were coming into their creative prime. Moreover, Tesler had imposed a new management structure to rationalize decision making in the company. Bennett had been excellent at spotting talent, and nurturing it through personal contacts; but he could not integrate the talent into departments. The latter demanded the kind of order which was anathema to Bennett's impulsive spirit. He was not keen to delegate and he encouraged individual producers to refer decisions to him. Tesler brought order to the programme division. He created a new layer of division controllers, to whom producers reported and who were responsible to Grade. This created the basis for a more systematic approach to programme making and it protected Grade for assuming Bennett's imprudent workload. Tesler created clear line-management in the company for the first time.

These new model departments became the foundation of a highly successful programming division. The new organization tightened up management procedures, created the foundation for forward planning, and went some way to meeting the IBA's mid-term criticisms of the company. Even before Selsdon, however, the drama department[4] was developing *Lillie* – the story of Lillie Langtry, Edward VII's most famous mistress. This series continued LWT's preoccupation and success with Edwardian tales and it contributed the station's highest ever rating for a drama.[5]

Selsdon provided Wharmby (who became Controller of Drama) and his department with renewed impetus and creative energy and, apart from *Lillie*, other series were well-received by the critics. *Love for Lydia* was a reconstruction of the H.E. Bates novel of that name; *Enemy at the Door* told the story of the German occupation of the Channel Isles; and *Just William*, based on Richmal Crompton's indomitable character, was evidence of a mild re-awakening of the company's commitment to children's series – pioneered so well by *Catweazle*.[6] Over the five years that followed, LWT had several major failures in drama, such as *Thomas and Sara*, the follow-up to *Upstairs, Downstairs*, and the Delderfield adaptation, *People Like Us*. But Wharmby and Grade also delivered LWT's best ever ratings performances in drama with *Lillie*, *The Gentle Touch* (which starred Jill Gascoine as a female detective and ran for fifty-six episodes), *The Professionals* (which featured Martin Shaw, Lewis Collins and Gordon Jackson as a Home Office armed criminal-intelligence squad, and which also ran for fifty-six episodes), and the Agatha Christie extravaganza, *The Seven Dials Mystery*.[7] Furthermore, Grade and Wharmby lured two of Britain's top television dramatists – Alan Bennett and Dennis Potter – over to ITV, the latter for the second time at LWT. Both delivered powerful and prize-winning plays: Bennett six and Potter three.

Grade, before his promotion, had planned several comedies and variety specials which, even without his advance, would have gone some way to rescue his reputation within the company. These included *It'll Be Alright on the Night*, LWT's most dependable occasional series in the ratings wars, and a vehicle for Irene Handle and Julia Mackenzie, *Maggie and Her*, which had the second highest rating for any LWT situation comedy. Grade also had in the can a new series of *Two's Company*, which starred Donald Sinden as a crusty old English butler to Elaine Stritch's equally cantankerous American author. This was a sound ratings performer.[8]

The most successful LWT situation comedy over the first 21 years was also their most controversial – *Mind Your Language*. Tesler suggested the idea that Leo Rosten's stories, *The Education of Hyman Kaplan*, could be adapted to London in the 1970s. The Kaplan stories captured the imagination of America in the 1930s with their depiction of the depression years and of immigrants striving to achieve recognition through becoming US citizens. They were also very funny. Kaplanisms, jokes based around broken English, abounded. LWT's idea was to produce a series about a language school in London in which similar themes could be explored about the problems of immigrants settling in London, and which would capture some of Rosten's robust humour.

The series was one of a number of pioneering but less than successful multicultural situation comedies. Others were *The Fosters* about a West Indian family, and *Mixed Blessings* about a racially mixed marriage with the, for the time, unusual twist that the black family was middle class.[9] *Mind Your Language*, however, entirely missed its mark, as Tesler pointed out in memo to Grade in January, 1978, during the first series:

> If we're not careful with this one it won't last the first series, let alone justify a second.
>
> It hasn't moved one step further on from the pilot. In fact, it's moved backwards: the premise is no longer credible (the characters all talk in perfect colloquial English until the lessons start): the facile mispronunciations are no longer *part* of the gag, they *are* the gag.

The series did not recover and Grade was savaged at the Edinburgh Television Festival for purveying racism. A series as successful in the ratings as *Mind Your Language* could easily have lasted for six or seven years. Grade, to loud acclaim from his fellow professionals, and some relief from Tesler, pulled it after the second series.[10]

Although he had these programmes as his potential bankers, Grade still had to learn how to schedule them and to replace them when their creative energy had become exhausted. He had a steep learning curve. In the space of five years he went from resurrecting the tired old situation comedy, *The Rag Trade*, to presiding over an explosion of innovative and interesting programmes. The nature of networking ensured that LWT continued to show uninspired game shows, situation comedies and dramas from the rest of the network which, added to LWT's own failures, concealed LWT's internal developments. In March 1980 Grade wrote to the IBA:

> Would that the system allowed us to contribute all the entertainment and drama for Saturday all the year round; but our mix of Category 'A' contributions has to be spread across the arts, current affairs,

features, adult education and religion, as well as the drama and entertainment programming on Friday and Saturday. This lack of peak-time Saturday offerings from the seven day companies has had very distressing consequences on the current quarter, where I have had no alternative but to throw a promising artiste in a new show to the Saturday night wolves . . . It certainly is frustrating.

The BBC dominated Saturday evening at the beginning of Grade's period. Among other shows the BBC's evening schedule contained an extremely successful game show hosted by Bruce Forsyth called *The Generation Game*; an Edwardian drama, *The Duchess of Duke Street*, which followed closely the *Upstairs, Downstairs* formula; an American crash and bang series, *Starsky and Hutch*; and the football highlights programme, *Match of the Day*. Furthermore, on Sunday nights Esther Rantzen's consumer programme, *That's Life*, garnered large viewing figures. Grade, who shared not only his uncle's habit of chomping on large cigars but also his predatory showbusiness instincts, decided that the best way of attacking the BBC was to buy the people who were causing the problems. He enjoyed the buccaneering, the intrigue, and the feeling of pulling off the high-profile coup. Over the next three years he brought over Bruce Forsyth, attempted to enter an exclusive contract with the Football League such that ITV would have sole rights to showing league football, and almost persuaded Esther Rantzen and her husband, the producer Desmond Wilcox, to produce a *That's Life* type of programme for LWT.

Grade so unnerved and irritated the BBC that he was publicly denounced by the BBC's then Director of Television and subsequent DG, Alasdair Milne, for running LWT like the 'mafia with a cheque book'. Grade loved it.

1 Gradie's Big Idea
In June 1978, Grade wrote a letter to Bruce Forsyth's agent, Billy Marsh, in which he noted his pleasure that three years of discussion with Forsyth were at last bearing fruit, and expressing his hopes for a prospective two-hour entertainment programme to be called *Bruce's Big Night*. 'There is no doubt in my mind that we have between us constructed a vehicle, the like of which has never been seen on British television.'

Grade's excitement stemmed from securing the man who was, in the mid-1970s, the most popular light entertainment star in Britain, teaming him up with David Bell, who had produced Stanley Baxter's prize-winning specials and whom Grade had appointed as Controller of Light Entertainment, and developing a *networked* sketch, review and song format which stretched across Saturday peak-time like the programme of a modern music hall.

The press pumped up the programme, giving lots of coverage, interviews and publicity, and the first show was aired to great expectation at 7.25 pm on 7 October 1978. The ratings for the first outing were excellent: it took the top spot in London and was number six in the national charts. The programme included a couple of game shows, one of which, *Beat the Goalie*, involved celebrities keeping goal against a machine which shot out footballs and which was supervized by viewers from home. The biggest game, *The £1,000 Pyramid*, was a quiz show format which Bell had discovered in the United States. The comedy side of the show was provided by a new duo, Cannon and Ball, and by the resurrection of two old series, *The Worker*, starring Charlie Drake, and Dennis Norden and Frank Muir's *The Glums*, starring Jimmy Edwards. Other elements of the programme included Forsyth's interviews and shared routines with major American stars such as Sammy Davis Junior and Bette Midler, and various variety acts such as the popular poet Pam Ayres, and the eccentric Rod Hull with his puppet, Emu.

Although the show began well enough, it immediately ran into heavy flak from the critics. More to the point, however, the audience, which sampled the programme in large numbers at the beginning, was quickly disenchanted. The viewers gave the lie to the, always suspect, notion that if they are hooked for one part of a programme they will stay with that channel for the whole night.[11]

The real problems began, however, when the press – especially the *Sun* – unleashed the hounds and not only ridiculed the show but ransacked Forsyth's past for scandal and gossip. The trade press, in the shape of Edward Durham Taylor at *Television Today*, was much more kind:

'Amuse me, make me feel good'; that is the challenge the light entertainment programme has to take up. The audience's demand to be entertained in this way is insatiable and its yardstick of success often hard to meet. London Weekend's new approach to Saturday evening's major slot was (even allowing for the considerable asset of Bruce Forsyth) confronting the challenge head on. Any light entertainment programme can be laid bare to reveal ingredients of not much individual value – not much value, that is, if you don't like light entertainment programmes or are not in the mood to watch one.

A show like this [*Bruce's Big Night*] is obviously very important to London Weekend, for entertaining in the public's main leisure time, and from the Metropolis, is what they should be good at. We hope that the company does not start doubting what it is doing. Any new look for the evening is bound to have a mixed reception. But the audience and the critics can't have it both ways; they can't condemn ITV's predictability and also summarily reject shows that people are trying. There is nothing essentially new, only different ways of presenting the same thing and the LWT show seems to have taken full account of that . . . What can be said is that the company is trying hard and shrewdly in the most difficult area of programming. That is commendable – they could have played safe – and we wish them luck.

This, however, was an oasis of praise in a desert of criticism.[12] The *Sun* ran a series of articles at the end of October in which they quoted the usual group of anonymous hatchet-men, witches and bitches who wish to contribute their own kick to a fallen man. Forsyth's wife and co-worker, Anthea Redfern, was humiliated by stories about her imperious and demanding attitudes behind the scenes, and stories were circulated that Forsyth's marriage was in deep trouble as a result of strain caused by the show's failure. Furthermore, despite spending most of his career with ITV, Forsyth was curiously accused of 'defecting' from the BBC – as if moving television channels was a moral decision.

Even without these gratuitous attacks, however, it was clear that the series was in trouble. The consultants who were brought in by LWT[13] to help them to assess the show after its first few weeks on the air noted: 'The main problem, is the choppy style of the show where there is very little inter-relationship between each section. By darting from one feature to the other in this way, the show lacks any climax, which is the vital ingredient to sustain audience interest.'[14]

These attacks undermined an already demoralized production team and the Network, easily frustrated by apparent, and more importantly, public 'failure', leant on LWT to move the show out of prime-time and reduce its length. In its earlier slot of 6 pm, audiences began to pick up, but everyone had had enough and, at the end of December, Grade wrote again to Billy Marsh outlining a new contract for Forsyth to revert back to a run-of-the-mill format. The big idea had failed.[15]

2 Snatch of the Day

In the middle of November 1978, the BBC was conducting a routine re-negotiation of their joint contract with the Football League. Grade and John Bromley had, however, been bargaining in secret with the League which had, for some time, felt that they were badly paid for the coverage of league fixtures. Grade, an ex-football correspondent, had quietly taken Jack Dunnett, a Labour MP and a member of the League's management committee, for a drink over which he outlined his new deal in which the ITV would offer the League £5 million for three year's exclusive rights to soccer. Dunnett passed the offer on to the delighted members of the Management Committee who, over the next few days, hammered out a new deal.

Although the other ITV managing directors were aware of the secret deals, as was the IBA, the men haggling over the formal contract were left in the dark and, therefore, gave no hint of impending trouble to the

BBC. The Corporation's management was astounded when, on 16 November, Grade and the League announced the new agreement. A ferocious battle ensued during which the BBC threatened court action and, with a fixation verging on paranoia, vilified Grade. Eventually, a new agreement was struck which was to allow both channels access to League football at a much higher price. The Football League, like a spouse receiving alimony from both lover and mate, was the only happy member of the triangle.

Grade's bold smash and grab broke the cosy, club-like relationship which had been building up between ITV and the BBC. The consequent ill-feelings remained both within the network and at the BBC for some time. The following year, at a dinner given by George Howard, the BBC's chairman, for senior figures of several ITV companies (Freeman of LWT, Forman of Granada, Windlesham of ATV, Thomas of Yorkshire and Buxton of Anglia) Howard was asked what had happened to foul up relations between the two channels, which had previously been more co-operative. After a certain amount of prevarication, Howard angrily blurted out that Grade's 'disgraceful conduct' over the football deal made it difficult to trust ITV. Freeman defended his Director of Programmes but was surprised that the other ITV executives, apart from Aubrey Buxton, steadfastly refused to join him in his justification of Grade. Big ideas make big enemies for their originator.

3 Potter's Gate?
At the beginning of 1978, Alan Bennett contributed a series of plays to LWT. Apart from the critical kudos garnered from this series, and the collective pleasure within the company at being associated with Bennett, the series was also notable for tempting Lindsay Anderson, the director of *If . . .*, to make a foray into television. Anderson's letter to Grade is illuminating in the light of the struggle which was to come with another playwright, Dennis Potter, and another director, Richard Loncraine.

Thursday February 23 1978

Dear Michael Grade –
    Thank *you* for the opportunity of working – and it doesn't happen very often – in such a friendly, supportive and stimulating atmosphere as I've found at LWT. I'm sure you understand that coming from cinema and theatre, one approaches the technical challenge of tv with some suspicion. And I'm sorry we didn't get through the shooting faster – partly of course my lack of experience, and partly I think the special challenge of a brilliant, highly original script.
    If I didn't get it done faster it certainly wasn't for lack of expert help and technical and creative work from a really splendid crew,

that went far beyond anything I'd been led to expect. I can't tell you how helpful it was to feel – not just that I had the benefit of really top class skill in every department – but that everyone on the floor and in the control rooms was committed to the project, doing all they could to ensure it success, and really appreciative of the effort. An extraordinary contrast to the atmosphere I've generally felt in British film studios . . .

Thank you again,

Most Sincerely,
Lindsay Anderson

Two years after this praise from Anderson, Grade was maligned by the Association of Independent Producers for his 'cowardly volte-face' in his dealings with Dennis Potter, arguably, Britain's most consistently interesting television dramatist. This fall from critical grace happened after a fiasco reminiscent, in a small way, of United Artists financial disaster with Michael Cimino's film, *Heaven's Gate*.

It had all started so well. In the spring of 1979 Dennis Potter, fresh from his triumph with the seminal drama series *Pennies From Heaven*, but smarting from the BBC's refusal to show his previous work *Brimstone and Treacle*, decided that the Corporation was not sufficiently committed to his next series. Furthermore, he and Kenith Trodd, Potter's regular producer, wished to take more control over their work and were interested in establishing an independent production company – a concept then in its infancy in television.

Grade, aware of Potter's concerns, set up a lunch at which a deal was sketched out which would bring the new company to LWT. This was the second involvement with LWT for both men, and Trodd recalls this lunch, and the days which followed, as the honeymoon period. He recalls, 'Everything seemed possible. It was almost as if we had the Midas touch; everything we wanted, and more, was offered to us. We were all caught up in a terrific euphoria which was created by Michael Grade, who has an ability to generate an atmosphere of great warmth.'

A deal was signed between LWT and Pennies from Heaven [PFH] Ltd – in effect a quasi-independent company which would appoint its own producers and directors but which would use LWT's crews and follow LWT's accountancy and production procedures.

The seeds of discontent were sown in this structural arrangement. Trodd argues, 'the first problem was that I did not know what an LWT pound could buy in the way of production values. It was an arcane costing system, and I needed someone to translate for me.' Translations are an imprecise art, and Trodd and LWT were often speaking a different language. The second problem was that there was a division of power and responsibility. LWT's crews answered to LWT's executives, whereas the producer, Trodd, had no direct authority over them. Moreover, Trodd was transient and the crews' superiors at LWT were permanent. Self-interest and loyalty merged.

Initially, the deal was for Potter to write plays for television, all of which would be shot on film. Trodd, however, suggested that PFH had a responsibility to other writers, and it was agreed that PFH would also produce plays from other sources. As promised, Potter delivered three scripts in the Autumn of 1979. The first glimmering of trouble appeared when LWT, which had taken a closer look at the budgets involved, invited PFH to consider making the first production – *Rain on the Roof* – in the studio and on tape. Although Potter was prepared to explore this possibility, Trodd was adamant that LWT should stick to its deal. 'Dennis was a reluctant convert to film', Trodd believes. 'I argued that we would only attract the best directors if we offered them the chance to work on film.'

Rain on the Roof, starring Cheryl Campbell and directed by Alan Bridges, was the first Potter to go into production, it came in on budget and without too many problems. Although the director complained later that 'five weeks (including rehearsal) is insufficient time within which to mount a film of even modest artistic aspirations', such complaints had been the stuff of directors' complaints since the invention of the moving image and were not unduly disturbing. Bridges' grievance was mild compared to the eruptions and fights emanating from the Isle of Wight, where *Blade on the Feather* – a study of spies and the corruption of the English ruling elite, starring Tom Conti, Denholm Elliott and Donald Pleasance – had started shooting.

Blade had a difficult birth. Joseph Losey, a director of international renown, was scheduled to direct the film, and PFH were hoping to secure David Niven and James Mason. This plan collapsed when Trodd was informed that the two men held an ancient grudge and would not set foot on the same set. Losey was committed to another production and, consequently, Trodd had to search for a new director. PFH invited Richard Loncraine, whose main experience was in directing advertisements, but who was desperately keen on moving to feature films, to take over from Losey.

Within days of arriving at the location, *Blade* was a tale of spies, confusion and disillusion among the production team. Filming began on 19 May 1980 and by early June stories were flowing back from LWT's team to Kent House which claimed that Trodd and Loncraine were extravagant and unable to work realistically within the budget. Moreover, it was also claimed that every time Loncraine was thwarted in his attempt to introduce something new into the schedule, he threatened to walk off the set. The production was, in the view of the crew, degenerating into chaos.

On 23 June, Vic Gardiner, who was protecting the backs of LWT's crews but who also was not unhappy to report on the inadequacies of programme-makers, wrote a memo to Grade:

For the record, I though you would like to know what Peter Cazaly and Tony Hepher have to say on *Blade on the Feather*.

The former writes in his management report for Period 11:

'Dennis Potter's *Blade on the Feather* continues to cause difficulties and aggravation which is to be expected with the complete absence of Producer control over a Director acting like a spoilt child.'

Tony Hepher writes – 'The film production *Blade on the Feather* is affecting all departments and constant variation from the original planning has a disturbing effect on management and staff. The constant threats of the Producer and Director to walk out of the programme unless they have their own way on trivial issues places all managers in an untenable and debilitating dilemma.'

Not a happy state of affairs.

Not only were the crews unhappy with the producer and the director, the cameraman was a freelance and was a personal friend of Loncraine. Moreover, freelance cameramen were the bane of unionized crews. LWT had its own staff cameramen, whom Trodd refused to use on the principle that the cameraman can be as important to the look of film as a director.

Grade was faced with a tricky problem: he could not alienate Potter and Trodd in the middle of three productions in which he had invested so much, but, at the same time, he had to prevent PFH setting off a spiral in production costs. Furthermore, he had to be tough otherwise LWT's production managers would have considered him weak and unable to control his programme-makers. He signalled to Trodd that problems were building up and that he had to be seen to control Loncraine; he also warned Gardiner about fuelling the fires of discontent. To Trodd, Grade wrote on 24 June:

A great deal of rumour and disquiet is circulating by word of mouth in the building about the production methods used on the *Blade* film. There are all kinds of horror stories about profligacy and lack of control on the production. I am particularly concerned to avoid the perpetuation into folklore of these rumours, which, assuming them to be untrue, can only be less than helpful to the relationship between the company and PFH. If there is any substance in any of the rumours then we need to take the appropriate action for the future for the same reason.

On the same day Grade wrote to Gardiner:

. . . I am very anxious to ensure that the valuable contract with Pennies from Heaven does not become a source of rumour and prejudice over the next few years. It is a matter of the highest priority to me to ensure that the same rules of law apply on these shows as everything else we do. I cannot however act on rumour and generalizations and, therefore, two weeks ago I instigated 'an independent panel' to report on the stories emanating from the Isle of Wight. Secondly, I asked Caz in confidence to supply me with as much factual information as possible. Once I have a decent case, if there is one, I can go to bat.

Having said all that I am very anxious that nobody lose sight of the importance of these plays to LWT.

Cazaly felt that Loncraine and Trodd were not playing by the rules and that they were not willing to compromise. PFH for their part felt that LWT were not taking into account the problems with the weather, which was awful, nor the need to allow the production the chance to breath and to develop. If these had been isolated blow-ups then it could have been contained without too many difficulties, but one problem after another emerged to add further grit to the wounds. Trodd recalls that his relationship with LWT's production executives was 'ragged and deteriorating'. Each item of extra expenditure became a source of conflict. For example, a storm and rain scene, which Loncraine ordered to match up some other shots, required a generator and wind machine, adding another £6,000 to the production. Furthermore, Loncraine demanded alterations to the house and garden in which they were filming and insisted on props which would add to the faded opulence of the interior of the house. These were typical requests and added to the production values, but again they added unexpected costs.

One item of extra expenditure added more fuel to the flames. Loncraine wanted a small bridge to be built in the grounds of the house. LWT pointed out that union agreements meant that in order to build the prop, a new man would have to be drafted in from London. Trodd and Loncraine said that if LWT had industrial difficulties then that was its problem and not theirs.

The tension came to a head, as far as Grade was concerned, over a flashback scene which Loncraine insisted was necessary to the film. What began, however, as one day and one night's filming in London turned into a proposal for two night's shooting in Cheshire, the sudden introduction of a sequence with a train, and one day's filming in a Zoo in Dudley. The flashback, which had not been included in the initial costs, would have added £65,000 to a budget which had already gone way over its initial estimate of £307,785. Grade, by this time fully conscious of the extent of the problems, simply refused to sanction this new scene. However, he did allow for the initial one day flashback to be shot at a cost of £30,850.

Meanwhile *Cream in My Coffee* (which went on to win Europe's most prestigious television award, the Prix Italia) starring Peggy Ashcroft, Lionel Jeffries and Martin Shaw, was also causing some financial problems. The first draft budget for *Cream* was £297,320. This allowed the director, Gavin Millar, an extremely tight schedule of 22 shooting days for a complicated tale which involved flashback sequences to a 1930s hotel ballroom, with all the period costumes and decor entailed. The film eventually exceeded its budget by over £45,000, most of which went on extra cast members, overtime, costumes, sets and props. More to the point, LWT's production divisions did not know how to adjust to the demands coming from the producer. Used to much tighter budgeting and closer controls, they were unhappy with constantly readjusting their estimates. This contributed to the unhappy and tense relationship between PFH and LWT.

In retrospect, to have produced three highly regarded feature length films on such limited shooting schedules should have been regarded as one of the highlights of Grade's period. As Trodd points out, 'by every creative index the films were a success'. However, the structure of the deal with PFH undermined the achievement.

If Trodd had not been such an abrasive and aggressive character the films might not have had the quality necessary to win awards. Trodd felt vindicated when, at the following year's BAFTA's, two of the Potters and one of his BBC productions – *Stranger on a Train* – competed for the top drama award. He sees the whole affair somewhat differently from LWT. Twenty years later he feels that Potter and Grade entered into a rather grandiose plan without proper planning or foresight. When it proved extremely difficult to bring the vision to life, Trodd was left trying to pick up the pieces. Consequently, he had to fight tooth and nail to realize Potter's scripts and his director's vision.

In a letter to Grade, after the dust had settled slightly, PFH recognized the problems:

> There are undoubtedly habits and styles which can appear to be unnecessarily abrasive when not properly understood. It was perhaps only to be expected that a new and, as then, unexplored 'creative' relationship should have more than the usual number of teething problems. You, in turn, had the right not to expect those 'teething' problems to be too literally translated into what might almost be called actual *bites*!

Before this relatively calm and reflective judgement, however, a final, traumatic disagreement occurred between LWT and PFH. As part of the deal, LWT was to produce a Jim Allen play, *The Commune*, to be directed by Roland Joffe. This 'small epic' (as Trodd called it) was set in Oldham and had a huge cast, including 400 Oldham school children. The project involved two 110 minute films and had a prospective budget of £780,000. If this had been the first of the films then perhaps the conflict which ensued would have been resolved without too much blood being spilled. However, as it came after the battles over the previous three productions, it became a point of managerial principle. Grade had to make a stand.

On the morning of 30 June Grade met representatives from PFH to discuss how to produce the plays. PFH suggested various financial permutations, including 'loaning' LWT some money in order to start the production in the summer of 1980. Grade pondered on the idea overnight and on the following morning the meeting reconvened, this time with Dennis Potter in attendance to add the force of his personality. Grade informed PFH that he could not accept the 'loan' and wished to postpone the production. By this time Trodd was regarded by most people at LWT as a resident demon. The accounts from the company suggest that at this point, Trodd exploded and had to be kept in check by Potter. Potter gruffly informed Grade that PFH 'might have to go to the press and the IBA, because that would be the only course left to us . . .'

The conflict seemed resolved when the warring parties agreed to a settlement suggested by PFH. The films would be shot in two stages and LWT would put up £500,000 in 1980 and £175,000 – the balance of PFH's revised budget – in 1981. Grade's sigh of relief was cut short when PFH phoned that afternoon to say that the revised budget was insufficient, partly because of fees for contracting artists over a split period.

On the following day, Roy van Gelder, LWT's Director of Personnel, extracted a favourable deal from the actors' union Equity which reduced the cost of the fees; however, LWT's production supervisors, by now deeply suspicious of PFH's budgets, decided to re-assess the costs from scratch. They produced a figure of £712,000 *plus* additional cast additions *plus* the inflation on the £175,000 earmarked for 1981. Kenith Trodd met the supervisors that afternoon to discuss the discrepancy. His combative approach – in which he threatened to 'produce a cheaper film which will be the last thing we ever do for LWT' – did not inspire confidence that an amicable solution could be worked out.

On Thursday the conflict came to a head. Potter was due to give a press conference that morning and Trodd issued a threat that 'if we are not spending money on the production by 12 o'clock then Dennis will spill the beans'. At a meeting between LWT's production staff, Trodd and Joffe, it was agreed that the final budget was to be £692,000, which had to be agreed by Grade before 11.30, otherwise, Trodd reiterated, 'we're out!' John Howard, who was overseeing the budget for LWT, reported this message to Grade who, irked by the constant barrage of threats, and unwilling to give, told Howard 'tell them it's off'. Five minutes later an incredulous Trodd was informed of the decision. Grade, however, was not quite finished. In the afternoon, he asked Howard and the others present at the meeting to repeat Trodd's ultimata. After the story had been confirmed he wrote to PFH a letter condemning Trodd's behaviour and indicating that LWT would find it difficult to work with him again.

On Friday morning, Trodd flew into Howard's office and denied that he had ever threatened LWT and told Howard that he was unprofessional and a liar to boot. In the presence of Howard's secretary, he issued a warning that if Howard persisted with his accusations then Trodd would sue him for slander. By the end of the meeting, however, Trodd had calmed down and was discussing the possibility of shooting a new Dennis Potter production.

Although he remembers little of this conflict, Trodd remarks 'I suppose the atmosphere would have been strong and heated. I was an outsider, and I had no intention of playing the company game. I wanted the films to be made and I had a passion for the work which bred a kind of arrogance. Also, I suppose I have little respect for company bureaucrats, and I cannot operate by taking people out for a drink and wooing them.'

A month after the Trodd–Howard meeting, 400 disappointed Oldham schoolchildren were threatening to descend *en masse* to confront Michael Grade – a.k.a. Scrooge – who eventually drove up to Oldham to placate the children and to pay £1500 to the Oldham Theatre Workshop (which had recruited the children) as penance. The *Commune* eventually was made at the BBC where it went by the name of *United Kingdom*.

Although LWT withdrew unilaterally from the contract to produce any further PFH films, the latter was not yet finished and they offered a Dennis Potter scripted series (in 12 parts) as well as four studio plays. In the offer, PFH acknowledged their own contribution to the débâcle:

> It is important to note that this series would be predominantly STUDIO based, with the smallest possible amount of filming. Potter was originally contracted to write FILMS only, and would prefer to do so still, but is hereby signalling both his desire to continue the PFH/LWT relationship and his acknowledgement of the onerous production costs of filming for television.

Grade, who wished to retain Potter, was interested in the idea. However, eventually the experiment with PFH ingloriously petered out with echoes of recrimination bouncing around in the trade press.

Diverse Productions

Apart from Grade's innovations, another consequence of Selsdon was the emergence of a unified features department. This idea was born out of Tesler's lunch with Brian Young five months before Selsdon. More resources had to be pumped into features in order to raise the station's profile (and placate the IBA). Consequently, Tesler decided on the creation of a department which would fully integrate features with current affairs under a single head. Tesler's own experience as Head of Features at ABC had made him aware of the restrictions that a weekend franchise imposes on feature and documentary programmes. There was no network equipment in the weekend schedule for local documentaries. But there was a *mandatory* requirement in ITV for religious and adult education programmes. Tesler wanted an integrated features and current affairs department which would have the resources to take advantage of this opportunity; it would also provide John Birt with a suitable job in the reshuffle that followed Grade's promotion.[16] Birt was promoted from Head of Current Affairs to lead the newly unified Features and Current Affairs department (with two others from the ex-Granada Cosa Nostra – Barry Cox and Nick Elliott – becoming, respectively Head of Current Affairs and Head of Features).[17] This group, and their co-workers, were about to generate a number of series which were consistently well received by the critics. This new department reduced the conflict for resources between Features and Current Affairs, and offered Nick Elliott the chance to leave *Weekend World*, which he had been with since joining the company.[18] Furthermore the unification encouraged the cross-fertilization of ideas and personnel and convinced ambitious producers and directors that working on a religious programme was a good career move.

Barry Cox, Elliott's counterpart at Current Affairs, recalls:

> When Nick started he took his people from Current Affairs, and so Features became an extension of Current Affairs which was its great strength for all those years. It stopped being a ghetto area which could not attract the best people and became an opportunity to move away from a very narrow diet of programmes. The integration enriched the department, it gave ambitious people the chance of promotion, to do new things. It became a virtuous circle. At a later stage Current Affairs got back people who had done quite different things – for example a documentary series which lasted 18 months – and this broadened their experience and made them better producers and researchers.

John Birt, the first Controller of Features and Current Affairs, is one of the few men to have written their signature on British television. Apart from the BBC's first Director General, John Reith, John Birt is the only person in British television to be credited with a doctrine.

The term 'Birtism' was coined when John Birt became Deputy Director General of the BBC in 1987. Initially it was used by his enemies who wished to type him as a dry theoretician. The men and women who had stood in the pouring rain outside coroner's courts, dodged bullets in the Lebanon, or covered skateboarding ducks were not at all keen to acknowledge the authority of a man who, in their eyes, knew little of real, gutsy news-gathering. Birt refuses to accept the doctrine which bears his name. 'I am not a Birtist', he states categorically. He sees himself as a programme-maker first and foremost. The theorizing and system-building is a means to an end rather than an end in itself; all of his efforts are bent to making, or causing to be made, programmes which demonstrate an original and inquiring approach to the questions which they raise.

As a programme-maker Birt has been involved in a number of different types of series: *Nice Time* was light satire, Frost was topical discussion, and *Weekend World* was an intense, analytical programme. As a programme executive Birt encouraged the development of programmes as diverse as *Jesus, the Evidence* and *Blind Date*. However, no matter how much Birt disclaims Birtism, many of those who worked for him took his ideas and created their own version of the 'thesis'. Television is hardly awash with interesting ideas about how best to make programmes; conequently, strong theories, well-expressed, will attract followers. It was inevitable that Birt's arguments, which he may simply have seen as a method for achieving good programmes, would become fetishized; the system outlined by Birt became, for some producers and researchers, more important than the programmes to which it was being applied.

The rudiments of what became known as Jay–Birt at LWT, and Birtism at the BBC, were first outlined publicly in an article in *The Times* on 28 February 1975.[19] This article, and the three that followed, which were co-written with Peter Jay, argued that television news was dominated by the twin historical influences of the newspaper newsroom and the documentary film. These prejudices led to a preoccupation with dramatic images and with film as the medium in which to convey a story. There was a directors' lobby in the news, wrote Jay and Birt, for whom 'an ideal programme is one which has an exciting location and lively situations with animated talkers in-between.' This approach may have been adequate to human interest stories, so the thesis ran, but was incapable of explaining and putting into context the social, political, economic and international forces which, for the most part, determine people's lives. This news tradition led, the authors contended, to a 'bias against understanding'.

In place of the obsolete structures and outmoded values of the newsroom, the renegades wished to erect integrated news and current affairs departments, staffed by specialists, which would focus on the big picture rather than stumble through numerous small stories which ultimately left the viewer unenlightened about processes and structures. The 'thesis' – Birtism writ large – dominated the thinking in LWT's features and current affairs departments. You may have been against it but you could not ignore it.

In the debate that followed the promulgation of Jay–Birt the two men were derided as desiccated elitists with no understanding of the needs of the 'ordinary' viewer (whoever that is). Critics, however, failed to grasp something quite important to the practice of Jay–Birt: the mechanics may well have emerged from Birt's analytical training in mathematics and engineering, but its power was generated by its dramatic force. Take, for example, the set of *Weekend World*: the interviewer and his guest were dwarfed by an imposing, almost overwhelming, background map of the earth; human beings, the set proclaimed, merely had bit parts in the moral and economic drama of the world. Moreover, the interviews and explanations in *Weekend World* – which were pre-scripted and rigidly controlled – were a form of theatre; the programmes were at their best in the hands of an interviewer whose style lent itself to the dramatic gesture or phrase.[20] This was, in part, why the programme found it difficult to sustain itself week in and week out.

Paradoxically, the *Weekend World* machine, which was designed to churn out explanations for everything, required the high octane fuel of climactic national or international events – such as the two miners' strikes in the early 1970s and the oil crisis of 1974 – to work at its best. Even the stagflation of the 1970s was the subject of excitement as *Weekend World* self-consciously pioneered the introduction of debates about new or refreshed intellectual positions, such as monetarism. With boring subjects, however, *Weekend World* could be like a dull Friday afternoon seminar on the Schleswig–Holstein question.[21]

The features and current affairs department moved into high gear in the late 1970s. It developed and sustained a creative momentum which took ITV into areas which had not successfully been tackled before. The first of these was the arts.

1 The South Bank Show

The roots of the *South Bank Show* lie in conversations between Nick Elliott and John Birt at the beginning of 1977. In February of that year, Birt outlined in a memo to Tesler his programme plans for the department. He reaffirmed his commitment to *Aquarius* but indicated that he would initiate:

A shift towards documentaries which will examine the work and the thinking of substantial artists with a body of work behind them; and which will have a bias towards, though they will not be exclusively concerned with, the more *consumed* arts – cinema, television, popular music, literature, architecture.

This idea took root before Selsdon. Birt had been asked by Bennett to take a look at *Aquarius*, and Birt had concluded that as the programme was a direct expression of Humphrey Burton's idiosyncratic enthusiasms, it often produced charming, insightful and, occasionally, brilliant, shows. However, Birt pointed out that LWT could not rely on the knowledge of one man for one of its premier series. This was confirmed in Birt's mind when Peter Hall took over as presenter from Burton, and Derek Bailey became the driving force behind the series. Birt believed that the format could not survive Burton's departure, and, moreover that the programme did not match up to the model of a series which would analyse and dissect the careers and works of major artists and artistic movements. After Selsdon, when the arts became their responsibility, Birt and Elliott brought this alternative model into being.

Nick Elliott, as Head of Features, had direct responsibility for creating the arts programme, and he thought long and hard about the type of programme that he would like to see. The new series would have to deal with the modern as well as the classic, pop and rock as comfortably as opera and ballet, Bauhaus as comfortably as Adams. The basic ideas for this series were hammered out between Elliott and Birt before they set out to recruit someone who would realize their plans. Somewhat fortuitously, they stumbled on a novelist and BBC presenter, Melvyn Bragg.

Elliott and Bragg had a mutual friend, Mike Wooller, an ex-Granada documentary-maker who had moved to the BBC. Bragg was at that time editor and presenter of a book programme, *Read All About It*, and he had expressed a strong interest in developing his own general arts programme along the lines of Hugh Weldon's *Monitor*, on which Bragg had worked after leaving Oxford. Wooller told Elliott that Bragg was champing at the bit at the BBC, and Elliott and Bragg met for several lunches at which they discussed the profile of the series which had been developed in February. Bragg, who agreed with the framework, was concerned that the programme should have sufficient weight and he wanted more time – one hour rather than 45 minutes – and more programmes – 25 as opposed to *Aquarius*'s 18. Furthermore, he wanted the series to be properly networked (*Aquarius* was scheduled at different times in each ITV region.) Finally, he wished to have a measure of autonomy and to have control over the producers and directors who worked for the series.

After Elliott had reported these conversations to Birt, the latter met Bragg and discovered 'someone who was down to earth and wasn't pompous about the arts'. Bragg's northern antecedents may also have contributed to the ease with which the Liverpudlian Birt accepted Bragg.

Bragg and Elliott, after going through all of the usual permutations of arts-type names, decided that they wanted something straightforward. They came up with *South Bank*, which contained references to the National Theatre, National Film Theatre, the Hayward Gallery and the Royal Festival Hall. Then they added the title's final word – *Show* – thereby grafting on a sense of entertainment on to a name which might have otherwise have seemed unduly 'arty' and metropolitan.

Great hopes were placed in the programme. Grade fought for, and won, a full network slot for the series, and they waited for the reactions to the first programme. Almost inevitably the first shows were a mess – a mixture of reviews, a bit of dramatization, odds and ends of interviews – and Bragg was attacked by the quality press for failing to force ITV to come up with a decent series on the arts. Grade was solidly behind the show and was extremely supportive while Birt, Elliott and Bragg struggled to work out the dimensions and structure of the series. They spent many hours working out why some parts of the show worked and others did not. In a department which believed in the single-minded pursuit of subjects it was inevitable that they would settle on a single-item format. Bragg recalls:

> In those older shows there were some smashing items, but they were rather slapdash. We were trying to do three programmes in one until we settled down and said: 'OK, I'd like to do those three different programmes, but I'm going to do one at a time.'

Out of the pummelling which they took in the first few programmes the *South Bank Show* established three rules which have sustained it over the years. Bragg notes:

> First, you have to respect the integrity of the subject – if you make a film about Arthur Miller it has to be something Miller would respect for its intellectual striving, its seriousness and its research. Secondly, you have to respect your own professionalism: the programme has got to be well made and well crafted. Third, you have to respect the audience. The interesting thing is that it's a series of parallel audiences – you are talking at one and the same time to experts and people whose enthusiasm you have to assume otherwise they would not be staying with you, but whose lack of knowledge verges on the absolute.

This formula, which, according to Bragg, makes the 'programme lucid and accessible to people who are enthusiastic without being patronising or watering it down', produced the great triumph of the first season – a two hour special on Kenneth MacMillan's ballet, *Mayerling*. This programme – which combined ballet, history, documentary, interviews and criticism – won the Prix Italia and was acknowledged as a landmark in the television coverage of performance art. Moreover, it immediately established the style and authority of the series.[22] Another Prix Italia award came to the show in 1980 for Tony Palmer's profile of Benjamin Brittan, *A Time There Was*, and in 1981 a protrait of William Walton, *At the Haunted End of the Day*, won for the programme an unprecedented third Prix Italia.[23]

Bragg, supported firmly by Elliott, established techniques and methods independently of the Jay–Birt thesis (again, this is one of the paradoxes of Jay–Birt: the author of the thesis was involved with the programme from the beginning.) In particular, Bragg felt that he had to maintain the celebratory aspects of the arts over against what was perceived to be Jay–Birt's constant desire for exegesis. The power of the arts, their resonance and ability to summon passion and evoke awareness, had simply to be acclaimed on occasion.

The *South Bank Show* settled into three broad approaches: first, the end-of-career programme in which an artist's life-work was put into historical and psychological perspective; secondly, the mid-career programme in which an artist who had produced a consistently interesting body of work, but who was in the process of change, was invited to speculate on his or her future. Finally, the show tracked the development of a major production from rehearsals through to performance.

If the intellectual framework was set early in the first series, so also was the management style. After the initial struggles to hammer out the format, and to allow the series space to develop, Nick Elliott by and large left the show to its editor. Bragg is a muscular impresario who loathes the fey, elitist, other-worldly image of the arts. He enjoys the feeling that he is creating Europe's foremost arts show on a limited budget and in competition with the BBC. He has strict shooting ratios – five days per show being the norm; programmes which were delivered in, say, 12 weeks for the BBC's *Omnibus* were delivered within five to six weeks at LWT. On foreign trips – especially to the United States – Bragg bundled together subjects, and was unhappy if he did not return with the bones of at least four programmes.

This tough approach to budgets suits ITV, and it persuades LWT to allow Bragg extra resources for programmes to which he is committed. For example, in 1988, he did a special on Gore Vidal. He needed more money to take a crew to Rome and, because of his track record, the funds were released. The images of Vidal in the ruins of Imperial Rome fitted in perfectly with the subject of the interview – Vidal's reflections on US imperialism. Similarly, when the RSC began its production of *Nicholas Nickelby*, Bragg approached Grade for an extra £50,000 to shoot the rehearsal and to follow the production to its conclusion. Bragg's consistently canny attitude to money allowed Grade to justify the extra resources and Bragg was able to produce another excellent *South Bank Show Special*.

The *South Bank Show* developed into Bragg's barony. The show's consistent success, and sheer longevity, allowed him the freedom, within budget constraints, to develop the show without much guidance or interference. But although the arts programme was in safe hands, there were many other aspects of the features output with which Birt, Elliott and Cox had to deal.

2 Weekend Worlds

John Birt's new and wide-ranging responsibilities allowed him to explore the limits of the arguments advanced in the Jay–Birt thesis. Furthermore, the amity between Birt and Grade, and Tesler's determination to allow his programme executives the creative freedom which he had always demanded, and for the most part received, at Thames, ensured that there were few institutional barriers to the development of the experiment in Birtism.

David Cox, who became editor of *Weekend World* in the 1977 reshuffle, was very conscious of the strategy. 'John's solution to the new areas . . . was to do a *Weekend World* about religion, a *Weekend World* for children, a *Weekend World* for the arts, and a *Weekend World* for broadcasting policy.'

The programme on broadcasting policy emerged from discussions which Birt had with Rod Allen, the editor of the trade journal – *Broadcast*. The programme, *Look Here*, presented by Andrew Neil of the *Economist*, a rising young journalist, was issue journalism in the Jay–Birt style. It placed television within an economic and political context and explored the resulting structural pressures and tensions. It was also greatly disliked by the rest of ITV.[24] Even within LWT it caused some problems. *Look Here* ran an item on the failure of *Bruce Forsyth's Big Night*, on which David Bell supposedly confessed that the show was dreadful. Bell was clear that he had been misquoted and that *Look Here* had not done the decent thing.

Grade read the script, saw the preview, and refused to block the programme. He was, in Allen's words, 'scrupulous'. He was also furious and his language turned the air blue *after* the programme had been screened. However, this was regarded as part of the give and take of argument, rather than as pressure to lay off LWT.

Look Here demonstrated, in fact, the divergence within Birt's division. Apart from Bragg and Andy Mayer, the producer of *The London Weekend Show*,[25] almost every one in the department pursued to varying degrees what they saw as Birt's line. Some did so from conviction, others from fear or in the hope of promotion, and several had been trained in Jay–Birt and knew no other method. However, in practice, there was not a simple Jay–Birt 'line'; it was adapted by different producers in various ways. At the softer end, Rod Allen felt that Jay–Birt hinged on a very simple point:

> It was the words that mattered. We were all very interested in words, and in arguments and in logic. As soon as people misunderstood that and start cartooning it as 'You've got to know the story before you interview the people', then you misinterpret what John is saying. John is saying: 'Ring them up, find out what the argument is. Is it worth talking to them. Its cheaper to ring them up than to take a camera along and film them while you ask them what they think.'

Barry Cox had filtered Birt through his Granada training, and *The*

London Programme retained a gritty, current affairs feel despite following the rigorous pre-scripting, editing and theory-building characteristic of Jay–Birt. If an item was developing into a type of arcane televised sociology as the result of its thesis, then Cox was likely to drop it in favour of something which was good television. David Cox, on the other hand, took the thesis out to extreme lengths. One of his colleagues characterizes him as 'the master of the re-write': 'He had a fetish for scripts. He would cross out definite articles and replace it with indefinite articles. He would underline commas.' Another recalled: 'David took Birt–Jay to the frontiers of austerity, and that started people in the department wondering if that was the right way to do things.' David Cox was considered by his colleagues to be bright, indeed brilliant, but some felt that under his stewardship of *Weekend World* and of the current affairs department the thesis was promoted with too much vigour.[26]

Birt's theories were being tested at the sharp-end, and were, more often than not, turning up successful programmes. Although competing interpretations of the thesis existed, Birt himself retained a strong editorial control of the department despite retreating from personal contact with the line producers, researchers and editors. Birt believed that if authority had been delegated then it should not be usurped by constant appeals over the head of the man whom he put in charge. He became, as a result, a somewhat distant and austere figure, and the day-to-day management was handled by Nick Elliott and Barry Cox.

Birt did not respond warmly to programmes which deviated from the style which he had developed in practice and subsequently conceptualized in theory. However, his department was not hidebound or doctrinaire. Birt encouraged the lighter end of current affairs. From the seat of Jay–Birt emerged a number of chat shows and quirky features, and the department harboured and delighted in a coterie of eccentric, smart, singular presenters, including Janet Street-Porter, Clive James and Russell Harty. These three presenters were involved with series that met with varying degrees of success; but LWT tried the impossible and brought them all together on the one show, *Saturday Night People*. This was something of a throwback to the style of *Nice Time*. Therefore, when Barry Cox presented at Selsdon an idea for a late night chat and review show, Birt offered firm support. Cox lit the blue touch paper and stood well back while the three garrulous presenters fought to dominate the show. All did not go smoothly, as Janet Street-Porter recalls:

The first couple of episodes were just disastrous because Russell really did not like the idea of doing the show. He had his own talk show, and had done *Aquarius* and was a big star. Clive hadn't done much television before and he used to write all of his jokes out on his wrist. We all wanted the camera at a different height to protect double-chins and bald heads. I couldn't get a word in edgeways for the first few shows, which is extraordinary for me, and I went to John to tell him I couldn't handle it. He told me to fight my way in, which I did. Everybody was neurotic about their performances but the show was very, very funny and I loved doing it.

The show did not last, but the breezy style emerged in several later LWT productions – most noticeably in the *Six O'Clock Show* in which Janet Street-Porter also featured, which emerged from Birt's department, and which became the cornerstone of LWT's Friday night schedule in the early 1980s.[27]

3 London Calling
One of the most pressing problems for Birt's Current Affairs and Features Department was identified by the IBA's Chairman, Lady Plowden, after her visit to the station in July 1978. In a letter to Tesler, she wrote of LWT's despairing view of how to broadcast programmes with a sense of community in the disparate area covered by the station. LWT set out to discover London. The current affairs section of Birt's department was already delivering *The London Programme*, but the features department began to turn up stories which reflected the ethnic and sexual politics of London in the late 1970s. *Wedding Day* celebrated diversity by focusing on the most hopeful of the sacraments, whereas the seamier side of London life was exposed in the series about *The Salvation Army*.

The problems of making programmes about London were legion. The capital has no single identity. It has three major ethnic groupings and hundreds of small immigrant populations. There are myriad temples, churches, mosques, ashrams, meeting rooms and assemblies; a complex network of business and cultural centres; and physically LWT's area encompasses depressed inner cities, commuter towns, historic market towns and farmland. Although this is true of almost every city, the sheer size and complexity of London makes it impossible for any sense of solidarity or belonging to emerge. What does someone who lives and works in Guildford share with someone living and working in Tower Hamlets? For the most part, there is little sense of community in large cities. At best there is a patchwork of interacting ethnic, geographical and occupational culture, but more usually there are disjunctions, a lack of common ground. Metropolitan culture is blasé and personal relations are remote, superficial and transitory. It is little wonder that LWT happily thought of itself in national rather than regional terms. Both the *South Bank Show* and *Weekend World*, for example, focused on London as a European capital or world centre rather than on the internal rhythms and realities of the city and region. Even the *London Programme* dealt with national crime and national scandals, inevitably so given the London focus.

At the end of 1977 Grade indicated that it was unlikely that viewers considered LWT to be a local station but, he said, this 'doesn't matter. What does matter is that they watch ITV and think that it gives them the service they want.' He did say, however, that he would have a word with Wharmby, faced with a similar challenge in his department, remarked 'I think it might be dangerous to particularize or to gear one's thoughts too much to London. That way you become insular and ingrown.' This could be thought to be somewhat cavalier, given that LWT received the franchise on the basis of the idea that regional cultures were important and that television had a responsibility to reflect them. John Birt accepts the charge:

> The problem was that the factual programme department was not commuter-based. We all lived in the city, we were all interested in the City and finance, politics, entertainment, theatre, cinema and so on – and so we naturally translated our own experiences into the programmes.

This metropolitan bias, which left the suburbs and London commuter towns unserved, did expose the programme-makers to the daily reality of London's cultural and ethnic diversity. This, and the injunction to make more local programmes, provided Birt and Barry Cox with the ammunition to argue for the creation of a unit, within the Current Affairs department, solely committed to making programmes about minorities. The London Minorities Unit (LMU), headed by Jane Hewland, came into being in 1979. It was confronted with the classic dilemma that its programme-makers were part of a cosmopolitan cultural elite who were translating the alien experiences of diverse ethnic, political and sexual minorities into a language with which television viewers would be comfortable.

Inevitably, LWT's programme-makers began as anthropologists and as outsiders, noting the quaint, eccentric and curious ways of the minorities who surrounded them. However, the Birtist style forced the programme-makers to think more seriously about the theses that they were pursuing. Producers had to take seriously the sustained quality of thought needed to make sense of, say, why more West Indians are Roman Catholics than Rastafarian. The programme-makers who were to carry forward Birt's plan were not trained urban anthropologists, however, and many researchers lacked the intellectual tools required to make sense of the complex behaviour and cultures of the minorities about which they were making programmes.

During the late 1970s the anthropological programmes were as often simplistic as they were insightful. Jane Hewland puts the point forcibly: 'The first year was a nightmarish process of working out what we were supposed to be doing. John was very clear that because it was on ITV, the programmes had to be about these minorities more than it was for them. The programmes were for the whole audience. But we quickly discovered the problem with that. The minorities became violently angry if the programmes were not sympathetic to them.'

The full impact of factionalism within minorities was felt when, during LWT's series on gays, a large number of lesbians picketed the lobby in Kent House with placards proclaiming 'lesbians are people too'. The ever diplomatic Barry Cox invited them up to LWT's restaurant to try to restore some order. He and Hewland were soundly barracked by the protestors who, given a rare opportunity to make their feelings known to a television executive, did not spare the rod. Hewland remarks, wryly, 'It was very consciousness raising.'

The focus of the programmes became clearer when members of the minorities themselves began to make inroads into production, thereby adding an insider's perspective. Towards the end of LMU's first series, Hewland and her team began to understand 'what the agenda was and how different it was from the mainstream agenda.' Birt was unhappy with the first series and hauled Hewland over the coals. Hewland, determined to make a success of the unit, fought back with a list of complaints that the unit lacked proper staff, and sensible structure and a realistic perspective. These arguments became academic, however, when stories overtook quarrels about methods and techniques.

In the early 1980s, when London spewed out racial conflict and racist incidents, LWT had a team ready and able to make sense of what was happening on the streets. *Skin*, a series on black life, dropped the outsiders role and identified more clearly with the groups which they were covering. Black journalists, recruited and trained by the LMU, produced an alternative to mainstream stories news stories about Brixton and Southall.

Although the spirit of the LMU moved away from rationalist disengagement with the minorities that they were covering, the framework and the techniques of the Birt style remained. It was only a matter of time, however, until the doubts expressed in the late 1970s were to erupt into full-scale re-evaluation, and in some cases, repudiation.

The LMU – which produced over 120 programmes – represented an attempt, more or less successful, to break away from anthropology and special pleading, and led eventually to *Black on Black* and *Asian Eye*, both LWT productions for Channel 4, which, to this day, are the most fondly remembered programmes of the minorities to which they were aimed.[23]

Although Birt's department produced some of the most exciting television in ITV it also disturbed the balance of, and harmony within, LWT. It forged resentments and dissatisfaction among the production staff (who were wedded to glossy light-entertainment spectaculars and large-scale drama) which simmered for a long time. The bogeymen for LWT's older staff became the features and current affairs researchers. These young, university educated, impudent young men and women appeared in Kent House like an infestation. The other staff felt that the glamour of LWT was being tarnished and that Kent House was becoming like the South Islington branch of the Fabian Society. The sense of being part of a family company which was so assiduously cultivated by LWT's management, and firmly believed in by the majority of the technical staff, was undermined by the feeling that the station was being taken over. In reality, however, the proportion of drama and entertainment programmes increased relative to features throughout Grade's tenure as Director of Programmes, and the post-Selsdon emergence of features and current affairs.[29]

Diverse Acquisitions

Grade, Tesler and Birt were not the only ones diversifying in the late 1970s. Freeman and the Board, suddenly cash rich, decided, as had many ITV franchise holders, to widen the base of the television company and to buy other leisure enterprises. On 21 June 1977, LWT became a public company and was traded on the Stock Market. Most analysts had earmarked a price of around 80 pence but the shares – on the strength of the increase in first quarter revenue of 38 per cent and the strong expectation that LWT's franchise would be renewed – traded at 90 pence on the first day of dealings and increased to 103 pence in August. On the foundation of this £14 million flotation Freeman finally had the chance to buy into other companies and to damp down his mistrust of ITV's fragile advertising revenue. Freeman noted:

> We were flush with cash and it still appeared to me – perhaps I was wrong – that the buoyancy of TV revenue was a cyclical thing: you could do very well or you could go into a two or three year period when you could do rather badly. This narrow revenue-base obsessed me almost from the day I arrived at LWT, therefore it appeared that instead of just holding the cash in the bank that we should invest it. However, it became extremely difficult to get any agreement among board members on what kind of diversification should be undertaken.

Freeman overcame the Board's doubts and invested in two companies. In May 1978 LWT bought the publishers, Hutchinson, and in 1979 LWT paid £1.95 million for a 60 per cent share of the travel company, Page and Moy.[30] Hutchinson looked good. It published a good mixture of educational books and popular authors, such as Frederick Forsyth, Norman Mailer and Kingsley Amis and the Pope, and it returned excellent profits in the year before LWT bought it. This, as it turned out, was the best year it was to have for a long time and LWT's board became enmired in difficulties as it tried to push out Hutchinson's management and to make redundant one quarter of the staff.[31]

Page and Moy was not consistently profitable during its ten years as part of the group. Despite the failure of the diversification programme the television company continued to expand at a steady pace: overall ITV's revenue increased by 21 per cent in 1978, and LWT continued to perform better than the other ITV companies – with an increase of 28 per cent. As a result of an eleven week strike throughout ITV which began in October 1979, ITV's revenue decreased by 4.5 per cent (for the financial year which included the strike LWT's revenues increased by 2 per cent). By 1980, however, the boom had returned: ITV's revenue increased by 52.6 per cent in the calendar year 1980, and LWT's income grew by 23.5 per cent for the financial year.[32]

It was on the back of this financial security that Tesler was able to convince the Board to invest more money in programmes and to allow Grade and the programme division the freedom to take chances and to make expensive mistakes. These relatively carefree financial conditions did not prevail for much longer.

Renewing the Franchise

LWT prepared for the franchise round of 1980 with meticulous care. The folk memory of 1968 was strongly ingrained in the company and it was determined not to suffer the same fate as that which Frost and Peacock had inflicted on Rediffusion. Moreover, Freeman and Tesler were well aware that if the franchise round had taken place in 1973, as had been the original intention, or even in 1976, which was the first extension to the contract,[33] LWT might well have lost or been merged with a new company. Furthermore, even in 1980 it was obvious that the IBA was shaping up to divest someone of their franchise – if for no other reason than to encourage the others. (As it turned out the Authority felt that it had good reason to cashier at least two franchise holders – Southern and Westward.)

Freeman took no chances. In late 1979, he recruited Jeremy Potter, Managing Director of Independent Television Publications (publishers of the *TV Times*), as a director with special responsibility for overseeing and co-ordinating the franchise application. Tesler, equally determined, promoted another creative conference and encouraged the programme division to outline their long term strategies. This conference, held in Brighton in the spring of 1980, was marked by Tesler's systematic analysis of many of the programmes produced by his own company. In particular, he dissected, with the ferocious composure of an Oxford don, Wharmby's drama series. Tesler pointed out that the characters in Wharmby's series were seldom afforded the opportunity to settle into a rhythm which would establish series for long runs. Series after series was subject to Tesler's scrutiny and, after the session had concluded, Wharmby immediately rushed to his hotel room with loud threats that he intended to resign. A crocodile of senior programmes executives trooped up to the bedroom to calm Wharmby down, but although the crisis temporarily abated, it was clear that Wharmby's cards were marked.

Brighton was also memorable for Jane Hewland's emergence into the spotlight. 'Jane was at her best', a colleague recollects, 'she was clear, sparky, articulate and, compared to one or two others, mercifully short.' Tesler took note of the rising star. It was also at Brighton that Barry Cox unveiled his plan to fill some of the new hour and three quarters which the IBA would be providing for the weekend contractor when the new franchises began. In a final effort to give the London weekend franchise a reasonable chance at sharing more of London's advertising revenue, the weekend franchise holder was to begin broadcasting at 5.15 pm. Cox, anxious that Current Affairs should make a significant contribution to the new time, outlined a plan for a topical, fast-moving show which would appeal directly to the Friday afternoon feeling of breaking free for the weekend.

The Authority announced that applications for franchises had to be lodged by May, 1980. LWT were delighted to note that its only competitors were a rather strange consortium called London Independent Television. This group – for whom Hughie Green, quiz show presenter and host of *Opportunity Knocks*, acted in the David Frost role of entrepreneur – was an uninspired mixture of former Assistants of this and Under-Secretaries of that. It even had Guy Paine as Managing Director. LIT had no chance of repeating the Frost–Peacock coup of the previous franchise round. LWT did not let up, however. They attended public meetings, presented well-written planning documents, outlined new programme ideas, and generally behaved with due deference to Lady Plowden and her colleagues.

On Sunday 28 December 1980, Freeman and Tesler – along with leading figures from thirty-three other applicants for a franchise – arrived at Brompton Road to discover their fate. The sealed envelope confirmed that LWT's franchise had been renewed for eight years beginning on 1 January 1982. The only bad news was that LWT and Thames had lost the use of the Bluebell Hill transmitter in Maidstone, Kent. This, along with the audience which it served, had been handed over to the contractor for the South and East.

The IBA decided to shake up the system in the 1980s: Southern and Westward lost their franchises, ATV was forced into major changes (from which it emerged with the new name of Central TV), and Trident was informed that it could not control both Yorkshire and Tyne Tees. Amidst these changes, LWT's success came as no surprise. The station had put a great deal of effort into drama, current affairs, local programmes and sport and this had hoisted it to the forefront of ITV. The IBA noted, with approval the emergence within LWT of 'diverse good qualities over recent years'.

The franchise process, however, came under strong criticism within
ITV and a debate began about franchising which has yet to be resolved at
the time of writing.[34] Complaints flooded in from all sides of television.
Lord Windlesham, Managing Director of ATV, noted that the process
was both arbitrary and capricious, and Alan Sapper, general secretary of
ACTT, accused the IBA of industrial hooliganims 'in the way it created
mayhem among the franchise holders and their employees with no
apparent advantage to either the public or the television industry.'

John Freeman's contribution to the debate prefigured many of the
later arguments advanced by those wishing to initiate change in ITV and
deserves to be quoted at length. It reveals not only the full extent of his
disenchantment with the IBA, but its splenetic tone spilled over
increasingly into LWT's dealings with the IBA over the next five years.
In a memorandum circulated to his Executive Directors at the beginning
of August 1981, Freeman wrote:

> Based on the experience of last year's advertising and award of
> contracts, the reasonable argument could be made that a very large
> part of the disruption and damage to the system lies not in the
> procedure as such, but in the dotty way in which the existing IBA
> applied it.
>
> The cursory dismissal of Southern TV, the injuries done to ATV
> and Yorkshire (possibly fatal for the former), the imposition of
> unwanted local news on London at the weekend, the irresponsible
> appointment of a rival (and probably unsuitable) contractor for
> breakfast time, the failure to think through the implications of many
> of the decisions so lightly taken – all can be ascribed to the amateurish
> and unrealistic attitudes of an Authority, most of whose members had
> little qualification for the job beyond, no doubt, assiduous reading of
> the *Guardian* and *Observer* newspapers . . .
>
> The essence of the problem, however, lies . . . in the ideological
> dispute about the concept of fixed-term contracts. It is easy to see why
> this was widely accepted in the Fifties and Sixties. And given the
> intellectual indolence of most politicians and bureaucrats, it is not
> surprising that it has now passed unchallenged into the cannons of
> 'unalterable law'. But it must be challenged.
>
> Basically it rests on three presuppositions: first, that no self-
> perpetuating elite of publicists – Grade, Bernstein, etc. – shall be
> allowed permanent control of British television output; secondly that
> the profitability of television is too great for any single group to be
> given unrestricted access to it in perpetuity; thirdly that no single
> commercial group shall be able to acquire a long leasehold on a scarce
> public asset which ought to be open to all. I think one must
> acknowledge that there is some theoretical validity in all three. But the
> environment has totally changed over the period of the present

contracts – and beyond doubt the change is permanent. So that the public objectives on which the doctrine of fixed-term contracts was based are now achieved by other means. It is the IBA today which has and exercises control over the general content of what appears on the screen. The idea that any board of directors is in a position to give a particular bias to ITV's use of a mass medium is palpably absurd. The profitability of ITV is controlled by the Government and Parliament. At present it is too low to confer any privilege on those who invest in it; but in good times or bad the reward available to share holders is no more than our elected representatives chose to decree. Does there then remain validity in the general principle that nobody ought to be given a long leasehold on a scarce public asset?

I think not. For such a principle conflicts with what has become a more important public requirement: that, given the mixed ecology of British broadcasting, the public requires above all the highest possible professional and administrative standards in the commercial wing of broadcasting. These are incompatible with fixed-term contracts – at least of the length which are now considered appropriate. And given that public control is exercised, as it now is, by other means, the theoretical objection to the long leasehold must give way to practical need for high standards. It is worth noting that in real terms ITV is now funded by private capital; and the control exercised over it by the Government and the government-appointed public authority is in many ways more rigorous and more detailed than that which applied to other nationalized industries, including the BBC.

Within such an environment, the question which has to be asked is whether Company X is doing its contracted job properly and playing its full part in raising the standards of broadcasting. If it is not, it may properly be chopped and, provided the consequences to the rest of the system are carefully weighed, the public interest may well be served if it is. If the answer to the question is affirmative, I can see no reason whatever why its contract should not roll on indefinitely, so long as the methods of control which have developed over the last decade remain more or less as they are.

Bridget Plowden put her finger on the nub of the problem – characteristically reaching the wrong conclusion – when she said of (I think) Southern Television 'we are not saying that Southern has not done an excellent job, only that we think another group might do it even better'. That sort of haphazard selection is a luxury which broadcasting can no longer afford. If Southern was doing an excellent job, it should have been allowed to continue.

If a touch on the tiller – or the throttle – was needed to guide it into new channels, the Authority should have taken the responsibility of applying it. If a company consistently failed to acquit itself adequately or properly, it should except to be dismissed regardless of a fixed term of contract. The BBC, which is a credit to broadcasting, has like any other institution, public or private, its ups and downs in terms of performance. Can any body imagine that, if it happened to be reviewed during a comparatively lean period, the Board of Governors and the top management would be collectively dismissed in the hope that somebody else might do better? Such a course of action could be contemplated only in circumstances of grave public dereliction or scandal, and in any other circumstances could do unimaginable damage to the public interest. With a publicly controlled ITV, there is obviously a distinction in scale since one is presumably thinking of the possible dismissal of only a handful of the 16 contractors. But the disruption applies to the whole system and the argument in principle applies to a 'nationalized' ITV as to a publicly owned BBC.

Thus in my view arguments about detailed procedures for the award of contracts are all secondary (though important in detail) to challenging the central doctrine of fixed-term contracts followed by open public tender. The public interest and the quality of broadcasting would best be served by a system under which all contracts were either indefinite or rolling; all were subject to constant review; and all subject to summary termination if, after due warning, satisfactory performance was not achieved. The corollary in logic to the present system is that the IBA's massive apparatus of control should be substantially dismantled and short-term contractors should cease to be effectively nationalised and revert to being priate entrepreneurs, at risk and answerable to their shareholders.

I know that this view is anathema to the authorities both in parliament and in Whitehall and Brompton Road. But since I believe it to be sound, I think we should face the difficult job of changing opinion – and be thankful that we have perhaps five or six years in which to achieve it.

The type of opinion expressed by Freeman in this memo was not unpopular in parliament for very long.

THE CHINESE PUZZLE

Gentlemen, you can include me out!
Samuel Goldwyn

John Birt departed for his holiday in the summer of 1981 suffering from a malaise brought on by failing to become Chief Executive of Channel 4 – a post for which he had applied in July 1980.[1] Although Birt had a good relationship with Grade, he was keenly aware that the latter was only one year older than himself and, moreover, as Brian Tesler was only in his early fifties, he was likely to remain in position for at least another ten years. Birt's restlessness was diverted into action when, enticingly, Channel 4 appeared on the scene.

Although Jeremy Isaacs, Tesler's successor at Thames and a prize-winning documentary and drama producer, was the clear favourite to head the fourth channel, Birt was determined to apply. Favourites occasionally fall at the first hurdle, he reasoned; moreover, as a close follower of succession-politics, he wished to lay down a marker for the future.

Edmund Dell, Channel 4's first Chairman, felt that the broadcasting establishment was foisting Isaacs on him. Dell was not at all certain that Isaacs – who had stormed out of Thames in 1978, reportedly just before he was sacked for offering to the BBC interview material which the IBA had instructed Thames not to broadcast – was the ideal man to launch a new and inherently contentious channel. Dell was, on the other hand, favourably impressed by Birt's carefully crafted application. Birt meticulously prepared his campaign. Two of his colleagues – Sue Stoessl, LWT's Head of Research, and Rod Allen, producer of *Look Here* – helped Birt to draft, redraft, and draft again the document with which he presented his case to Dell and the consultants.[2] This submission followed the theme, articulated by Anthony Smith, the channel's intellectual father, that Channel 4 should be a publishing house for the programmes of independent producers. Birt was not a fair-weather recruit to this idea. In 1973, Birt and David Elstein – then editor of *This Week* – wrote to the Minister for Post and Telecommunications, Sir John Eden, outlining their ideas as to how the fourth channel might be organized:

> A programme controller running the fourth channel with departmental heads (but not departments) might be able to back hunches and allow *ad hoc* production units to form in a way that is just not possible within the present institutions.

Birt and Elstein proposed that ITV2 should be a national channel, run by a single controller and regulated by the IBA. The existing ITV companies would sell the new channel's advertising time in their own region, and this additional revenue would be extracted in the form of a second levy which would, in turn, pay for ITV.

This letter, his record on programmes for minorities as Controller of Features and Current Affairs, Tesler's recommendation, and the articles on the bias against understanding raised Birt's profile. However, although Dell was a reluctant convert, he was persuaded that the outcry which would have followed had Isaacs not been appointed would have made it extremely difficult for anyone else to succeed. Isaacs had the support of almost all of the consultants and in September 1980 he was duly appointed.

Birt was surprised by his intense reaction to this 'failure'. 'I underestimated the impact on my emotions', Birt recalls. 'I was bitterly disappointed, even though I didn't think that I would be appointed. I was upset because I had put so much effort into the application. Not that I was lobbying, but I was thinking, considering, questioning, etc.' Throughout the year which followed Isaacs' appointment, Birt continued to plan and to implement new programme strategies, but his department no longer provided the same stimulus and charge which previously had driven his career.

Throughout the first half of 1981, with the franchise in the bag and his department running smothly, Birt spent much of his time co-ordinating LWT's programme offers to Channel 4 and considering his future. When he arrived back at Kent House from his holiday, the decision was, in a sense, taken out of his hands. Michael Grade dropped in to his office to welcome him back and to invite him to join a meeting scheduled with Tesler and John Freeman at six o'clock. Birt was puzzled; generally he met the Chairman and the Managing Director only when he had to clinch a major financial deal – such as hiring Brian Walden. Grade noticed Birt's reaction and said 'don't worry there's no problem.'

At five to six, Birt took the lift to the thirteenth floor and walked through the doors of Directorate to Tesler's office; his career was about to take an entirely unexpected direction. Tesler told him that Grade had decided to leave LWT and to become president of a US production company, Tandem Productions.[3] Birt was shocked. He found it difficult to believe that his working relationship with Grade could be recreated with anyone else. As Birt was digesting the implications of Grade's departure, Tesler continued, 'This is happening a few years earlier than planned. I had hoped that in due course Michael would succeed me as MD and you would succeed Michael. However, we would like you to take over now, if you think you are up to it.' Birt's surprise doubled in its intensity. However, he asked Tesler for a few days to think over the offer.

He had never wanted to be Programme Controller of LWT. The position involved confronting the BBC at the red-nosed centre of the Saturday night schedule; and Birt, who was still pining after Channel 4, was not certain that Saturday peak-time was to his taste. He went home and churned over time and again the various possibilities, prospects and problems associated with the job. The thought occurred that if he did not take on the position then someone else would, and, consequently, he would have the difficult task of working under someone whom he might not like or respect. Two days later, Birt turned up at Tesler's office with his answer: 'I think I am up to the job and I would very much like to do it. As you are well aware, however, I am a very different person from Michael. I don't have Michael's instinct or gut-feeling for Saturday night's schedule, but what I don't have by nature I can acquire by analysis and applied intelligence. I'll arrive at the same conclusions, but I'll have to do it not just by my own analysis but by an infrastructure that will supply for me what Michael did instinctively.' LWT, a company reared on intuition, was about to enter the computer age.

The news of Grade's resignation and Birt's elevation caused great alarm on the studio floors, bars and offices at Kent House. Many of LWT's staff viewed Features and Current Affairs with suspicion and Birt, as Controller of the Department, with active dislike. As Brian Tesler had noted at the Brighton conference the year before: 'Current Affairs and Features . . . as a result of the massive, spontaneous growth it has enjoyed since Selsdon [is] seen by some as a cross between a cuckoo in the nest and the Incredible Hulk.' Birt's reputation on the studio floor was as a grey, austere, humourless man. It was inevitable that a company raised on the very open and endearing qualities of Bennett and Grade would not raise three hurrahs for Birt.

Birt was aware of the problem: 'I just wouldn't make the mistake of trying to do something that I knew that I was not equipped for. I wasn't like Cyril and Michael; they were comedians, they could have stood on a stage and told jokes. I wasn't that sort of person, so I didn't compete.'

Birt, although aware of the disapproval of others, did not shirk from becoming unpopular if it was an inevitable consequence of his ideas. During his five years as Director of Programmes he challenged the techniques, beliefs and values of the ITV network. With Tesler's support, Birt attempted to create a new way of looking at audiences and revenue in ITV; in effect, he tried to unlock the Chinese puzzle that was the network. LWT introduced new ideas, values and methods in order to solve some old questions.

By 1987, when Birt left ITV, many of his ideas had entered into the mainstream. He had unlocked the puzzle to his own satisfaction; however, his ideas were, in a sense, trumped by a major intellectual shift initiated by two neo-liberal economists – Alan Peacock and Samuel Brittan. These two were the principal architects of the Peacock Committee's Report on Advertising on the BBC which, in the late 1980s, became the touchstone for the Conservative government's deregulation of broadcasting. LWT's challenge to the network turned out to be preparation for a very different world from the one in which Birt began to formulate his ideas.

The Puzzle Man

John Birt spent much of his career in ITV commanding the respect of those for whom he worked and earning the warm friendship of some who worked most closely with him. However, he alienated a great many people in LWT. One of his closest colleagues comments, 'He was a very kind man who did not realize the effect he had on people. Often he did not realize the force of what he was saying; he didn't realize that he was making people feel stupid. Because he was so relentlessly logical he followed the argument all the way home to the humiliation of the person who had lost. Someone else would have let the guy off the hook long before.' He was thought arrogant, cold, hard and elitist by a considerable number of people at the station.

According to his close colleagues, one of Birt's assets was his ability to work through a mass of detail, absorb the patterns and trends inherent in data, reach conclusions about these trends in advance of most of his contemporaries, and act resolutely on his analysis. Those who rejected his answers, or even his questions, were in turn rejected – unless they could demonstrate that they had thought longer, harder, and had more data than he possessed. His respect was hard won and his disdain was obvious.

Born into a working-class, Catholic family in 1944, Birt was brought up in hard streets behind Liverpool docks. His father lived out one part of the working-class dream in the five years after the war. He became a salesman and he was able to leave the docks behind and buy a house in a suburb of Liverpool. Birt personified another aspect of the working-class ideal of those years. The year of his birth was also the year of R.A.B. Butler's Education Act, which guaranteed education for all up until the age of 15, and which signalled the beginnings of a cross-party commitment to meritocratic advance. A working-class, grammar school boy could, in the early 1960s, reasonably hope to enter Oxford or

Cambridge: there was room at the top for those bloody minded or lucky enough to climb there. Birt was both. He gained 3 A-levels – two in Mathematics and the other in Physics – and in 1963 was accepted, appropriately, by St Catherine's College, Oxford.

After many years as a Society (an associate college), St Catherine's became a full college in 1962. The new college, whose prize-winning, austere modernist buildings were in stark contrast to its old run-down location near a police station, was created, in part, as the result of the efforts of its first Master, the historian, Alan Bullock, but also in response to the expansion of higher education needed to service Birt's generation. It was an appropriate place for an upwardly mobile working-class boy to read for a degree in engineering.[4]

Birt could have easily have settled for a good degree and a steady job in industry, as did many of his contemporaries. In his first week at St Catherine's he became, instead, enthralled by the cinema. During the early 1960s undergraduates and cinephiles would gather round small screens, or sheets draped on walls, to watch *The Bicycle Thieves*, *Four Hundred Blows*, *Un Chien Andelou*, and anything by Fellini. French critics and directors, such as Truffaut and Godard, who wrote for the critical journal, *Cahiers Du Cinema*, made grandiose claims for cinema as the art form of the twentieth century. Such assertions found responses among many of Birt's generation. The new medium – the moving image – was to take the place of old, bourgeois art forms of the past.

Birt was omnivorous: he watched everything, developing and refining his taste. He ran a film society, directed a short film,[5] and acquired an education; in between times he finished his degree in engineering.

He decided to take the well-trodden path to the BBC television centre, and he applied to the BBC for a job as a trainee. To his dismay, he was turned down. His next application, to Granada, was successful. He was appointed as a production trainee and subsequently became a researcher on Granada's brash, young current affairs series, *World In Action*. Although he had no formal training in politics or economics, and he was not part of the Oxford PPE set who had so irked Michael Peacock at the BBC, Birt quickly established himself. He pulled off his major coup in July 1967 at the end of his first year with the programme. Somehow he convinced the editor of *The Times*, William Rees-Mogg, Bishop Trevor Huddlestone, and Frank Soskice, a former cabinet minister, to meet Mick Jagger – fresh from a court appearance for possession of cannabis. Jagger flew in by helicopter (carefully filmed by *World In Action*) to talk to the assembled elders about the problems of youth in the modern world. It was a classic piece of tabloid television twenty years before the term was coined, and Birt was on the first level of the greasy pole.

The following year Birt and a colleague, Andy Mayer, created *Nice Time* – a mixture of a chat show and parlour games which launched the television careers of Germaine Greer, then a lecturer in English at

Warwick University, and Kenny Everett. After two series of *Nice Time*,
Birt joined Gus McDonald as co-editor of *World In Action*. Birt was the
star tabloid journalist, brought in to add sparkle and a bit of energy to a
programme which Granada's management thought was in danger of
going stale. His experience at *World In Action* rapidly brought him face
to face with his limitations. He knew nothing of foreign affairs and even
less about the economy, but he gave himself a crash course in both, and
over the following two years he developed a solid reputation.

By the time Bennett invited Birt to join LWT (on the strength of *Nice
Time* as much as *World In Action*), Birt had undergone his first apparent
transformation. The man who created *Weekend World* would no more
have flown in Mick Jagger for an interview about 'morality' than he
would have dressed in breeches and performed a morris dance.

Birt's management style, in which he demanded a great deal of
autonomy from above but exercized considerable control on those below,
emerged over the next ten years. He had an overriding commitment to
hierarchy and to order. He spoke about programmes or strategy only to
those to whom he considered it appropriate so to do. Birt's personality
was as relevant to LWT in the early 1980s as Bennett's had been in the
early 1970s. Moreover, just as Bennett's Jewishness was a clue to his
editorial and business judgements, and his professional relationships, so
Birt's Roman Catholicism cannot be ignored.

There are myriad ways to be a Roman Catholic. The long historical
experience, and world-wide reach of the Church, encourages it to
sanction both those who take pleasure in life, and those who adopt a
more ascetic approach. There is a spacious humanism in one strand of
Catholicism; pleasure in the form of food and drink is a gift from God
which should be enjoyed to the full. However, the Church also sanctions
austerity and rigour. From St John of the Cross to Opus Dei, the current
champions of puritanical Catholicism, the Church has nurtured men and
women who elevate self-control to the first of the virtues. Catholicism
prides itself on the intellectual rigour of its great philosophers and
theologians. However, the great danger has always been that logic
overbalances into the pursuit of minutiae. The legendary instance of
medieval theologians arguing over the number of angels that could dance
on the head of pin is a picture of reason gone mad. At their best,
however, Roman Catholic grammar schools fostered long-cherished
styles of analytical thought. Catholicism also promoted the idea of a
hierarchy of valid judgements. Religious truth, the faith contended, was
validated by a tradition which was interpreted by the religious hierarchy.

After the war, children of Irish Catholic families, even those that
stretched back for several generations, slowly lifted themselves from the
sink to which they had been consigned by the host country. Each Irish
Catholic who made it into the English middle class and beyond was
profoundly influenced by his or her background, and had to make a

decision, consciously or not, as to which lifestyle was appropriate. Many responded by following the expansive style of Irishmen the world over, and despising the cold arrogance of the class into which they had entered. Others, however, choose public self-control; they mastered their instincts and their background.

Birt exemplified elements of each tradition. He followed the intellectual style of the church in his respect for detail and commitment to logic. His was the scholastic approach applied to television; he was a born paradigm-builder. However, this austere public face disguised great enthusiasms. He had a Liverpuddlian's commitment to football and his delight at scoring a goal in a charity match on Cup Final day at Wembley was undisguised. The Liverpool connection was exposed further by Birt's elated reaction to Cilla Black's decision to join LWT. The recruitment of Cilla – a member of the enchanted circle that surrounded the Beatles in Birt's teenage years – is considered by Birt to be one of his finest decisions.

Birt's asceticism was also belied by the pleasure which he took in his clothes. His style in the 1970s was that of an unredeemed hippy; a jangle of tie-die shirts, long hair, John Lennon glasses, and strange footwear. In the 1980s, this was replaced by designer jackets and expensive shoes; all studiously casual but extremely costly. When he left LWT in 1987 to join the BBC, the channel controllers asked him what he would like as a gift. 'An Armani suit', Birt replied. When he was relaxed with close friends or colleagues the Catholic style owed more to Liverpool than to St Thomas Aquinas. Birt's personality and style helped to shape LWT's response to the 1980s.

The Essential Tension?

LWT thought that it was entering 1982 in reasonably good shape. Almost immediately, however, it became clear that the company was heading into serious financial problems, and that any long-term plans which Birt had for the programme division had to be put on the shelf while he and Tesler dealt with the exigencies of the crisis.

Two events, in particular, sapped the network's and, consequently, LWT's revenue: the cost of launching Channel 4, and a dispute between Equity, the actors' union, and the Institute of Practitioners in Advertising (IPA), which represents the advertising agencies. The conflict between the agencies and Equity was, in essence, quite simple. The agencies wanted the actors to be paid less for advertisements which appeared on TVam and Channel 4 than for the same ad when it appeared on ITV. Equity pointed out that they had never before been paid according to the size of the audience, and it could see no reason why this principle should be introduced for the new channels. The agencies countered with the assertion that the new channels *inherently* had small audiences and were different from ITV in which small audiences were *contingent* on time and opposition from other channels.

As a result of this dispute, advertisements in which Equity actors appeared were not repeated on Channel 4 and TVam. This produced embarrassing gaps between the programmes, but the real effects were felt by the ITV companies which had relied on their Channel 4 advertising revenue to offset the costs of the new channel.

Channel 4 cost money. In the first year, each ITV company had to contribute 18 per cent of its advertising revenue to the new channel.[6] This was to be offset by levy relief and by selling the channel's advertising space. The IPA/Equity dispute meant that LWT was unable to sell much of its Channel 4 time, and the amount it did sell was heavily discounted.[7]

LWT's sales department had sold the weekend airtime with their usual enthusiasm. They had anticipated on average that five per cent of viewers would watch Channel 4's programmes and were somewhat shocked to discover that the average rating was less than half of this figure. Consequently, LWT suffered a shortfall in advertising revenue of around £3 million in 1982. Eventually, the IBA allowed the ITV companies an extra two minutes in peak-time to compensate for the losses which they were making on their Channel 4 airtime. However ITV was suffering. By July, six months into the new contract, LWT's profits had fallen to £4 million – £200,00 down on the previous year.

LWT took Channel 4 very seriously.[8] Birt was asked by Grade to organize LWT's productions for the new channel and the station became the biggest single contributor to Channel 4. In May 1982, all of the hard work came to fruition: Channel 4 commissioned £6 million worth of programmes. Sue Woodford, Channel 4's Commissioning Editor for Multicultural programmes, bought two series on the strength of *Skin*. These programmes – *Black on Black* and *Eastern Eye* – were derided by many black intellectuals for not concentrating on 'serious' issues, but they were greatly loved by the communities at which they were aimed. *Black on Black* became *the* programme to which people referred when they were discussing ethnic television. Other series included the drama, *A Married Man*, adapted from the novel by Piers Paul Read; the game shows, *Babble* and *Tell the Truth*; and Clive James' eccentric chat show, *The Late Clive James*. LWT produced 198 hours of television for Channel 4 in 1982–3.

ITV companies often claimed at the beginning that it cost them money to produce programmes for Channel 4. This was, by and large, an accountancy trick. In strict terms LWT did lose money; when it was in dispute with the IBA over programme cuts, LWT calculated that it was subsidizing a series of 20 *Black on Black*'s by £217,500, and overall that they had discounted their Channel 4 productions by £1.2 million. However, this was not a real subsidy; it was based on an assessment of total costing, which is the amount that a programme would have cost if the share of the price of plant, fixed studio costs, the electricity bill, and even the canteen and the company secretary, etc had been built in. The other way to calculate the figure was to look at the marginal costs: how much it actually cost LWT to make the programme, excluding the majority of the below-the-line expenditure. On that basis, LWT did not lose money on its Channel 4 programmes.

As well as the Equity dispute and the cost of Channel 4, LWT's financial future seemed blighted by the Thatcher Government's broad-casting policy. In 1982, Kenneth Baker, the Minister for Information Technology, asked the Government's Information Technology Advisory Panel (ITAP) to produce a report on cable services. ITAP pointed out that unless action was taken, overseas companies would come to control the provision of systems and equipment. The Government took this report – which scandalized the television industry – and turned it into the grandiose strategy of an entertainment-led information revolution. The Hunt Committee, under the chairmanship of the former Cabinet Secretary, Lord Hunt of Tanworth, was asked to explore means of financing and regulating cable. The committee was established on 6 April and reported on 28 September 1982. It recommended that cable systems be allowed in the UK, and that they should be funded, in part, by advertising.

On 27 April 1983, the Government published a White Paper, *The Development of Cable Systems and Services*, in which it announced that ten to twelve pilot licences would be granted to cable operators, and, on 26 November, eleven franchises were duly awarded: Aberdeen, Belfast, Coventry, Croydon, Ealing, Glasgow, Guildford, Liverpool, Swindon, Westminster and Windsor.[9] This was the first breach in the duopoly and, within the next four years, it was followed by a flood of criticism from the Conservative Party and right-wing intellectuals which engulfed the ITV system.

In 1981 Tesler and LWT's board established a working party to explore the implications of cable and satellite services. This report fed into their long-term plans but, in the short term LWT had prepared for the expense of the Channel 4 subscription and for the problems of launching the new channel. They did not, however, anticipate the seriousness of the shortfall in advertising revenue. By the winter of 1982, Tesler and Birt were becoming worried. Tesler recalls, 'We were hit by a recession, and I had to set up a task force which met several times a week to make economies and, inevitably, we had to make programme cuts.'

Birt was particularly perplexed. He had been developing a plan to force the other major companies to make more suitable programmes for the weekend. He, along with his team, had spent a considerable amount of time working out why whole quarters could go by in which LWT had to rely on feature films and repeats in order to shore up their schedule.

The team had come to four conclusions. First, the ITV regions in the south of England were, for reasons to do with the uneven distribution of economic growth in the UK, taking an increasing share of ITV's advertising revenue without bearing the cost of network production. It was clear that TVS, for example, would eventually outstrip Yorkshire in revenue. Secondly, American series no longer pulled large audiences and therefore ITV could not rely on relatively cheap imports to maintain the schedule when it did not have sufficient material of its own. Thirdly, the BBC's weekend peak-time schedule cost more than that of ITV, and delivered better ratings because it relied on home-grown drama, comedy and variety. The BBC's weekend peak-time seemed to Birt to be more rich, varied and solid than that which had been delivered by ITV. Fourthly, as a result of the success of Brian Young and Lady Plowden's policy of forcing ITV to spend more on off-peak minority programmes, the amount of revenue available for peak-time was not sufficient to generate the type of schedule which the BBC was producing. IBA policy, Birt felt, was slowly strangling the life out of the source of finance for minority programmes. Without *Game For A Laugh* there would be no *South Bank Show*. Birt did not want ITV to revert back to the early 1960s; however, he was desperate to see the financial balance between minority programmes and peak-time recalibrated.

Although he had the rudiments of this strategy worked out, he was unable to bring any of it to immediate effect. Instead, he found himself at the centre of a major financial crisis. He had, simply, less money to make more programmes. Consequently, instead of producing the kind of varied diet of drama, comedy, features and current affairs which would have been in keeping with his long-term aims, he believed that the only way to keep the company going was to assemble an emergency schedule of comparatively inexpensive, high-ratings programmes.

Some years later, reflecting on LWT's response, some ITV people, including a few within LWT, expressed the belief that the short-term approach was muddle headed. If ITV had kept its nerve, the critics argue, and not converted the weekend to a clearing house for game shows then LWT would have been able to build the kind of high ratings and strong revenue performance which Birt himself delivered in 1986 and 1987. Birt and Tesler are unrepentant; to use one of the slogans current in 1982, they are convinced that there was no alternative to their approach, and that any one else faced with their problems would have taken the same route. They point to two reasons for their version of TINA. First, LWT was not alone in its problems, the rest of the network were suffering. As ever, when ITV was in trouble, the companies sought to maximize their revenue during the week, rather than expose their programmes to the intense competition of the weekend. Consequently, not only were LWT's own financial resources stretched, the company had to fill the gaps left as the network pulled out of producing drama and situation comedy for the weekend. LWT had no choice, Tesler and Birt believed, but to develop a short-term fire-fighting schedule.

Secondly, LWT's – and the network's – crisis occurred during a major structural shake-out of British industry. The country was struggling to cast off the effects of a deep recession. High unemployment and public sector cuts resulted in a pervading sense of gloom in Britain. It is against this background, and the government's cable policy, that LWT's game show period should be evaluated.

When faced with these fiscal problems, Birt began to apply some of the lessons that he learned while co-ordinating LWT's Channel 4 productions. In order to assess the cost of LWT's productions for the new channel, Birt set LWT's accountants the task of working out the cost per hour of making certain programmes. He was astonished when the accountants delivered their first thoughts on what was known as total costing. Instead of including simply the above-the-line costs – such as the stars, non-staff directors etc. – a total costing budget for a programme included a share for the below-the-line costs such as electricity, studio costs, the rates, the wages of the cameraman, and the receptionists etc.

Total costing is not a precise science. A great deal of the expenditure is difficult to apportion to programmes and, of course, the studios would have to be open, and staff employed, regardless of whether a programme was being made. However, the total costings procedures revealed that, for example, instead of an average drama costing say, £80,000 an hour – the above the line costs – the actual price was, say, £160,000. Armed with this information, and aware of the extent of the cut-backs, Birt was able to calculate that situation comedies and dramas cost more per hour than any other type of programme. Moreover, with the network cutting back too, and with more holes appearing in the schedule, Birt had to fill them as best he could. He resorted to making game shows which, like fast food, had an initial appeal which was quickly burned off. In his opinion, his schedule, for the duration of the financial crisis, had to be dictated by LWT's need to produce as many strong ratings performances as cost effectively as possible.

Birt feared that if he did not plug the revenue decline then LWT would enter a vicious circle in which lack of money would produce an impoverished schedule, and a threadbare schedule would result in a further loss of advertising revenue. However, in order to make the cut-backs, and to react to the crisis, LWT needed the backing of the IBA. On 23 December 1982, Tesler wrote to the IBA's new Director General – John Whitney:[10]

Most expenditure in any television company flows from [programmes] and we have instituted selective cuts in the budgets of most of the programmes we are due to make before the end of our financial year in July 1983. But the only really significant economy we can make is in the actual cancellation or postponement of programmes. And it is here that we need to seek the Authority's understanding and approval.

Tesler and Birt asked that the IBA sanction the cancellation of several programmes. LWT wanted to cut two local series – *London Talking*, which was a kind of *Right to Reply* for London programmes, and a series of social action programmes. It also wanted to drop a local documentary, *Inner City*, seven editions of *South of Watford*, seven editions of the *London Programme*, and to reduce the running time of *The Big Match*. These programmes would not have disappeared permanently, but their cancellation would have necessitated a reduction in LWT's local output to 2 hours 50 minutes a week – 10 minutes below the 3 hour minimum required by the IBA.

Tesler also asked for permission to reduce *Weekend World* by six editions, and to drop three plays from a group of ten. In drama, Birt was willing to hold over the transmission of a drama called *Mitch*, starring John Thaw, until the next financial year.[11] Finally, LWT wanted to close down transmission at 12.30 am.

Whitney responded cautiously to this unwelcome Christmas gift. On 6 January he informed Tesler that, 'Members [of the Authority] were concerned to hear about your situation, but they have asked for a study to be made of your position before a decision is taken.' Most of the IBA's senior staff were deeply sceptical of LWT's plea of poverty. They had seen ITV cry wolf so often that they were immune to further appeals.

The IBA's suspicion was revealed to Tesler by Peter Rogers, the IBA's Director of Finance. At the end of January, Rogers and Tesler met at a Channel 4 conference. The latter took Tesler aside into a quiet corner and explained that Colin Shaw, the IBA's Director of Television, was extremely unsympathetic to LWT's proposals and, moreover, that members of the Authority were leaning in Shaw's direction. Rogers was, himself, in something of a quandary. He had recently become Director of Finance and, indeed, John Whitney had recently beaten Shaw for the post as Director General. LWT was Whitney's and Rogers' first major test, and the rest of the Authority – along with its senior staff – was waiting to see if they had the stuff to stand up to ITV.

Over the next forty minutes Rogers cross-examined Tesler. Rogers pointed out that his colleagues were unhappy for three reasons. First, if the Authority accepted a reduction in LWT's local programmes, there would be a long queue of others behind them; secondly, the reduction in programme supply would have an impact on network arrangements; thirdly, and most importantly, LWT had had a long and very successful run. 'What's wrong with one bad year?', Rogers asked.

Tesler pointed out that LWT was particularly badly hit by the problems associated with the launch of Channel 4; that if the financial problems disappeared, LWT could readjust their commitment to the network from programmes in stock; that if the Authority did not accept LWT's proposals, then LWT might have to cut back further. Tesler argued his case forcibly: 'the economies we have already made in overheads, in capital expenditure, in staff, and in programme budgets, have seriously damaged the company's morale and jeopardized its longer-term ability to sustain the ITV system at the weekends, as it had done for years almost single-handed.' He continued: 'if we are forced to devote more time to local programmes than we think right, not only will the number of our peak-time contributions to the schedules reduce, but the quality of our local programmes will suffer. There will be fewer *London Programmes* and more London talking heads.'

Tesler felt that he might have won the battle with Rogers, but he would be lucky to win the war with the IBA. He was right; three days after his chat with Rogers, and the day after the Authority met to discuss a paper presented by their senior staff about LWT's problems, John Whitney wrote the following reply to Tesler:

Members well understand and are deeply concerned at the damage which the IPA/Equity dispute is causing throughout the industry and they appreciate the nature and magnitude of your own company's difficulties. At the same time, Members are reluctant to allow any company to depart from its contractual obligations except in the most extenuating circumstances. They believe strongly that a company (and its shareholders) must do its utmost to marshall its own resources in order to remain within its contractual obligations. This must, I believe, include an examination of the extent to which non-television activities within the LWT group might have a part to play, even if that should involve the realization of assets or disengagement from some of the activities involved.

I would not wholly rule out the prospect of some limited and temporary contractual adjustment, but you will appreciate that the IBA will press you to dig very deep into your own resources before this stage is reached.

Whitney's offer of 'some limited and temporary contractual adjustment' offered some hope, and Tesler asked his staff to provide him with more information to complete his case to the IBA. Peter McNally, LWT's financial director pointed out to Tesler that 'there has been a significant erosion of profits in real terms over the past six years', and moreover, that although a large part of the variance between Channel 4 income and Channel 4 subscription was mitigated by a reduction in the Levy, it did leave LWT with a substantial deficit.

At the end of February, having made its general point that it would not accept the principle of cuts to offset financial difficulties, the IBA accepted that LWT did have problems and it offered its own version of the judgement of Solomon. It permitted selected cuts while insisting on an increase in other programmes. *London Talking*, the social action programme (which was to be about local unemployment), and one hour of local documentary disappeared. However, although the IBA accepted that seven editions of the *London Programme* could be dropped, it insisted that only two *South of Watford*s be omitted. Furthermore, it asked for an additional three programmes on pool, and three more editions of the local review and chat show, *Sunday, Sunday*.

On the network front, the IBA allowed LWT to hold over John Thaw's *Mitch*, to cut three single dramas, and not to transmit some repeated series. It was adamant, however, that *Weekend World*, the IBA's Holy Grail, should retain its full run.

This attempt by LWT to make cuts which it considered necessary in order to live with an externally imposed cost (the Channel 4 levy), demonstrates the tension inherent in the ITV–IBA relationship, but also examplifies the reasons for ITV's frustrations with the IBA down the years. It was the IBA's constitutional responsibility to ensure a properly balanced television service which reflected the diverse cultures of Britain's regions. The IBA was integral to the maintenance of a proper commitment to local programmes. However, LWT's history shows that when revenue is flowing and the company feels secure, then the IBA's immediate and day-to-day pressure was not essential to the creation of local current affairs and features. The weekend contract ensures, however, that when ITV feels a draught, LWT catches a cold. This was clearly the case in the winter of 1982.

The essential tension between the IBA and the companies may have resulted in stability, but in the short term LWT was still in the middle of financial problems. Birt's old department bore the brunt of the immediate shearing, and his survival tactics over the next two years resulted in an increased commitment to game shows and people shows, and, as a result of the cut-backs, a reduction in resources allocated to drama and variety spectaculars. The internal strains and pressures within LWT continued to build through 1983. However Birt, being Birt, was not responding simply to short-term financial tensions; he had already begun to work out a theory of how the network should operate.

Conjectures and Refutations

Running an ITV company used to be a relatively simple business. You made your programmes, decided where to put them, and hoped that the audience and the advertisers liked them. Occasionally your profits dipped, but this tended to be random and it was difficult to plan ahead. You could wing it; play your hunches, back unpredictable projects, and protect irascible, expensive and sensitive programme-makers. The

Grades, the Bernsteins, and the other great ITV figures enjoyed themselves. They took the business extremely seriously, and were successful at it, but they were, in spirit, closer to Hollywood than to Pension Funds.

Contrast this with a typical day for a fictional old-style ITV executive in the mid-1980s. His day starts with a conference at which he cannot escape from people who speak about 'the footprint of a geosynchronous satellite in the "Clarke Belt" ', or who hint slyly the Germans will regret their decision to go with DMAC. Not only does a new technological jargon free-fall into his conversations with a dull thud, but the audience – which previously had seemed clearly defined, if in reality unpredictable – is described to him as 'a series of targeted, sub-demographic groups'. Back at the office, he scurries to a dictionary to discover that demography 'is the statistical study of life in human communities' (The Little Oxford Dictionary). Not much enlightened, he phones a friend in advertising to ask what the dictionary means. The friend explains that basically it refers to the various distinctive groupings of which a society is composed. Male and Female are demographic groups split by sex; age and class may be divided in the same way: the usual market research classifications were AB=professionals, C1=white collar workers, C2=skilled working class, and DE=unemployed, unskilled and those on state pension. The friend points out that the multiple sub-divisions are bewildering in their complexity and he begins to wax lyrical about 'lifestyle analysis', at which point the executive makes his excuses and drops the phone in disgust.

Somewhat clearer as to how the Clarke Belt relates to AB men aged between 16 and 24, he drops in on the Head of Research to ask how last night's new situation comedy fared. 'Well', the researcher replies, looking up temporarily from his IBM series 2 personal computer, 'the AI's were good'. 'But did people enjoy it?' asks our by now irascible executive. 'It had an AI of 80', the researcher answers before bending once more to his computer. At this point our executive discovers that not only is the word 'audience' no longer acceptable in adult conversation, the word 'enjoyed' is suspect. (The Appreciation Index [AI], which is a scale from 1–100, on which a sample of viewers indicate their approval of the programme, is the operational definition of enjoyment. Schedulers increasingly relied on AI's as the 1980s progressed.)

Nowhere is safe. Our executive is invited to dine with the Prime Minister – a somewhat daunting encounter at the best of times. Over the port, the Prime Minister asks him whether Friedrich von Hayek's thoughts on the market have any relevance to broadcasting. Our ITV executive is dismayed to discover that Hayek did not play left back for West Germany in the 1974 World Cup, and he bluffs furiously, hoping the Prime Minister doesn't notice (she does). That night, his dreams are invaded by a softly spoken Scottish ghost who, with devilish grin, beckons him into a world of computers, marketing men, financiers, fibre optic cables, aerials, squarials, LNB's, TVRO's, SMATV's and peritelevision sockets. 'I am the ghost of broacasting future', the ghost intones. The following morning our executive hires an academic to provide him with a thorough briefing on market economics.

The old conceptual, financial and programming tools which had sustained ITV for nearly thirty years were becoming obsolete. Even Tom Margerison's slide-rule would not have been much help in sorting out the combined effects of video, cable, satellite, Channel 4, Channel 5, sub-demographic targeting, and whatever else had to go into the econometric model which ITV became. New values, new beliefs and new solutions to the puzzles had to be brought into play. Unfortunately, it was difficult to achieve such breakthroughs and to maintain the cosy, collegiate atmosphere which, for all the stresses and strains, had pervaded ITV for many years. The system was ripe for change.

In May 1983 John Birt began to put into practice the changes which he, and his teams, had sketched out in theory. The first shot across ITV's broadsides occurred when he threatened to do the unthinkable; he was prepared not to show a network drama production – Granada's *Shades of Darkness*. Most companies took advantage of their right to schedule a production outside of peak-time if they felt that it did not play well in their region; no one, however, refused to show a network drama once it had been accepted. Birt had already exercised his right to reschedule a programme when, in April, he transmitted a Central series called *Pictures* at 10.30 pm when the rest of the network was showing at at 9 pm.[12] Although *Shades of Darkness* was eventually broadcast in London, it was transmitted after the 10 o'clock news. Birt had made the first point in his wider struggle to make the network aware of the specific needs of the weekend schedule.

The network controllers realized quickly that Birt, although a new boy, was not about to bide his time, listen to sage advice, and speak only when spoken to. He was convinced that his own analysis was clearer, superior and sounder than those of his colleagues.

In July 1983 Birt stirred up the hornets nest with a presentation, complete with pie charts, at the annual meeting between the network controllers and the members of the IBA. This paper, *Competition and Change*, was the first fruit of the infrastructure which Birt established to help him make his decisions.

This infrastructure consisted mainly of two committees: the resources planning committee and the transmission planning committee. The latter contained the Controllers of Research, of Programme Planning, and Programme Organization, and it became the think-tank within which LWT's schedules and ideas were hammered out. Warren Breach, Controller of Programme Planning recalls the reason for establishing the committees:

Before 1982, each company exchanged their programmes on a quarterly basis, and the system was about two quarters ahead at any one time. There did not appear to be any strategic planning, whereas John thought that we had to have an entertainment plan, a religion plan and so on. We needed a basic schedule outline for the whole year, but it wasn't easy. We had to drag ITV out of the world of quill pens and swinging light bulbs into the world of computerized offices and schedules. Now we as a company are planning three years ahead – which is what you have to do with drama. Furthermore, now that we are commissioning independent producers we need to be in a position to identify vacant slots. This means knowing what the whole year's schedule will look like.

This committee was looked on with some disdain by programme-makers who thought that it slowed up the process of decision making, and, moreover, that it squeezed the creative juice out of television. However, it provided the information and the strategic thinking which, at the meeting with the Authority, allowed Birt to attack the way in which the network allocated its resources.

Surrounded by puzzled members of the Authority, network programme controllers who were imploding with fury, and the officers of the IBA – some of whose teeth ground silently as their policies came under attack – Birt outlined his position. He began by emphasizing that, in the long term, television – and ITV in particular – had problems:

> Television watching as an activity seems to be declining . . . We can speculate on the reasons. Our viewers are richer and less home-bound than they were twenty years ago; and, with the growth of leisure activities of all kinds, they have other ways of spending their time. But nevertheless they *will* stay at home and watch television, *if* they like what they see.[13]

Birt continued with an explanation of the reasons for ITV's relative decline *vis-à-vis* the BBC:

> What explains the relative decline of ITV in audience terms? First, there's no doubt that over the past ten years the BBC has tried increasingly to be competitive in peak-time and most of all at weekends . . . But the second reason for the worsening of ITV's fortunes may be the intrinsic weakening of ITV peaktime.

Birt's research team had identified the weaknesses in the ITV schedule: on an average spring weekday ITV won the early and the BBC the late evening; the audience dipped between *Crossroads* and *Coronation Street* where a factual programme was placed; and the audience further declined when a documentary was scheduled at 9 pm. LWT's research identified an average Saturday in which ITV won early evening, drew the late evening, and were trounced in the middle. This research led Birt to conclude that 'the best domestic material is more popular than all but a handful of new films' and, therefore, that 'the way now to build a successful peak-time schedule is to place together a number of strong, first run, domestic programmes.'

Building a strong peak-time schedule was important, Birt argued, because 75 per cent of ITV's revenue was earned in that period. The problem was that although ITV spent some 30 per cent more than the BBC making programmes for the average Sunday, the network spent *less* money than the BBC on peak-time programmes. Only 13 per cent of ITV's expenditure was spent on peak-time programmes; therefore, Birt argued, ITV would have to spend 70 per cent more – or £50 million – if it was to build a sufficiently strong peak-time schedule. The extra money would come from savings on off-peak programmes.

The problem, as Birt pointed out to the members of the Authority, was the IBA's policy of insisting on an overabundance of local, religion, adult education, current affairs and other minority interest programmes. This ensured that the ITV companies, in search of credit with the Authority, spent twice as much on off-peak as they did on peak. Birt called on the Authority to sanction his survival tactics. He asked some hard questions, and introduced uncomfortable conjectures:

> [I]n the light of Channel 4 . . . is there any longer a case, for instance, for expending money and talent on education programmes which can only be placed on Sunday mornings? Could some of the majors' existing programmes in other areas of minority interests be transferred to Channel 4 and be financed by Channel 4 out of its own budget?

Secondly:

> From where else can we free resources? . . . There is scope for reducing the amount of local programming made within ITV – by the majors and by the regionals – without sacrificing the regional characteristics of the system and the local identity of ITV companies.

Having found the money, Birt then decided on how it should be allocated. He offered two options: first, that the regionals should make a concerted effort to contribute to peak-time programming. This would present problems however: 'The programme experience of the regionals is rooted in their local programming. They *have* made occasional forays into peak-time; but *large scale* production is another matter.'

The other approach open to the Authority would be to ease the obligations on the regionals to make local programmes; but to ask them to carry a greater share of the burden of Channel 4 and the rental than they do now. This would in turn free the majors to increase their provision of peak-time programmes.

Birt asked for a reduction of 11 per cent in expenditure in off-peak programmes, and for this revenue to be reallocated to the majors for investment in peak-time programmes. He concluded:

All that is needed is the will to strike a new balance within our programming; and the energy to galvanize into action the whole of the ITV system.

ITV was undoubtedly galvanized into action; everyone scuttled off to find ways of attacking Birt. The IBA's television division under its new director David Glencross, set about examining critically the figures upon which Birt based his analysis.

Several people inside the IBA were torn between their concern about Birt's analysis and their commitment to challenge ITV. Colin Shaw, Glencross's predecessor who had moved across to join the Independent Television Companies Association, long held the view that ITV was far too conservative in its programme policy, and was sympathetic to Birt's challenge. However, Shaw felt that Birt's attack was too wide-ranging and that it was in danger of dispensing with solid achievements as much as moribund policies.

TVS, which was emerging as the most powerful and ambitious of the regional companies, took on itself the task of attacking the assumptions which were at the heart of Birt's paper. Finally, TSW, the contractor for the South West of England, developed a long and detailed criticism of Birt which it hoped would allay any possibility that his paper would be taken seriously.

The arguments rumbled on for six months. On 7 October, Whitney wrote to Tesler:

When John Birt came with the Controllers' Group to talk to the IBA, we listened to his thesis with interest. The issues that he raised were important ones. However, we were, upon reflection, very doubtful about the figures upon which most of John's prognosis was built, and the staff there have had discussions with LWT staff about them. It soon became clear, to both sides I think, that the figures were not just slightly awry, but so substantially wrong as to make them of little value. Indeed they were misleading.

Tesler, Birt and McNally were disappointed that the IBA chose to ridicule the figures on which LWT's analysis was founded. Their gloomy prognosis of ITV's advertising revenue and audience share convinced them that a radical approach to peak-time was necessary, and that Birt's paper was an important contribution to the debate. Tesler responded immediately to Whitney; on 10 October he wrote:

First, it is *not* the case that both sides accept that 'the figures were not just slightly awry, but so substantially wrong as to make them of little value' . . . John Birt's paper stated explicitly that the figures were estimates and had been compiled without access to confidential information held by other companies. So we were grateful for the opportunity to refine our calculations with the information available to the IBA but not to us. But our delegation at the discussions argued that the IBA's own information in the area of assigning indirect costs and overheads to programmes was in fact not as developed as our own. This is an area of which LWT has made a special study in the past three years, in the process of developing what we believe to be the most sophisticated total costing system in British television. So the LWT team did not and does not accept, on the basis of the discussions so far, that the figures were 'substantially wrong'.

Tesler did accept, however, that newly released information on ITV programme costs revealed that LWT's calculations were 'awry' as to the amount that the regionals' local programmes cost. The IBA, and the other companies, were missing the point, Tesler argued. Birt's case was not built on pie charts. His argument was that ITV's peak-time, especially at the weekend, needed to be strengthened if competition from the BBC and from cable and satellite was to be countered. Tesler continued, 'He (Birt) argues that ITV will be able to compete successfully only if more domestic material of popular appeal is placed in peak-time. He estimates, roughly, that £50 million per year needs to be found to make these extra programmes. This is the heart of his argument; and it does not rest on pie charts.'

The brickbats from Tesler's network colleagues came flying at Birt's head. In October James Gatward, TVS' managing director, produced a characteristically boisterous response. 'It is now necessary', he wrote, 'to respond to what was a not too significant paper as it may gain credence from "leaked" publicity, particularly when an "IBA spokesman" is quoted as saying "Such proposals should be ones in which the IBA would certainly take an interest." ' Gatward was not to know that the IBA was preparing an attack on Birt's argument.

Gatward set out to defend his position as a major regional and to make a pitch for further access to the network. His principal objection was as follows:

We would challenge the assumption that because the major regional companies have a responsibility to local programming they would be, in John Birt's words 'faced by problems in making a significant and concerted contribution to the network.' The contrary is true. A rationalization of ITV effort would free the major regionals to re-direct resources to provide support for all areas of network programming. There is considerable weight of network expertise within the major regional companies. At present this talent is under-used.

We believe that in the long term, *all* regional companies are going to have to provide *some* support for what will be a lengthening daily schedule. This will require a radical change in perspective right across the ITV system.

Although Birt's second option was unacceptable to the vested interests of the IBA and ITV, his first option – of including the regionals in network production – became, a few years later, the foundation of network policy. Gatward was a prime beneficiary of Birt's challenge to the network. The change, dawning slowly in Gatward's mind, was that TVS, whose advertising revenue occasionally outstripped that of Yorkshire and LWT, would become a major. The big five would become the big six.[14] Gatward's splenetic response captured the mood of the smaller ITV regions:

It is bad enough that the regionals have to earn their revenue on a schedule over which they have little or no say, but to suggest they be given a larger proportion of fixed outgoings whilst the majors have an even greater control of the variable programme expenditure, which would be compounded by the larger regionals suddenly being left with underutilized staff and facilities, must represent profound business naivety. This proposal is totally rejected by the regional principals.

New Times, New Strategies

Despite the criticism from the IBA and the network, LWT pressed on with their short-term policy to save money and their long-term strategy to change the system. In October 1983, five months after the Conservative Party had been re-elected and had embarked on wide-ranging economic and political changes – including a concerted effort to impose new, and powerful controls on the trade union movement – LWT returned to Selsdon Park for a management conference. Selsdon 1983 took place in a very different atmosphere, and had very different consequences, from Selsdon 1976 or Brighton 1981.[15] Hard and uncomfortable financial decisions were the order of the day; discussions focused on industrial relations and cut-backs. Programmes were part of an industrial process, not an end in themselves. The Thatcher Agenda penetrated into ITV just as much as other British industries.

Peter McNally, LWT's Finance Director, and Craig Pearman, the Controller of Sales, opened the conference. McNally made it clear to the programme-makers that there was little connection between money spent on programmes and money earned in advertising. However, Pearman emphasized the very direct relationship between ratings and revenue. Moreover, he pointed out that LWT had become too dependent on the autumn quarter, in which it placed most of its own programmes, which left it at the mercy of the BBC and the seven-day contractors in other periods. One consequence of LWT's reliance on one quarter was that the company was at risk when the autumn coincided with a recession or a dispute. The IPA/Equity dispute produced intense problems in the autumn and winter of 1982, and led to the economy-drive outlined above, which had created the unrest in the company.

John Birt followed Pearman and McNally's gloomy financial analysis with his explanation of LWT's special needs. He tried to explain that, with the financial cut-backs, if LWT had continued to make situation comedies and drama they would not have been able to fill the gaps left by the rest of the network. Although it was clear that this was to be a temporary arrangement, it was also clear that Birt felt that game shows and real people were the cement which was necessary to hold the schedule together. It was a question of judgement, and Birt made up his mind and carried the policy through despite the deep reservations of the majority of people in the company.

The key theme of Selsdon 1983 was, according to Birt, that the company's programme policy had to be driven by its transmission needs.[16] Birt explained what he meant by this. LWT's accountancy procedures meant that programmes were not charged to the profit and loss account until they were transmitted. In the period leading up to Selsdon, LWT could not afford to transmit some dramas; therefore, they remained in stock awaiting transmission. Consequently, any new drama would be put into stock to await transmission in future years. As this would have tied up resources without delivering audiences, Birt diverted resources, which otherwise might have gone to drama, to programmes which were produced as close to the time of transmission as possible. These programmes – such as game shows and real people shows – delivered more ratings for each pound spent than drama and sitcom.[17] LWT's need to transmit a schedule which delivered consistent audiences had, in the immediate future, to drive the production process.

In the light of this financial predicament, Nick Elliott, David Bell and Barry Cox each took the floor to list the cuts which they had made in their departments. Bell pointed out, however, that he had gone as far as possible in paring down creative costs. He gave as an example a game show called *Punchlines* which, he pointed out, was being made with a minimal programme team. Further savings would have to come from the production side. The same story of cut-backs could have been told about almost every series.

Barry Cox, at a separate session, reported on a working party which he was chairing which had developed the prescient argument that the way to cut costs *and* maintain programme quality was to turn the programme and the production division into separate profit centres. This would, he argued, create an internal market within LWT which would highlight inefficiency – particularly if programme-makers could go to outside facilities for the productions. Cox's argument was slightly ahead of its time, and was criticized by his colleagues; nonetheless it lurked in LWT's thinking and provided impetus to radical thought about the structure of ITV which served LWT well in planning for the uncertain broadcasting environment of the late 1980s.

This conference spawned three working parties: Working Practices, Planning, and Management.[18] In the rhetoric of the time, LWT aimed to be a leaner and fitter company. There were, of course, some blocks to LWT's plans – not least the unions and the other ITV companies.

Persuasion

Tesler and Birt took themselves off on a whistle-stop tour of Central, Granada and Yorkshire to explain LWT's views as to the needs of the weekend. They presented their evidence based on ratings, appreciation indices, and revenue, and they began the task of convincing their colleagues of the need to make programmes specifically for the weekend.

Programme-makers in the other network companies had traditionally made programmes and then found slots for them. LWT argued that there was insufficient time to experiment or to build audiences for weekend programmes. They had to hit quickly or not at all. Therefore, ITV had to make specially designed programmes for particular time-slots in order to beat the BBC and to hold off cable and satellite.

Each of the companies, to varying degrees, understood LWT's point and they tried to meet LWT's requests for weekend shows. For example Granada, whose record at the weekend was particularly weak, came up with an idea at the beginning of 1984 which looked like a certain winner. With its unrivalled experience in making a long-running soap opera, Granada offered to make a twice-weekly series for the weekend. They developed two options: *Castlehume 8*, which was based on a doctors' group practice, and an as yet untitled show was to be set in a street market – possibly built around the Eddie Yates character from *Coronation Street*.[19] This latter option became *Albion Market*, which was launched in the autumn of 1984 and was, from the first, regarded by the critics and by the audience as dull and uninspired. LWT thought that the series was a millstone around its neck.

Birt and Tesler were aware that it would take the majors some time to develop the strategy for the weekend. In the meantime LWT still needed more programmes than its NAR share would allow it to make.[20] The solution was to bring Anglia and TVS into a satellite relationship.

These two companies were based in affluent regions which were similar in attitude, voting behaviour and social background to LWT's audience. The South East was benefiting from Conservative economic policies while most other regions were haemorrhaging jobs. The audience in the South East had considerably more disposable income, was younger, and was more likely to be employed in sunrise industries or white-collar occupations. It made sense, therefore, for the companies clustered in this area to pool their resources; particularly when three of the big five were located north of Watford Gap, and were based in regions which were experiencing the worst of the recession.

LWT could not guarantee network spots for Anglia and TVS. However, if LWT decided to take a programme for the weekend, it was unlikely that the other companies would opt out. While Tesler and Birt were planning this strategy, fate offered a helping hand. In the course of a long conversation during a break in a conference about ORACLE in Jersey, James Gatward made it clear to Tesler that he was not entirely happy with the performance of his controller of programmes – Michael Blacksted. Tesler and Birt, sensing the opportunity, knew of the ideal person who would facilitate the introduction of the new relationship between LWT and TVS – Greg Dyke.

Greg Dyke had left LWT to become editor in chief at TVam in May, 1983. Over that summer, by fair means and mostly foul, he dragged the moribund and divided station out of the mire. By mid-August Dyke had increased audiences from 300,000 peak quarter-hour viewing to 1,750,000, and he had incurred the wrath of *The Times* in so doing. In an editorial, which in late 1989 seems a little ironic, the Thunderer declaimed, 'When Mr Dyke rode to the rescue, there were fears that he would take an exclusively low road to recovery. This he has done.' Despite this success, Dyke was not comfortable at TVam and was open to other offers. Birt, who had maintained contact with Dyke, was aware that the latter was in negotiation with the BBC. Both Tesler and Birt were keen that Dyke remain within ITV. Tesler had a long-term plan for Dyke which involved Birt taking over as Managing Director and Dyke succeeding Birt. If Dyke became entrenched in the BBC, Tesler reasoned, it would be much more difficult to prise him out.

LWT had much to gain from convincing Gatward to install Dyke in place of Blacksted. Gatward did not need much convincing and, in 1985, Dyke duly joined TVS. There was, as expected, a close relationship between the two Directors of Programmes and the two companies.[21] Dyke recalls: 'the others in the network were saying that we piloted for LWT and that was probably right. But they weren't telling us which shows to do. I would go to John and say: "What do you think of this; do you fancy this, or that?" It was that type of relationship.'

The argument between Birt and the other controllers rolled on into 1985. When the programme controllers met at Hambleton Hall in June 1985 to review the previous year, Birt repeated his claim that apart from a series entitled *Connie*, starring Stephanie Beecham, the majors had produced no drama for the weekend. Granada's Mike Scott explained that as the seven day companies could not get a mix of their programmes into the weekend, it made it extremely difficult psychologically for them to be helpful to LWT.

Birt offered his customary response to such charges. The BBC, he pointed out, was simply too competitive at the weekend to allow for experimental programmes. Yorkshire's John Fairley took the argument to Birt. He argued that LWT spent too many of its tariff points on current affairs, leaving insufficient for light entertainment and drama. Birt was undaunted: even if *Weekend World* were to be transferred to Channel 4 – and there was little possibility of the IBA permitting or Channel 4 accepting the transfer – this would free only thirteen hours for drama.[22] Birt indicated that the solution was for the regions to do more for the network.

The other controllers did not accept Birt's analysis. 'I was naïve in many ways' Birt recalled, 'I thought that all I had to do was to work out the various problems and the rest would begin to put this theory into practice.' Instead, the controllers launched a concerted attack on Birt's scheduling policy. In particular, they complained that Birt's changes to the scheduling of the game show *The Price is Right* and to *Game For A Laugh* had undermined their ratings. Andy Allan, Central's acerbic Director of Programmes, pointed out that when ABC was a weekend contractor it had maintained a regular scheduling pattern which audiences had trusted. This covert reference to Brian Tesler's period as a programme controller was met by Birt's simple rejoinder, 'The evidence does not support your criticism.' Allan replied: 'There is a contrast between my reliance on Mrs Allan Senior and yours on your mainframe. I know which I depend on more.'

Birt's mainframe was churning out information which called for a long and difficult argument within ITV over the next few years, and which was first raised formally at this meeting at Hambleton Hall. Birt argued that the viewer south of the M4 was more sophisticated and better educated than their counterparts in the North and consequently that the artists and drama on which ITV's success in the North was built were loosing audiences in London and the South East. Greg Dyke was to give popular expression to Birt's analysis when he exclaimed that, 'If I see another comedy starring Molly Sugden, I will die.'[23]

In 1984 and 1985 Birt revised his strategy in the teeth of the worst recession ITV had known for ten yeaars. His new approach was a complete reversal of his fire-fighting policy of 1982 and 1983. Birt recalls that in the first phase of his controllership:

I was just shovelling in the numbers, and so was everybody else. Everything was driven by ratings, and I played that game and did quite well by it. I began to understand that things like *The Price is Right*, which I had been very glad to have in the beginning, did not produce the right kind of audience profile. These shows were wrong in every way: wrong commercially, wrong in audience appeal. The penny started to drop that ITV was weakening among the very age and class groups that advertisers were trying to reach. The average Brit was 34, has a car, goes on holiday, is quite well off. And I thought that ITV had to expunge the memory of 20 or 30 years ago. As I began to sense this, I began to change. I changed my mind about entertainment and drama, and certain acts were dropped, and I began to understand the North–South split.

Birt asked his researchers to produce demographic profiles of programmes and of channels, and to relate these to similar economic and social profiles of London, the South East and the other network regions. On the basis of this information his understanding of how to attract and keep audiences deepened. Moreover, LWT began to receive a better supply of programmes from the network, which was beginning to understand how to target the weekend audience.

The first fruits of this strategy emerged after yet another financial downturn in May 1985 which had brought forth an uncharacteristic doom-laden response from Colin Shaw. 'It is the worst crisis to hit the ITV companies in at least a decade. We do not know at present when the situation will improve and, of course, many productions are being postponed and others stockpiled to try to counter the effects.' Other ITV people were speaking of some of the smaller companies going to the wall, and of a merger between Thames and LWT. Moreover, not only was the revenue failing, the BBC had unleashed its secret weapon in the ratings' war – Michael Grade. Grade had returned to Britain to become Controller of BBC1 in 1985. He carried with him an intimate knowledge of ITV and of how to schedule weekend programmes. ITV knew that it had a fight on its hands.

Between October 1984 – when the crisis surfaced – and March 1985, revenue actually declined by 6 per cent. The reasons for the decline were mixed. Some analysts claimed that the problem was high interest rates and a weak pound which had hit American and Japanese advertisers. Others pointed to a new measurement system which was introduced by the Broadcasters' Audience Research Board and which resulted in an increase in measured audiences – shows which had ratings of, say, 10 million under the old system, were revised upwards to 12 million.[24] A key problem was that with the coming of TVam and Channel 4, the amount of cheap and attractive advertising airtime had increased. This had an impact on ITV as agencies began to experiment with their advertising packages.

Whatever the short-term reasons, it was clear that ITV had to revise its selling strategies. Ron Miller had long before identified that the packaged goods market, with its safe and predictable expenditure cycles, could not sustain LWT. In 1985 the rest of ITV reached the same conclusion. Cars, newspapers, financial services and expensive electronic goods were emerging to dominate the market. Not only were these advertisers unpredictable in their spending pattern, they also demanded an audience which was not the traditional mass audience of older, soap-powder buying, vacuum cleaning housewives, which ITV had prided itself on delivering.

Just as LWT's sales strategy finally hit ITV, so did its tactics. Many of the other companies adopted Miller's non-pre-empt rate card.[25] LWT's sales department, backed by the research staff, had long worked on the theme that advertisements had to appeal to certain lifestyles and should clearly target the audience to whom it wanted to sell a particular product.

In 1986, a report from LWT's sales department pointed out that while advertising on what the business calls fast moving consumer goods (FMCG) – food, drink, cosmetics, etc – had declined by almost one-quarter between 1975 and 1985, new advertisers had entered the market: financial services had increased by 268 per cent, office equipment by 1,455 per cent, and cars by 85 per cent. Advertisers wished increasingly to target middle class men, or young adults, or single women. Campaigns aimed at housewives had declined from 60 per fent of total advertising in 1975, to 23 per cent in 1985.[26]

Ron Miller's sales policy involved selling complicated sub-demographic groups, and he invested heavily in a supplementary analysis of the audience other than that provided by the straightforward BARB data, to demonstrate that LWT's programmes delivered such audiences. His problem was that the programme policy from 1983–5 did not produce the affluent audiences in sufficient numbers. Shows like *Surprise, Surprise* and *Albion Market* did not attract middle-class viewers, whereas others such as the BBC antiques and detective series, *Lovejoy*, were more successful.[27] LWT was in the curious position of making shows, such as *Cannon and Ball* and *Surprise, Surprise*, which performed better outside of London. It was extremely difficult to create shows which convincingly crossed the divide at Watford Gap.

Eventually, such thinking penetrated the Chinese walls between the sales and programmes departments – perhaps because both relied on the same research evidence. Birt did not develop his theory of targeting because of sales policy; but it did feed into his calculations. Shovelling in the numbers was out, and was replaced by hitting precise audiences (without alienating the mass audience). Not only was LWT making programmes for slots in the schedule, it began to make them for specific audiences who might be enticed to watch a programme at a specific time.[28]

Birt's revised strategy, which took shape during the financial crisis, came to fruition when the panic was over. The recovery began in the middle of 1985, just in time to facilitate Birt's new thinking, and in 1986 income from advertising increased by 21 per cent. Advertising through-out the industry, and LWT's revenue in particular, was buoyant for the rest of Birt's period at LWT.[29]

Peacock Puzzles

The other major event of the mid-1980s, of which Birt and Tesler had to take account, was the publication of the Peacock report. Each of the major reports on broadcasting in Britain have reflected the ebb and flow of ideas about wider, grander themes, such as democracy, representation, national identity, cultural integrity. These reports have been ideological battlegrounds. John Reith forced his way on to the very first committee of inquiry on broadcasting – the Sykes Committee – in April 1923. By sheer force of will and intellectual authority he ensured that the BBC dominated broadcasting for thirty years. Reith demanded the 'brute force of monopoly', to use his celebrated phrase, in order to promote the views of 'people of education.'[30] The BBC was to be the 'servant of culture' and would make no appeal to 'vulgar' taste or base emotions. 'It is occasionally indicated to us', he wrote, 'that we are apparently setting out to give the public what we think they need – and not what they want, but few know what they want and very few what they need.' 'In any case', he concluded, 'it is better to overestimate the mentality of the public than to underestimate it.'

Sixty-three years later, the Peacock report rebuked Reith's heirs as arrogant, self-serving and undemocratic. The Committee was established as a political manoeuvre by the Home Secretary, Leon Brittan. In 1985, the BBC had asked for an increase in its licence fee at a particularly bad time. It was embroiled in various political arguments with the government, and its credibility was severely dented when it showed an American mini series up against Granada's worthy adaptation of *Jewel In The Crown*. Conservative MPs were baying for blood, and were unwilling to grant the BBC any increase at all. Furthermore, as part of the assault on the state and quasi-state institutions, the government expected the BBC to slim down its workforce, and to become more like the independent sector.

Brittan invited Peacock to head an inquiry into advertising on the BBC, which at the time most commentators and industry figures imagined was simply a smoke-screen for government policy. Peacock – a renowned welfare economist, with pronounced liberal economic views – had other ideas. He began with the assumption that advertising on the BBC was feasible and inevitable, but it soon became clear that neither supposition was sufficiently robust. There was insufficient advertising to fund both a fully functioning BBC and ITV. Moreover, economic models demonstrated that an expansion in more advertising time would result in a drop in the price which could be charged for the time. The result of introducing advertising on the BBC, might have been insufficient revenue to maintain the existing quality of broadcasting.

The Committee recommended that the BBC should not be funded by advertising. However, this was not the end of the matter. Peacock, Sam

Brittan and Peter Jay, who acted as principal adviser to these two, hijacked the committee, and presented their own view, premised on liberal political theory and free market economics, as to how British broadcasting should develop. The report made two significant points:

> The fundamental aim of broadcasting should in our view be to enlarge both the freedom of choice of the consumer and the opportunities available to programme makers to offer their wares.

Consequently:

> British broadcasting should move towards a sophisticated market system based on consumer sovereignty. That is a system that recognizes that viewers and listeners are the best ultimate judges of their own interest, which they can best satisfy if they have the option of purchasing the broadcasting services they require from as many alternative sources of supply as possible.

The consumer was to be king, and his or her sovereignty was to extend over a range of services provided in the long term by a fibre-optic grid of cables which would deliver myriad choice.

Sir Alan Peacock was later to comment on the misconceptions surrounding the report.

> The . . . misconception of broadcasters is based on the failure (or refusal) to recognize that creating a market which gives viewers and listeners much more control over what they want to watch is not synonymous with the introduction of complete laissez-faire. Viewers and listeners cannot give full expression to their preferences if channels are financed primarily by advertising revenue, although a marked increase in the number of radio or TV channels can make advertisers much more responsive to differences in consumer tastes. This is the case for the introduction of subscription or 'pay-per-view' methods of financing. Nor can viewers and listeners develop their tastes and preferences unless these are challenged by a wide range of alternative forms of entry into the programming business. The creation of such a market entails government intervention in order to prevent 'horizontal' integration (concentration of ownership in TV channels, for instance] and 'vertical' integration (concentration of ownership in programming, scheduling and transmission of pro-grammes).[31]

Peacock's real problem was not the misconception of broadcasters, but the misapplication of the report in the Government's White Paper on Broadcasting which followed on two years after the publication of the report.

In common with much free market thinking, the Peacock Report – which was so critical of the broadcasters' inability to define public service broadcasting – failed to provide a convincing and clear account of what a consumer actually is. In free-market thinking the consumer often appears to be what is left when you take the emotions, confusions, deceptions, ignorance, stupidity, avarice and greed out of a human being and replace his or her blood with rationality. The prevailing image in the report was of the consumer as a clear-sighted individual, who had distinct preferences which were freely arrived at and clearly articulated in the act of making a choice. This cavil – as it would seem to free market thinkers – would probably strike Alan Peacock as vaguely amusing; in liberal economics the consumer is, by definition, making the correct choice – even if the cumulative effects of such choices produce a market dominated by shoddy, badly produced, inarticulate programmes.

Despite the many problems with the report, it was a document of great originality which seemed a little other-worldly. Most broadcasters felt that it would have been improved by the presence of someone who had been a senior executive in a broadcasting organization and who had some experience of the actual broadcasting market. Peacock deserved, and continues to merit, a serious and sophisticated rebuttal. Unfortunately for those committed to public service broadcasting this refutation has yet to appear. Most of the critics of the report – many of whom misunderstood or had never read the philosophy or economics which underlay Peacock's thinking – responded with restatements of vague eternal verities; some simply blew raspberries.

The IBA was furious to discover that someone in LWT had written a briefing document for Peacock which stated:

> The IBA should, in the next franchise round, make it a condition of all franchises that no company holding a franchise can make programmes (except, possibly, the quota of local programmes demanded in the franchise) nor can it directly own production facilities.
>
> This reform would transform ITV at a stroke into a dynamic, open competitive market for programmes and facilities; yet it need not be massively disruptive.
>
> It should, for example, be possible for the existing ITV companies to equip themselves to meet such conditions by turning their present programme and production departments into wholly-owned sub-sidiaries, if they chose to. (They could of course sell these to their staffs or to other buyers if they preferred.) The one absolute necessity is to break the link between transmission (with the sale of airtime) and the other aspects of production, so that those who commissioned programmes and wrote the schedules were constrained only by the public service objectives laid down by the IBA and the commercial imperatives of building audiences for advertisers – not, as now, by the additional need to make a range of programmes themselves.

A copy of this document fell into the hands of David Glencross at the

IBA. Glencross was keen to find out which LWT executives were breaking ranks and taking tea with the enemy. He scrutinized the document and, as he expected, it was written on John Birt's very distinctive word processor. Birt was, on this occasion, not guilty. Glencross was correct about the typist but wrong about the author. Barry Cox wrote the piece and his wife Katy, John Birt's secretary, typed it on Birt's processor. The precariousness of the weekend franchise seems to drive LWT's executives back to the network blueprint time and again. Cox's paper was in a long tradition which began with Michael Peacock and is continuing with Greg Dyke.[32]

After Peacock

ITV soon felt the full effects of the Peacock Report, which provided a rallying point for those who wished to see the duopoly broken up. Although derided initially it became the ideological touchstone for government policy on broadcasting.

LWT's solutions to the interlinked puzzle of programme-making, scheduling, networking, advertising and production took five years to develop. By the end of 1985, in the face of cyclical downturns in advertising revenue, tumultuous and sustained attacks on the duopoly, and a general uncertainty as to what government policy would entail, LWT had in place the thinking which will take them into the 1990s. This analysis was based on two key components – total costing and complex demographics. The station attempts constantly to monitor the changing economic and social character of London and the South East and to relate the programme policy to potential audiences. The underlying idea was simple – to retain the interest of youngish, mobile, reasonably affluent, South-East, white-collar workers, without alienating the mass audiences. In practice, as we shall see in the next chapter, this is a devilish undertaking.

Not only did the programme strategy reflect new thinking. Barry Cox's notion of separate profit centres within the company, and of an internal market within LWT, percolated away. Tesler, for so long a doyen of the old ITV, established working parties whose express aim was to find ways of cutting down costs, of streamlining production, and of generally moving away from the rigid demarcations and overtime payments on which the company's staff had relied for many years.

The mood of ITV's management in the Thatcher years – particularly after the miners' strike and Rupert Murdoch's transformation of union agreements at his new plant in Wapping – was very different from the cosy days of beer and sandwiches in the boardroom. Union agreements, against which ITV had railed for many a long year, but which had seemed rock solid, began to dissolve. LWT was, unusually, at the forefront of this challenge to the unions. As well as these changes in production and programme-making, the LWT group was being re-structured. John Freeman retired in January 1984, but, as ever, he had his successor in place:[33]

> Once Tesler, Birt and Miller were in position and operating on all legs, it became clear to me, particularly after the successful re-application for the franchise, that I had done all that I could for LWT, and that the sooner I got out the better. There was a whole new team in place, and I was operating as a 5th wheel – I hope I wasn't actually getting in the way – but the sooner they were free to run their own business the better.
>
> I decided what they needed was a business man to look after the affairs of the company. I decided on Christopher Bland, who was young, go-getting, ambitious and exactly the right sort of person to give the company a commercial fillip, and to make sure that the programme people did not run away with the funds.[34]

Although Bland took over from Freeman as chairman of LWT (Holdings), Brian Tesler was appointed as chairman of the television arm – London Weekend Television.[35] This was an awkward arrangement, but Freeman was adamant. 'I wanted the TV company to run with its own separate chain of command right to the top. Answerable to the Holding's Board, but not otherwise answerable to anyone. I just believed that.'[66]

Freeman's own control of both the television company and the holdings company was, in his own mind, 'an accident conditioned by temporary unfortunate circumstances.' Freeman's decision to split the chairmanships was not welcomed with any enthusiasm by his board; however, in deference to Freeman's success with the company, they acquiesced. Bland was brought on to the Board in 1981 – without the offer of the chairmanship but with the understanding that he would be a serious contender – and he became chairman in 1984.

Bland in some ways represents the coming breeds of entrepreneurial chairmen of ITV companies. In the late 1960s he was a Conservative councillor on the Greater London Council, and between 1971 and 1972 he edited *Crossbow*, the magazine of Edward Heath's rising young stars in the Tory Party. However, he has a mixed background in both public and private sectors. He was a director of the Northern Ireland Finance Corporation between 1972 and 1976, and was deputy chairman of the IBA from 1972 to 1980. His private sector experience came mainly from the publishing company – Sir Joseph Causten and Sons – of which he was chairman between 1977 and 1985.

Bland introduced a different style to the company. He believed that LWT had overextended itself and should concentrate its energies on its core business of making, selling and transmitting television programmes. First, though, he had to sort out Hutchinson's and Page and Moy.

Page and Moy had spent considerable amounts trying to sell holidays to high street travel agents. This had soaked up profits and diverted the company away from its main source of revenue – business travel. Bland persuaded and cajoled the company to turn back to its original base, and revenue and profits increased.[37] In 1986–7, profits grew by 23 per cent to £902,000, and in 1987–8 profits were up to £998,000 – another 10 per cent. Nonetheless, Bland was delighted when, in 1988, Barclays bank brought the company for £8 million, of which LWT received £5.4 million.

Hutchinson's was more of a problem. Bland believed that it needed a new and vigorous managing director. One of the people in whom he was interested decided to take up a position with the publishers, Century. This led Bland into discussions with Century which in due course produced a merger, in which LWT reduced its holdings to 25 per cent. Despite these changes, the company made a loss in 1985–6, and less than half-a-million pounds' profit in the following year.[38]

This activity on the part of Tesler, Bland and Birt was subordinate to one simple fact: LWT had to make good programmes. As we shall in the next chapter, strategies, restructuring, theoretical speculation, paradigm building and debate ultimately boil down to a programme and its audience.

THE ENTERTAINERS?

Hello Playmates!
Arthur Askey

Every year, in September, a few privileged television executives disappear to Italy for the television equivalent of the Venice film festival, the Prix Italia. LWT has enjoyed considerable success at the Prix Italia; three *South Bank Shows* and Dennis Potter's *Cream in my Coffee* have picked up awards. At the festival in 1981, Nick Elliott took time off from the round of screenings, debates and drinks to sit by a telephone and wait for a call from John Birt.

The phone rang and Birt confirmed the news that Elliott had suspected would be forthcoming. Birt had become Director of Programmes and he wished to discuss with Elliott a new position for him at LWT. Elliott had planned to leave the station. In 1980, Peter Jay, with whom Elliott had worked on *Weekend World*, invited him to become Director of Programmes of TVam. Elliott was ripe for change. He had been at LWT for eight years and, with Birt and Grade as his superiors, both of whom were around his own age, further advance within LWT would have been slow. Furthermore, the excitement of the franchise chase was too much to resist.

He spent much of late 1980 helping to win the franchise, and most of 1981 working on the programme strategy for the new breakfast channel. However, the chaos at TVam had already taken its toll; his position as controller of programmes was severely compromised when Jay appointed Michael Deakin – a co-founder of TVam – as Director of Features. Deakin, although second in command to Elliott, was, in fact, in sole charge of his own area. This unhappy compromise, and his long-standing interest in drama, persuaded Elliott to remain with LWT when Birt offered him the opportunity to run the drama department.

Elliott had a strong background in drama. He had been a member of the National Youth Theatre at the age of 15, and of the Oxford University Drama Society; moreover, he had begun his career at

Granada in the drama department. His appointment, however, increased resentment within the company. Tony Wharmby, his predecessor, was a hands-on producer of the kind loved by the old Rediffusion staff who were the self-appointed conscience of LWT.[1] His 'resignation' made it appear as if Birt was picking off the old guard and replacing them with his own men. Birt felt that Wharmby was essentially a drama director, by temperament and inclination. The drama department, in Birt's opinion, was in reality a loose confederation of programme-makers; he felt that Wharmby spent too much time on shoots or in the studio rather than at his desk running the show. Consequently, Birt looked for someone who could actually run the department as Birt thought a department should be run. He thought immediately of Elliott. Birt knew that it would be a controversial appointment and he consulted Michael Grade, who readily concurred with Birt's choice. The rest of LWT's staff were not so easily convinced. When Elliott arrived back from lunch, not long after taking over in January 1982, he found a note pinned to his door which suggested that he go back to whence he came (or words to that effect). It took four years, and the development of high-profile, successful drama series such as *The Charmer* and *London's Burning*, before the drama department settled again.

A new executive team took shape in the winter of 1981. Nick Elliott became Controller of Drama and of Arts (the *South Bank Show* was moved out of the features department), and Barry Cox followed Birt as Controller of Features and Current Affairs.[2] The third senior programme executive, David Bell, remained as Controller of Entertainment. However, he was effectively sharing the department with a man whose programmes became closely identified with LWT in the early and mid-1980s – Alan Boyd.

David Bell originally tried to poach Boyd – who had produced *The Generation Game* – to work on *Bruce's Big Night*. Boyd considered long and hard before remaining with the Corporation.[3] Bell made a second attempt in 1980, by which time Boyd had developed *Blankety Blank*, and was working on various entertainment specials. Boyd was at a low ebb. The BBC, after many promises, would not allow him to concentrate on the development of new ideas. Bell, aware of Boyd's frustration, lured him to LWT in August 1980 with the promise that Grade would back new approaches.

Boyd entertained a robust view of his own talents. His language was peppered with references to 'putting the Boyd stamp' on programmes. He believed firmly that he had an inborn feeling for what the public wanted to watch on Saturday nights. In short order, he added to LWT's stock of game shows – which extended only to Bruce Forsyth's *Play Your Cards Right* – by introducing *Punchlines* and *The Pyramid Game*. Moreover, using a mixture of parts of various American shows and his own ideas, he developed an audience participation show, *Game For A*

Laugh, which set the tone for light entertainment in the early 1980s.

Boyd was prepared to back his judgement. When Michael Grade threatened to schedule *Game For A Laugh* outside early peak-time, Boyd threatened to resign. He saw the show as the next stage in a cycle of light entertainment shows which he planned to unveil as his career progressed. Boyd, in this sense, was similar to Birt; once he was convinced of the value of a programme, he fought and clawed to ensure that it was produced.

The new executive team inherited a roster of programmes, most of which were in stock awaiting transmission, in the process of being made or were actually on the screen. On the basis of the previous five years, however, the programme-makers thought that they could look forward to an enjoyable and creative time developing their own shows. As we saw in the previous chapter, life was not to be that simple.

Under Pressure: Shovelling in the Numbers

There are several reasons why a department suddenly takes off and begins to dominate the company, or to stand out from the pack of network equivalents. First and foremost it requires secure funds. Without adequate money, experimentation and development are impossible. However, finance is not the end of the story. A small department can stand out if the controller of programmes believes in it enough to fight for its programme-ideas in Network committees. Moreover, the department needs leadership; it requires someone who either believes in himself or herself, or who is deeply committed to the programmes which are emerging from the department. Fourth, the programmes need to find, and to keep, an audience; it has to be in tune with whatever cultural changes are taking place. Finally, if the department does not have talent then leadership, money, funding, and a benign controller of programmes will be of no avail.

ITV is full of examples of moribund departments which were galvanized when the above conditions were met. Similarly, when a department goes into reverse, the reasons are not hard to adduce: it is starved of funds, loses sight of the audience, and the controller of programme's attention is elsewhere. This produces a crisis of confidence, and a sense of insecurity among those running the department. Tried and tested programmes are churned out, and few experiments take place. Experimentation and renewal are important not only to drama and the arts, but also to variety, chat shows, current affairs and situation comedies. Without innovation and change, the audience, which is itself changing, will leave the department behind.

Some departments rise because of the whim or the caprice of the controller of programmes; others through sheer bullying on the part of a single-minded head; yet others as a result of interpretations of where the audience is going. In Birt's period, departments rose and fell in time to Birt's response to the short-term crisis and, subsequently, to his strategy of targeting and demographic analysis.

Birt's regime began with a bang. The *6 O'Clock Show*, which launched the new franchise in January 1982, was an immediate hit; furthermore *Game For A Laugh*, with its mix of presenters, its games, and its *Candid Camera*-like stunts, was a great success.[4] Greg Dyke, who was the first editor of the *6 O'Clock Show*, does not remember the pilot programmes with any affection:

We made three of the most disastrous programmes ever seen in the history of television. The third one was truly unbelievably bad. A monkey escaped in the studio and all the bloody electricians were chasing after it. The director decided to stay with the guests and not to go with the monkey. The whole thing was a shambles.

With the monkey business out of the way, the series settled down.[5] Dyke stole some ideas from *That's Life*, injected humour based on class divisions ('I discovered that the working class and the upper class were very, very funny, but the middle class were a pain – you couldn't get a line out of them'), and generally made it appear that London was an enjoyable place in which to live.

Dyke faced up to LWT's hardy perennial: which London was he supposed to be representing? In those early days, the London with which Dyke identified, was not 'Havering and Milton Keynes, not in a million years – you only went there if you had to. It was Central London and different bits of working-class London.' This was exemplified by the presenters: Janet Street-Porter played the chirpy Cockney act to perfection,[6] Fred Housego – the cab driver who won *Mastermind* – appeared as a traffic announcer, and the studio was protected from incipient chaos by the ever calm Michael Aspel.

The *6 O'Clock Show* was one of a string of successful programmes bequeathed by Grade's regime (although, of course, it was developed in Birt's department). Among the situation comedies was *A Fine Romance*, which starred Judy Dench and Michael Williams as awkward and disorganized lovers and was every critic's favourite comedy.[7] Two other comedies, *Metal Mickey*, which starred an anarchic robot, and *Whoops Apocalypse*, a burlesque on the end of the world, both appealed strongly to their target audiences. Finally, Birt was bequeathed *The Goodies* – Tim Brooke Taylor, Graham Garden and Bill Oddie – whose brand of comedy had been a success at the BBC.

Birt also inherited Bell's glossy variety and entertainment specials as well as Boyd's game shows and people shows. The company had a roster of established stars, such as Stanley Baxter, Bruce Forsyth, and Clive

James, all of whom were starring in, or were lined up for, expensive and polished spectaculars. Moreover, LWT was cultivating rising talent such as Russ Abbott and Cannon and Ball.

Several drama series still had life in them. These included *The Gentle Touch*, which starred Jill Gascoine as a successful policewoman and which was a solid, and occasionally excellent, performer in the ratings; *The Professionals* – produced by Mark 1 Productions for LWT and starring Gordon Jackson, Martin Shaw and Lewis Collins – had been a notable success but was, after four years, at its end (the last series had still to run when Birt took over, but the stars no longer wished to continue with the series); *We'll Meet Again*, starred Susannah York in a story set in a town next to an American airforce base during the Second World War; Grade had intended it to run for at least four or five years. Also produced but not yet transmitted was a co-financed series called *Marlowe* based on Raymond Chandler's world-weary private detective; *Partners In Crime*, based on Agatha Christie short stories; and *Mitch*, starring John Thaw as a crime reporter.

In the late 1970s, this roster of programmes would have provided the platform for several good years in the ratings. As we saw in the last chapter, however, the financial cut-backs of 1982, ensured that while some departments prospered, others languished.

In Birt's first few years his attention and LWT's resources were focused on variety, people shows and game shows. He was fascinated by the way is which these programmes generated revenue, turned over very quickly, and captured the public's attention. Current affairs and features, which had benefited greatly from the explosion of the late 1970s, were, in Birt's mind, settled; any further expansion would take place on Channel 4. The big losers were situation comedy and drama. These did not deliver consistent ratings, would not fit comfortably into planning schedules, and were extremely expensive.[8]

Humphrey Barclay, the Head of Comedy, left in disgust early in 1983. Barclay and Birt found it difficult to reach agreement on anything in Birt's first year in charge. Tension was locked into the relationship even before Birt became controller of programmes. He and Barclay had fallen out over the tactics for selling a multi-cultural situation comedy called *No Problem* to Channel 4. This went on to achieve cult status and to run for three series. However, Barclay felt so incensed by the negotiations over this programme that he almost resigned: 'It was one of the most emotional experiences of my entire life,' he was later to recall.[9]

When Birt took over as Director of Programmes, Barclay feared the worst. He could not adjust to Birt's policy of dealing only with the man immediately below him on the hierarchy – in Barclay's case, David Bell. Barclay liked to make snap judgements and to have direct access to the controller of programmes. This privilege had been granted by Bennett, and was passed on by Grade – who almost made it a condition of Bell's contract. Birt was different. Most of the time he required a thorough briefing and close examination of an idea. 'I am not the sort of person who, when someone comes into a room and says – "Shall we do [a] or [b]?", replies, "Well, [b] seems right to me." '

Not only was the decision-making process and the hierarchy different, the financial conditions had changed vastly from the days when Barclay felt that he was being encouraged to make the most inventive situation comedies in the network. The financial problems of late 1982, combined with Birt's view that he needed safe, long-running bankers in order to settle the schedule, and that in a crisis comedies drained resources without a sufficient return in revenue, ensured that Barclay's type of situation comedy could not flourish. Between 1977 and 1981, Barclay made on average twenty-three hours of situation comedy a year; in 1984–5, this dropped to five hours.[10]

Matters came to a head when Birt accepted a series about milkmen, which Barclay had put forward. *Bottle Boys*, which starred Robin Askwith, an actor who had made his name in a series of bawdy film comedies, such as *Confessions of a Driving Instructor*, was the last desperate act of two men who simply failed to communicate. Birt recalls, 'Out of a deteriorating relationship silly things happen. *Bottle Boys* should not have been offered to me by Humphrey and I shouldn't have accepted it.' In Barclay's mind, the dreaded days of *Yus, My Dear* had returned. He resigned.[11]

The gulf between Barclay and Birt was a consequence of the weekend schedule, the financial crisis, Birt's long-term objectives, and personal misunderstandings between the two men. Moreover, Barclay could not deliver the type of high ratings garnered week in, week out, by BBC comedies.

The Corporation was able to bring comedies into weekend peak-time that often were nurtured and protected in weekday slots. By the time that the series arrived on Saturdays or Sundays, they had a strong following and a high profile. Moreover, these comedies were aimed squarely at the middle ground; they were built to attract large audiences. Barclay's talent lay with comedies that were quirky, clever, urban, and smart; such comedies could not survive in red-nose, Saturday prime-time. Barclay's programmes needed time to breath and to develop in safe havens rather than in the slots into which they necessarily were thrust. Consequently, although many of LWT's comedies in the late 1970s and early 1980s were memorable, few were major ratings gatherers. They were not made to last year in and year out as were their BBC equivalents. Barclay was not fighting like with like and Birt, looking to match the BBC, wanted a comedy which would help to shore up his fire-fighting schedule, and on which he could rely for several years. (Cyril Bennett was fortunate in having the various *Doctor* series, *Please Sir!*, and *On the Buses.*)

Barclay recognized the problem of matching his talent with the demands of the weekend schedule:

I had no pretensions at all when Michael asked me to become Head of Comedy. My first protest was that I didn't have a broad enough range of humour to come up with the commercial goods, and, indeed, that was proved in the six years I was Head of Comedy. We raised the tone of comedy because we had sunk to the *Yus, My Dear*'s of the world, and Michael wanted to put us in a bracket where people said the most interesting comedy was coming out of London Weekend. This was terrific for me and it allowed me to do lots of wonderful things, but I never achieved a long runner except, curiously enough, with *A Fine Romance* which, because it started small, would never have happened under any regime other than Michael's. I also left them with *Me and My Girl*, which was planned to run for five series and did.

The shop-floor was confused. 'Where is the glamour?', people asked themselves as they made game show, after chat show, after talking heads. It was difficult for the workforce to adjust to, or even to understand, the need for the rigorous planning, research and financial stringency which Birt considered was necessary to guide LWT out of its financial problems and into an uncertain future. In August 1983, LWT's ACTT shop steward, Gavin Waddel, articulated the rest of the company's feelings: 'Morale is very low here. We were told some years ago that drama was expensive and that the company was only likely to go ahead with major projects on a co-production basis . . . There had been a sharp decline in drama on the shop floor, and the workers don't like this.' Part of the problem was that people had to revise their opinion of Birt. Instead of elitist dramas and current affairs, which it had been feared that he would deliver, he was fighting in the rough-and-tumble at the other end of the market. We are always doubly hard on people who force us to change our mind about them.

When the financial crisis hit them, Tesler and Birt believed that there was no alternative but to cut back on drama. Real people shows and game shows delivered more ratings and more revenue for every pound spent on man-hours, studio-time, above- and below-the-line costs. Consequently, the two men believed that in a revenue recession, with companies cutting programmes across the entire network, LWT had to keep its ratings and revenue going with more and more holes appearing in the network schedule and fewer resources of its own production, LWT could make either X hours of drama or Y hours of game and people shows. In these circumstances, and as long as the crisis lasted, Birt felt that he had no choice but to concentrate on the latter and cut back on the former.

This was small consolation to Elliott who had to chase around the world looking for co-production money. At the beginning of 1983, Nick

Elliott had enticed one of the BBC's top producers to join his drama department. Robert Banks Stewart had been responsible, as producer, for successful drama series such as *Shoestring* and *Bergerac*. Banks Stewart spent eighteen months developing the type of expensive series on which he had worked at the BBC. Birt, and a reluctant Elliott, vetoed each of these ideas as too expensive. Birt insisted that any major investment in drama had to be accompanied by co-production funds. Although Elliott spent innumerable, tedious hours in planes to and from the US, Banks Stewart's ideas simply did not take. (Subsequently, none of the ideas have emerged as major series.) The series for which Elliott managed to put together co-production funds was what Banks Stewart called 'caper rubbish' – namely, *Dempsey and Makepeace*. This was co-funded with the US Tribune Group and it made LWT a great deal of money in overseas sales. Banks Stewart returned to the BBC in October 1984.

Elliott did not have far to look for his troubles between 1982 and 1986. He had to wait for several years before some series were taken out of stock. *Mitch* eventually crept on to the air in 1984 – four years after it was produced.[12] Moreover, *We'll Meet Again*, the series which Grade believed would become a banker, was dropped.

Elliott's first major series as Controller of Drama did little to rescue his ailing reputation. *Drummonds*, which was set in a private boys' school in the 1950s, was widely considered by audiences and critics alike to be dull and uninspired. One of his colleagues pronounced the ultimate curse on it: 'It could've been made by Granada.' Moreover, it was difficult to take chances, and to learn from his mistakes. The funding for drama simply dried up, as the following table demonstrates.

Date	Production Hours
1977/78	66.50
1978/79	58.00
1979/80	47.25
1980/81	47.50
1981/82	44.25
1982/83	19.75
1983/84	16.58
1984/85	19.58
1985/86	25.00
1986/87	27.00[13]

Under Grade, the number of hours of drama declined from the high point of Bennett's last schedule. However, this slow slide turned into a massive drop during Birt's first year as controller of progammes. Birt's short-term tactics of producing programmes that had a fast turnover made it extremely difficult for Elliott to maintain morale within his department. Two one-off productions – *Blue Money*, a film made especially for television, and William Boyd's *Dutch Girls*[14] – helped a little, but a despondency set in which lifted only when the financial pressure on Elliott was released.

Elliott's major consolation was that the *South Bank Show* – over which he retained nominal control when he moved from Features to Drama – remained vital and dynamic. The award-winning form continued into the 1980s. In March 1983 it won a BAFTA for *Laurence Olivier – A Life*, in September 1984 it was awarded the RAI prize for *Ralph Vaughan Williams – A Symphonic Portrait*, and in September 1986 it was rewarded with a Primetime Emmy in the States for the Olivier special. Between times the show produced an eclectic record of art (in the widest sense) and artists which is rivalled in the history of British broadcasting only by *Monitor*.

After the traumatic budget cuts in 1982, features and current affairs carried on much as it had done in Grade period. Barry Cox believes that 'We were a victim of our own success. We had established our style, made a success of the *6 O'Clock Show* and of our Channel 4 programmes, and there were few other challenges. John had a clearly defined schedule, and we could not expect any more time on ITV.'

The work of the department, however, continued to win awards and plaudits. Network series included *Breadline Britain*, which explored the impact of mass unemployment and drew high praise from the IBA, and *Shadow of the Gun*, a four-part series on Northern Ireland which won a silver medal at the New York International TV and Film Festival. Local features included *South of Watford* which, in many ways, began to establish the style of 1980s youth programmes, and an exhaustive account of London's recent past, *The Making of Modern London. Sunday, Sunday*, an early evening chat and review show for London, produced by the Light Entertainment department, was presented by Gloria Hunniford and was well-received locally.[15]

On Channel 4, the department produced *The Making of Britain*; the companion to the history of London, and various one-off specials – such as *Bad Times at The Times*, a report on *The Times*' distressing history in the early 1980s. *Jesus, The Evidence*, proved to be a controversial inquiry into the life of Christ. Birt triggered the series by passing on to Julian Norridge, the editor of religious features, a newspaper clipping about set of Gnostic papyri discovered in Upper Egypt. David Rolfe, whom Norridge hired as a producer, turned the idea into a series which included filmed inserts with American academics striding purposefully around in Israeli deserts, and dramatic reconstructions of various debates in the Church; the sets included a Roman Arena, Constantine the Great's palace, and Christ's burial chamber. Inevitably, it produced storm in church circles.

LWT's other contribution to unsettling the religious establishment was *Credo*, which approached religion with a seriousness of purpose not typical of televised religion. Its moment of national fame arrived when it conducted an infamous interview with David Jenkins, the Bishop of Durham, in which he expressed his doubts about the Virgin Birth. The series was transferred to Channel 4 in 1984 and did not return to LWT when, after two further series, Channel 4's Commissioning Editor for Religion no longer wished to take it.

At the end of 1981, Jane Hewland produced a report which reflected on her experience with minority programmes. In particular, she commented on her worries about *Skin*.

Skin ha[s] developed towards policy programmes and away from programmes which show a slice of black or Asian life. We recognize the dangers in that bias. It isn't simply that endless shows on policy and about problems can become tedious to watch. The most serious problem is that, by focusing on unemployed black youth, on clashes with the police, on rioting and so on, we present to the bigot the very image he already has of blacks . . . But although we want to change the profiles of our shows to make them more people- and less problem-oriented, the task is not an easy one. We have a limited number of slots. There are always important policy issues on which it would be absurd for *Skin* to fail to report . . . Inevitably these sorts of shows squeeze out the 'softer' looks at black and Asian life.

We now feel that this change of direction is probably best achieved not on *Skin*, but on year-round nationwide, multi-item shows for blacks and Asians. Such shows would have space not just for news and policy items but for the kind of social and cultural stories *Skin* has had to neglect. With this kind of service, the portrait that *Skin* has painted of black and Asian communities, would be deepened and enriched, as it now ought to be.

LWT submitted this idea for a news and current affairs magazine to Sue Woodford, Channel 4's first commissioning editor for multi-cultural programmes. The series – *Black on Black* and *Eastern Eye* – were the first ethnic programmes to be commissioned by the new channel. The series were staffed and presented by Asians and Afro-Caribbeans, and Beverley Anderson, the formidable and charming presenter of *Black on Black*, ensured that the series had a strong identity.[16]

The series garnered praise from, among others, the European Broadcasting Union, and the High Commissioner for Bangladesh, who wrote to the IBS in May 1985 applauding the programme and hoping that 'the Independent Broadcasting Authority and *Eastern Eye* in particular will continue to protect the needs, activities and aspirations of the Bangladeshi community resident in Britain.'

Furrukh Dhondy, who replaced Sue Woodford, had other ideas. At

the end of 1984, he informed LWT that he intended not to renew the
commission for the series. This decision stirred up a great deal of fury at
LWT, which could see five years of experience going to waste. Birt
called the verdict 'galling, unjust and absolutely infuriating.' Dhondy
was unrepentant. The shows, which won posthumously the top prize at
the black TV awards in the US, and which set the style for the BBC's
later attempts at ethnic programmes, died. They provided many of the
staff for the BBC's ethnic programmes, which carried on the *Black on
Black* style.[17]

Birt spent the early part of his controllership learning about light
entertainment from David Bell and Alan Boyd. Bell, however, was
increasingly uncomfortable as the balance swung decisively away from
the high-gloss spectaculars with which he had made his reputation, to
chat shows, game shows and real people shows. He recalls, 'You have to
remember that producers like me came in almost off the street.
Therefore, when a scientist like John came along we had to listen.
However, I became fed up with "ABCs" and all that stuff.' In 1979,
LWT made fifteen hours of game shows; by 1985, it was making almost
forty hours.[18] In October 1984, before this high point was reached, Bell
resigned as Controller of Entertainment and returned to production.

Stanley Baxter, whose recruitment was one of Bennett's great coups,
and whose early prize-winning programmes were produced by Bell,
returned to the BBC in May 1985. He cited as his reason, '[LWT] looked
at the budget for the series I had already started to write and decided
they could not afford it.' (Birt had been informed that in total costing
terms, one Baxter special took over £500,000 of LWT's resources.) Two
weeks later, Russ Abbott, whom LWT had nurtured into a major star
but who required the kind of resources which Baxter sought, also moved
to the BBC. When the Baxter switch was announced to the press, James
Moir, BBC's Head of Variety, sniffily commented, 'London Weekend
seem to be investing most of their money in game shows. We are
investing in people.'

In the mid-1980s, LWT launched a massive publicity campaign based
around newspaper cartoons, photographs taken of its stars by Lord
Snowden and an award-winning animated film by Pat Gavin.[19] LWT
needed an identity. It had a stable of celebrities, well-known and
respected presenters and interviewers, and chat-show hosts which
could promote. However, what did these people have in common? Well,
for one thing they appeared at the weekend when people wanted to relax
and forget about the working week. Therefore by definition the public
wished to be entertained by LWT's stars. The message was simple.
LWT was the channel of 'The Entertainers'.

The advertising did not discriminate between Melvyn Bragg, pictured
by Snowden sitting in a producer's fold-away chair glancing up to heaven
for inspiration; Cilla Black, shown surrounded by teddy bears; Jimmy

Tarbuck, clinging on to a set of golf clubs; Brian Walden, looking on the verge of contempt; or Bobby Ball, whose photograph worked against type: he was depicted wearing a dinner suit, with the braces outside his jacket and clipped into his breast pocket at the one end. Not the glimmer of a smile was on his lips or in his eyes. In what sense were these people the same? Were they doing exactly the same job? Could Walden be called an entertainer without stripping the word of any meaning or, more dangerously for LWT, without equating *Weekend World* with *Play Your Cards Right?*

The lack of discrimination showed up more clearly in a cartoon which was used as a newspaper advertisement in September 1983. Beneath the banner title of The Entertainers, a jumble of caricatures of LWT's performers and presenters jostled for space. Brian Walden peeped out from under Dickie Davies's armpit, and Bragg looked as if he was being head-butted by Jeremy Beadle: not quite the place for the sober face of LWT.

This campaign was the climax of the schedules which were the result of Birt's short-term reaction to the financial cut-backs. However, it left a sour taste in the mouths of many of his programme-makers and there are revisionist views around in LWT which claim that even if the cut-backs were necessary, Birt need not have denuded the schedule. 'The Entertainers', it is claimed, unnecessarily set up LWT as the game show station; a reputation which has taken a long time to live down. Birt and Tesler, for all of the reasons outlined in the previous chapter, while aware of the pitfalls, could see no alternative to the path which they took.

Whatever the arguments about the tactics pursued in 1982–5, by the middle of the latter year LWT began to edge towards a mixed, balanced schedule in which each of the different aspects of television and of life was explored.

Happy Days are Here Again: Hitting the Target

Drama was the first to benefit from the upturn in LWT's financial fortunes when the financial storm of 1985 had abated. Birt loosed the purse-strings somewhat and Elliott recruited Linda Agran who, as head of scripts at Euston Films, had contributed to the success of series such as *Minder*. This partnership, with sufficient finances, produced as string of successes in 1986 and 1987. LWT made *The Charmer* which starred Nigel Havers in an unusually tough role as a murderer, and which, when transmitted in 1987, was a major success. *London's Burning*, a single two-hour play written by Jack Rosenthal, worked well on its first outing in 1987 and went on to become a successful series. *A Little Princess*, a children's drama starring Maureen Lipman and Nigel Havers, was set in familiar territory for LWT – Edwardian Britain. It too was an important critical success in 1987.

Bust, starring Paul Nicholas, a popular situation comedy sta explored a central pre-occupation of the 1980s, making money. It w made in 1987, transmitted in 1988, and it became a solid rating performer. *Wish Me Luck* and *Piece of Cake* (an independent productic for LWT), were commissioned by Elliott in 1987 and broadcast in 198 Both were set in another of LWT's home territories, World War Tw The former was concerned with women spies in France, and the latt with an RAF squadron during the Battle of Britain. In 1989, the seal w set on the revived drama department when John Alderton and Pauli Collins returned to LWT in *Forever Green*. This series attracted one the few audiences of 15 million garnered by LWT's drama output in th 1980s.

As well as these series, Elliott's department delivered, among oth things, a four-hour film based on J.G. Farrell's novel *Troubles*, a bad received adaptation of Evelyn Waugh's *Scoop*, and a critically successf feature film based on Waugh's *A Handful of Dust*.

This expansion in drama was initiated at the end of the financial cris of 1985, but Birt did not entirely lift the restrictions on drama. It w only when Greg Dyke replaced Birt that Elliott pushed his drama outp up to the levels which it had enjoyed under Grade. However, it must l stressed that this expansion was only made possible by the type increase in advertising revenue which was typical of Grade's period ar very typical of Birt's early years. From 1986, LWT's drama departme satisfied the four criteria for a burgeoning area: the Director Programmes was committed to its projects, money was made availabl the programmes found an audience, and its controller found his fee The man who led the entertainment division back from the world of ca games and practical jokes was the king of the game shows himself – Al Boyd. Boyd's track record ensured that he became Bell's successor January 1985. His first act, curiously enough, was to preside over th demise of his biggest success to date, *Game For A Laugh*. The ne series, which began on 20 January 1985, was ripped apart by the critic James Murray of the *Daily Star* fulminated:

> *Game For A Laugh* sank to even murkier depths of awfulness ar degradation. New presenter, Martin Daniels, screwing himself up do his masters' dreadful bidding, was required to ask a young girl fro the audience to place star stickers on the parts of a man's bo beginning with the letter B. The man with the body (in a little yello costume) twitched his muscles and hid his face while Martin goade and badgered the girl with cries of: 'You must be able to think of couple of things!'
>
> Then, heaven help us, the otherwise sensible-looking girl did just tha
>
> Whereupon a girl in a bikini was wheeled on so that a ma contestant could place stickers on her bits beginning with 'T.'

The raucous screeching from the audience was enough to make you despair of the human race.

This degrading spectacle, after its first show last week, in which a child was seen repeating a dirty joke, must make *Game For A Laugh* the most grotesque TV show of all time.

They even had somebody making a joke about the Queen's 'private parts.' The men immediately responsible for this show are Alan Boyd, the executive producer, and Brian Wesley, the series producer.

Watchdog, John Whitney, boss of the IBA, must take a close look at *Game For a Laugh* and tell these men that they have gone too far.

The trade paper, *TV Today*, commented:

Brian Tesler, managing director and chairman of LWT knew a thing or two about LE long before his current head of LE, Alan Boyd, ever saw a camera.

Being popular is one thing, he might say, but being smutty is not on. We wonder, therefore, if he said something like that to Alan on Monday after Sunday night's *Game For A Laugh*?

Alan is a shrewd cove and he will know very well that the show is played out. O.K. Alan, we understand that. But will you tell your producers not to scrape the bottom of the barrel again before you take the show off the air next year.

As ever with failures, everybody blames everyone else. In Boyd's opinion *Game For A Laugh* died because Birt moved it from Saturday to Sunday. 'I told John that the new schedule would kill it. I thought that you simply couldn't have custard pies on a Sunday.' Birt agrees: 'Alan is right to chastise me. I thought that I had good reasons; we were winning Saturday night and I wanted a strong Sunday night. However, it is doubtful whether the series could have survived the change of presenters.'[20] Whatever the reasons, however, the demise of the series created the space for one of the quintessential LWT shows, *Blind Date*.

Boyd had bought the format for *Blind Date* from its US producers a few weeks previously. He did not offer it to Birt, however, as this would have entailed killing off either *Surprise, Surprise* – which had brought Cilla Black back to television as a presenter – or *Game For a Laugh*. When the latter died from natural causes, Boyd put *Blind Date* in for evaluation.

Birt was cautious initially. It was almost time for the mid-term review from the IBA and he thought that the Authority might not appreciate the show. He decided, however, to pilot *Blind Date*. As host, Boyd hired a young, camp, comedian called Duncan Norvelle. The result was, in Boyd's words, 'hysterical. Duncan would rush out from behind the screen and say, "If you don't like him, I do!" '

It was impossible to stop the pilot show leaking to the press. In April

1985, the IBA, responding to press rumours, wrote to Birt expressing concerns that he was making a television equivalent of a contacts magazine. Birt offered David Glencross, the IBA's Director of Television, a copy of the pilot (codename: *It's a Hoot*). Birt pointed out that the winning couples would always be sent away on a treat which would allow them to return to their homes at night (unlike the raunchy Australian version), and that a researcher and still photographer would always accompany, and therefore chaperone, the couple.

David Glencross had reservations about 'several cringe-making points' in the show, and he requested further conversations with LWT about the programme. However, the problems dissipated when Boyd and Birt came up with the ideal host – everybody's favourite aunty, Cilla Black. Boyd bustled off to phone Cilla Black's husband, who acted as her agent, and who had just returned from Australia. After chatting about Australian television, Boyd said, 'We would like Cilla to do a new show.' 'Is it Australian?', Bob asked. 'It's similar to one that they show there', Boyd replied. 'We loved it too' Cilla's husband replied. 'You don't know what it is', Boyd said, somewhat puzzled. 'Yes, I do, Cilla watched *Perfect Match* when we were in Australia, and she said to me then, "I would love to do this show." ' The deal was done and *Blind Date*, which was first transmitted in November 1985, went on to become LWT's most successful show of the 1980s, and the third most effective ratings performer in the channel's history.[21]

Marcus Plantin, whom Boyd had recruited from the BBC to become the Head of Light Entertainment, followed Birt's directive to search out new audiences. First, he introduced 'alternative' comedians to LWT. At the beginning of 1985, Channel 4 broadcast a pilot programme made by LWT called *Saturday Night Live*. This was hosted by, and starred, many of the comedians from London's pub and club circuit. The pilot was a success and Channel 4 commissioned a series. Birt fought hard for the show to go out live, beginning at 8.30 pm, despite Jeremy Isaacs' feeling that he could build a better schedule around it if it was later in the evening. The excitement of live television allied to the harnessing of new talent ensured the series' success.

The show, which ran for several years, had all of the resources of LWT's main studio at its disposal. It encouraged the careers of Ben Elton, Hale and Pace, Fry and Laurie, and Harry Enfield, and provided a testing-ground for some comedians and comic actors who have now entered the mainstream. LWT benefited in particular from their connection with Hale and Pace who were given several Channel 4 series, tested out in an early evening Saturday show called *The Saturday Gang*, and eventually were given a prime Sunday night slot for their own series which won the Golden Rose of Montreaux in 1989.

Second, Plantin came up with new situation comedies which were aimed squarely at Birt's target audiences. *The Two Of Us*, written by

Alex Shearer and starring Nicholas Lyndhurst, fresh from *Only Fools and Horses*, was an update on the domestic sit-com, with the twist that the characters were co-habiting and were greenish in their politics. *Hot Metal*, starred Robert Hardy as a megalomaniac newspaper proprietor, and was outrageous in every way. It was planned as a one-off serial for six episodes in the 'cult' comedy 10 pm on a Sunday slot. Its brand of invective was applauded by both critics and target audience and a sequel was commissioned. (It was repeated, to further acclaim, on Channel 4.)

Another innovative pot-shot at a target audience was *Network 7*, a live two-hour programme aimed at teenagers and people in their early-20s. This was invented by Jane Hewland and Janet Street-Porter and was launched on Channel 4 in 1987.

It was surprising in many ways that it took LWT five years before they had a commission accepted for a youth programme. Street-Porter's and Andy Mayer's innovative programmes had been made in the features department for more than five years when Channel 4 went on the air. Street-Porter believed that they had unrivalled experience, and 1981 she had pitched some programme ideas to Mike Bolland, who had responsibility for youth programmes at Channel 4. 'We were very, very naïve. Because we had made *Twentieth Century Box* I thought that we would immediately get programmes on to Channel 4.' Bolland, however, had spent much of his career producing the BBC's access programmes, and he believed that not only should the programmes be about young people, they should be made by them. LWT's ideas were tainted by their source in an ITV fat cat.

Having failed with Bolland, Street-Porter spent a year talking to the Commissioning Editor for Music, Andy Park. When this too broke down, she pushed some ideas through LWT's arts department – again without success. In the meantime she and Jane Hewland began to construct the idea for 'a programme which would strip away the ghastly conventions of news and current affairs productions which were dreamt up in the late 1950s and 1960s. We wanted factual television to be as exciting as other programmes.'

Hewland reminisces about their sales pitch to Channel 4:

Janet and I had a tremendously close working relationship, and we complemented one another. We were due to meet John Cummins, a commissioning editor at Channel 4, and we were talking about the type of programme we would pitch at him. We more or less decided in the taxi to go for broke; to double the hours and go for the whole morning. We were on exceptionally good pitching form that day. Every question he came up with, we had an answer to. We could see the light go on in his eyes. We were saying: 'If you want to be innovative you have got to have a big space; if you want to be flexible you must have an established and big framework. Originally, John asked us to provide the shell, and he intended to drop into it shows which were made by other people. There was an agonizing eighteen months while we talked John out of it.

Although Hewland and Street-Porter won the contract, Cummins was keen that they do it as independents. LWT joined up with an independent production company, Video Visuals Ltd., run by Keith MacMillan, and set up Sunday Productions Ltd.[22] The show, with its quirky camera angles, deliberate amateurishness, and breathless interviews won as many admirers as detractors. The hecklers, hoping to wound, pointed out that Street-Porter and Hewland were forty going on nineteen, and that *Network 7* was an example of yobbish, illiterate television. The duo's flamboyant dress sense and abrasive manner left them wide open to criticism. However, much of the criticism simply resulted from their refusal to play the game by the old rules. Moreover, there are still relatively few successful women who are accepted in ITV. Television – and, for that matter, feature film production and direction – has been a bastion of male domination for almost half a century. During ITV's first thirty-five years only two women became programme controllers, and not one woman has chaired an ITV Board of Directors; indeed, few women have become programme executives. Feature film and television production, in common with many craft-based industries, have, consciously or not, excluded those who do not conform the standard white, male profile. Independent production is slowly breaking down this exclusivity but it may be that Britain will have a second woman Prime Minister before the BBC has its first woman Director General. Too many men have, down the years, patted women producers on the head and diverted their attention to shows about knitting and yoghurt making. Anyone who patted Hewland on the head would have had their hand bitten off.

Network 7 consumed itself very rapidly and lasted only two years; however, the style was resurrected in *7 Sport* and in several of the productions emanating from Janet Street-Porter's department of youth programmes at the BBC.[23]

The other determined attempt to break with established youth programmes was *Night Network*. This was inspired by an attempt to protect ITV's night hours from the government, which was considering selling them off to the highest bidder. However, Birt decided that instead of running a package of repeats and old films, as did most of the ITV companies, he would commission a programme which would be run by its own team, would broadcast in the night hours on Friday and Saturday, and which would be aimed directly at young adults coming back from clubs and pubs.

Night Network, which had a cult following, ran for two years. It was killed eventually because it was difficult to convince advertisers that the viewers to whom it was aimed were actually watching. The sample used by the audience research board (BARB), which publishes the ratings, was not big enough to contain sufficient young people to represent adequately the size of the audience.

Sport also was grist to the Birtian mill. *World of Sport*, which Brian Tesler had invented twenty years before, was finally laid to rest by his Director of Programmes in 1985. The old, down-market, audience profile was entirely out of keeping with the new look ITV network. Moreover, when horse-racing moved over to Channel 4, the spine of the programme – the ITV 7 – disappeared. Birt wanted sport that was, in the words of the advertising hype, 'live and exclusive'.

Two sports in particular have become the focus for LWT's sports policy: athletics and football. In 1985, ITV tapped into the athletics and running boom of the 1980s, and took over the contract for the coverage of British athletics from the BBC. Over the following three years LWT, on ITV's behalf covered, among other athletics events, the AAA Championships, the Talbot Games, the Westminster Mile, and the World Cross Country Championships.

Live football came to the LWT after many acrimonious arguments between LWT, the network and the Football authorities. In 1985, Birt and Grade – after taking over as Controller of BBC1 – decided that recorded football was dying on its feet. They felt that the public was bored with fragments of matches and that football was of declining use to television. The only way forward, they thought, was to restore the excitement and energy of the live game. However, Birt was determined not to pay over-the-odds for the new contract between ITV and the Football League. This put John Bromley – who was the Chairman of the Network Sports Committee as well as LWT's Controller of Sport – in an invidious position. The BBC and his other ITV colleagues wished to settle for a considerably higher amount than Birt was willing to countenance. Birt wrote to Bromley, 'Their [the League] proposition that live football increases ITV's profitability is ludicrous. Taking football as a whole, and including production costs, the opposite is the case: we will save money if there is no football.' He went on to state baldly that if the League did not accept ITV's offer 'I will immediately take football out of LWT's budget for the next year.' Birt's obduracy forced a deal which was satisfactory for everyone and eventually, in September 1985, the first live game – Tottenham against Nottingham Forest – was broadcast.[24]

The football conflict was typical of the ironies which multiplied in Birt's period as Controller. He thought that Kenny Dalglish walked on water, and his weekly five-a-side match was a fixture at LWT, and yet he was willing to drop football from LWT's schedules. He took great pleasure from drama, and the department was run by one of his oldest friends, and yet as a result of the financial problems which he faced when becoming programme controller he allowed it to be drained of finance for three years. He created *Weekend World* and LWT's features and current affairs department, and yet the first programme cuts were in this department. Moreover, if he could have moved *Weekend World* to Channel 4 he would have done so. His own tastes were simply not the point.

The Revolving Door

On the morning of 2 March 1987, an acquaintance of Birt's called him and asked: 'Would you be interested in becoming Michael Checkland's deputy?' Birt thought that this was just one more link in the chain of gossip which had begun when the BBC had sacked its DG Alasdair Milne and which Birt thought had ended when Michael Checkland had been appointed as DG a few weeks before. Birt assumed that the caller was simply floating an idea. A few days later, however, Birt received a call from the same person who told him that Checkland was waiting for an answer. Birt suddenly realized that he was being offered the job seriously, and he informed the intermediary that he would like to meet Checkland.

The two men met at the Howard Hotel, and Checkland came straight to the point. He explained that he wished Birt to become his deputy and also to take special responsibility for the fledgling News and Current Affairs Directorate. Characteristically, Birt asked for time to think.

The financial implications of the deal were troubling. His share options at LWT were worth a considerable amount of money; moreover, his future at LWT was secure. Tesler had offered him the position as Managing Director and they had gone as far as discussing Birt's new contract and reward package. Moreover, he enjoyed LWT. He had worked there for 17 years, many of his friends were his colleagues, and the company was on a sound footing; 1986 had been a good year in the ratings and, in keeping with the rest of the network, an extraordinary year for revenue. The BBC, by contrast, was alien and hostile territory, with its own rules, myths, and values. These thoughts rolled around his head for a few days and then he simply woke up one morning, with a mixed sense of foreboding and exhilaration, and thought, 'This is one job that I cannot say no to.' He felt that however painful leaving LWT was for him, he could not have lived with himself if he turned down the opportunity to help to guide the BBC through one of the most turbulent periods in its history. On 20 March, he announced his departure from LWT.

Birt's replacement was obvious to Tesler. He immediately put out the call to Greg Dyke. 'It was several years earlier than I had planned,' Tesler recalls, 'but Greg was always in my mind as an ideal Director of Programmes for LWT.' The revolving door clicked around a few more times as Alan Boyd left LWT to replace Dyke at TVS and Boyd's deputy, Marcus Plantin, moved up to take over from Boyd. Michael Grade, some months after Birt's arrival at the BBC, jumped the divide once more to become Chief Executive at Channel 4. All of these men in their new jobs were about to face the onslaught of a government committed to a massive reorganization of broadcasting in the UK.

— 11 —
UNFINISHED BUSINESS

It is impossible to write with any confidence about the events which have taken place inside LWT since 1987. Thus far, this history has relied on memoranda and personal recollections. These are neither reliable nor, in some cases, available for the period under review in this chapter. Many of the internal documents are financially or creatively sensitive and, no matter how willing people are to tell the truth, people do not have sufficient distance from actions to be relatively dispassionate about them. Furthermore, many of the programmes and series developed under Dyke's regime are still running and, it is difficult to evaluate the success of failure of his and his executives' strategies.

Several points can be made about Dyke's regime. First, he was greeted with great enthusiasm in the studios of LWT. He was in the Bennett and Grade mould of the fast talking, jack-the-lad (moreover, Tesler believed that he shared many of Birt's analytical abilities). Dyke has a nice line of self-mockery: 'If I hadn't left LWT, I would now be assistant to Jane Hewland in Current Affairs', he points out. However, like most successful people, he has a strong sense of his own value. For example, he left LWT because the company would not give him a company car. 'I was running their most successful current affairs show and they wouldn't give me a car and I was really irritated. When TVam came along with their offer, I jumped at it. I knew that audiences were so bad that I wouldn't be tagged with failure if I did not perform a miracle; but, if it worked I was going to made overnight, and that is what happened.'

When Dyke arrived at LWT, drama and situation comedy were slowly recovering from the cut-backs which Birt and Tesler had considered to be the only practical response to the financial crisis of the early 1980s. Dyke continued the tactics which he had developed during the LWT–TVS alliance; he encouraged Plantin and Elliott to develop more programmes and series which would target the audience in the South

East. Elliott more than doubled the number of hours of drama which were being produced under Birt.

It seemed to some at LWT that aspects of Birt's strategy in the early 1980s had been wrong; in order to maintain a large and faithful audience, so the revisionist version ran, LWT should have maintained its nerve in situation comedy and drama and should have preserved a rich and varied programme schedule. Dyke is determined that LWT should enter the 1990s with a commitment to popular drama and light entertainment which LWT will be able to sell to advertisers and which will attract large and varied audiences.

The department with which Dyke was most unhappy was the one in which he had begun his career, Current Affairs and Features. Dyke's most significant act in some ways was axing *Weekend World*. LWT had tried intermittently to convince Channel 4 to take *Weekend World*. However, the IBA indicated that it would have been displeased with this move. When Brian Walden left and was replaced by the ex-Conservative MP, Mathew Parris, the programme's flagging reputation and the IBA's sagging morale allowed Dyke to kill the show. Dyke continues to nod in the direction of Birtism, but he believes that the '*Weekend World* people did not take John's thinking on to the next stage. It is perfectly valid to do your research and work out what you want to say, but you've then got to make it visually interesting. The test is to try make your point in a way that people can understand it.'

Dyke unashamedly rejects the notion of protected slots for current affairs and documentaries. Each programme has to fight for an audience and, as Dyke believes there is an audience for current affairs, he can see no reason why such programmes should not take their chances in the general mix. David Cox, the ultimate *Weekend World* specialist, found it difficult to accept these new ideas, and, moreover, was not in good health. He resigned in 1988.[1]

Others within the Features and Current Affairs Department reacted differently to Dyke's arrival. Barry Cox had been promoted to Director of Corporate Affairs in October 1987, and his successor, Jane Hewland, developed a brand of 'infotainment'. She believed that LWT's features and current affairs had to take their position in a tougher market for programmes. 'I believe that public service broadcasting has killed serious journalism by protecting it,' she asserted not long after taking over from Cox. She summed up her own, and Dyke's, point of view:

I am developing a lot of popular shows in this department, but there is a sort of belief in the business generally, that if you want to appeal to a large number of people there must be something rather base and Murdoch-like about you; you must be intending to give viewers items on vicar's love tangles. In order to prevent this, and to preserve quality journalism, people put barbed-wire fences around saying, 'Do

Not Touch This Programme.' All the people inside the fence can give each other pats on the back and talk to each other and make programmes that no one wants to watch. There is no control on them. If you look at entertainment and drama, styles change and stars change. There is no pressure on Current Affairs to change and therefore it innovates incredibly slowly.

It never has to work for an audience, in fact it never has to get an audience – if it ever starts to build a large audience people look on it with a great deal of suspicion . . . The regulators should have said: 'Your target is to get ratings. Obviously not *That's Life* audiences, but high AIs, and it should show up in audience research as something audiences care about and want to watch. If you don't do that, we will withdraw protection from you.' That would mean something.[2]

David Cox looks at the debate somewhat differently:

It looks to a casual observer as though the whole Birt thing, which began in 1972 as far as factual programming is concerned, is now being reversed . . . There was a flowering of the public service broadcasting ideal in its guise within commercial television and this produced some distinctive and unique programmes. That's now been swept away. However, I don't think that it's the personalities of Greg Dyke or Jane Hewland or whoever that is responsible. It is historical forces that are changing ITV.

Most of those who grew up and learned their craft during Birt's, the two Cox's, and Elliott's regimes left when Hewland tried to drive the department forward into what she saw as the future.

The historical forces to which David Cox was referring emanated from a combination of technical developments (satellite dishes, optic fibre cables etc.) changes in the industry (particularly the rise of a burgeoning independent production sector), and a government commitment to transforming ITV. The most important innovation, and ITV's greatest fear, was the introduction of competitive tendering. Instead of the IBA's successor, the Independent Television Commission (ITC), awarding franchises on the basis of programme promises or performance, the government began to suggest that contracts should be awarded to the highest bidder. Moreover, the Conservatives' heavy victory in 1987 led to a sense among British management that the time to confront the unions had arrived – particularly when the Prime Minister scathingly referred to ITV as 'the last bastion of restrictive practices'.

Flowing off the high point of Thatcherism, and with the sure and certain knowledge that the government intended to institute measures to break-up the ITV network, LWT went on the offensive.

The management made provision to take on the unions. It bought programmes, and a long mini-series in particular, which were reserved in the library for emergency purposes. If the unions had shut down production then LWT intend to transmit more than old feature films and repeats. Its reserve schedule ensured that it would be able to withstand a strike for longer than the unions.

On 22 March 1988, with the reserve programmes in its back pocket, LWT's management set out the terms of new agreements with the broadcasting unions, ACTT, BETA and EETPU. LWT was extremely fortunate in the timing of these negotiations. The IBA's breakfast television franchisee, TVam had not long before locked out its staff and its management had produced the programmes. Tesler felt that he had to strike hard and fast. It worked. LWT's new agreements – known as The Document – seemed relatively reasonable compared to the hard-nosed behaviour of TVam. The plan was to reduce LWT's staff from 1600 to 1300, to institute agreements which would break down the demarcation agreements which had seemed almost frozen in time, and to allow LWT to use freelance talent, new technologies, independent producers, and to lease out its studios as a facilities house.[3]

LWT needed to open up its studios to independent product. The government has decreed that it expects ITV and the BBC to take 25 per cent of their productions from the independent sector and LWT wanted union agreements which would allow those who were making programmes independently for the station to use its facilities. LWT has already engaged in several high-profile independent productions: most notably its local news programme, and the dramas *Troubles* and *Piece of Cake*, a six part series based on a best-selling book about a squadron of fighter pilots in the early months of World War II. Needless to say, the aftershocks of The Document and the concomitant redundancies have left a sour taste in what was once a family company. It will be some time before LWT's staff will feel comfortable once more.

In the winter of 1989 the government laid a Broadcasting Bill before Parliament which will transform ITV. It will be impossible for anyone to stage a secret coup similar Frost's. LWT has prepared long and hard to meet the challenge of broadcasting in the 1990s. In August 1989, Christopher Bland masterminded a deal whereby all of the top executives and programme-makers in the company would be able to purchase shares on a basis which would, if the company continued to be successful, make it extremely difficult for a rival franchise bidder to prise them away.[4] Bland intends to ensure that there will be no parallel to the exodus from the BBC which helped to launch several of the 1967 franchise bids.

The broadcasting environment in the 1990s will call for a mixture of nerve, good sense and decent programme-making skills, and, just as LWT's first 21 years demonstrated the strengths and weaknesses of the IBA-ITV system, so LWT intends to be around long enough to act as an indicator as to the health of the new system.

NOTES

Chapter 1

1 The name was changed from the Independent Television Authority in 1972, when the government gave the Authority responsibility for independent local radio. Early in 1990 the IBA's successor, the Independent Television Commission, was established. The new body will allocate franchises primarily on financial grounds and it will be virtually impossible for a coup, such as the one outlined in this chapter, to again occur.

2 This was a generation of Parliamentarians who had experienced the worldwide benefits amassed by the BBC's war efforts, and by Churchill's radio speeches. However, radio had also been described as 'Goebbels' lips' when Hitler chief propagandist had used it to great effect before and during the war.

3 A public corporation is a body of people incorporated as a legal entity as the result of a Royal Charter of an Act of Parliament. The number of public corporations expanded greatly as Attlee's Labour Government brought private enterprises – such as coal and railways – into public ownership.

4 The first contracts were awarded for regions as transmitters came on line. Grampian and WWN (Wales) completed the network in 1961–2. In 1991 the contracts will be awarded by the ITC.

5 ATV provided the programmes for the weekend in London.

6 Bernard Sendall, the IBA's official historian and a former Deputy Director General of the Authority, firmly believed that ITV would have a considerably more difficult beginning if Wills had not held the line.

7 This natural distance was enhanced by social distance. As real wages increased, new skills were learned and higher education expanded, some members of the family benefited more than others. Affluence carried a heavy social price.

8 Bernard Sendall, *Independent Television in Britain Volume 2 Expansion and Change, 1958–1968* Macmillan, London, 1983. p. 86.

9 Sendall, op cit, p. 94.

10 Lord Hill of Luton, *Behind the Screen*, Sidgwick and Jackson, 1974, p. 16–17.

11 Along with Norman Collins – a former Controller of BBC Television – Fraser virtually invented ITV.

12 Sendall op cit. p. 229.

13 BBC2 was launched in 1964.

14 The regional companies all held seven day franchises.

15 Paradine is Frost's middle name.

16 Henceforth, if quotations are given without a source they are taken from personal interviews with the author, or from internal LWT memoranda.

17 A couple got away: the electronics group, Thorn, pulled out at the last moment and Iain Macleod, the former Conservative Home Secretary, who had recently retired from the House of Commons, decided not to continue after early interest.

18 The writers of *Steptoe and Son* – Ray Galton and Alan Simpson – agreed to write a series for the new station.

19 The LTC also recruited Bill Fletcher, the BBC's Chief Engineer, Operations.

20 As Peacock was still employed at the BBC, he took little part in these discussions until the final few weeks.

21 The only condition was that the *Observer*, the *Daily Telegraph* and the *Economist* should be offered shares.

22 'Thames' was taken by the ABC-Rediffusion merger as the name for their station.

Chapter 2

1 Cyril Bennett in fact dealt with the programmes exchanges in the Major Programme Controllers Committee.

Chapter 3

1 ITV's Share of the Audience in London, 1968.

	Weekdays %	Saturday %	Sunday %
August	51 (54)	38 (51)	47 (67)
September	51	38	43
October	46	38	41
November	48	42	46
December	47	42	49

The 1967 figures (shown in brackets) were collected by Television Audience Measurement (TAM) using a slightly different method of calculation. It is possible that TAM over-reported; however, the BBC figures for the period confirm that ITV dominated Sunday night in 1967.

2 The levy was calculated as follows in 1964: there was a 'free slice' of £1½ million; on the next £6 million there was a charge of 25 per cent; and above that 45 per cent. See Sendall Vol 2 op cit 190–201.

3 Year ended 29 July Net Advertising Revenue Before Levy (NARBL)

1965	£
1966 (i)	82,619
1967	82,017
	89,945

1968	£
1969	94,930
1970	98,623
	92,737

Source: NBPI

(i) Cigarette advertising was prohibited by the ITA from 1 August 1965. This had accounted for £8 million in the previous financial year.

4 Levy: 1964 – July 1969

Net Revenue (£m)	Scale of Levy (%)
Nil – 2	Nil
2 – 6	20
6 – 9	35
9 – 12	40
12 – 16	45
Over 16	50

Levy: July 1969 – April 1970

Nil – 0.5	Nil
0.5 – 1.5	7
1.5 – 4.0	25
4.0 – 10.0	35
Over 10.0	47.5

5 *Facing the Nation*, Grace Wyndham Goldie, The Bodley Head, 1977, p. 149.
6 Depending on one's degree of cynicism one can either regard these restrictions as beneficial to the community, in that they sustain moral frameworks among the practitioners of key symbolic occupations – such as the law, medicine and education. Or, one might view these qualifications as merely a device to disguise arrogance and greed.
7 Twenty years on Doreen Stephens recalls that 'It was a permanent fight with Cyril. I was at loggerheads with him all the time; I never felt comfortable with him. He was taking the old independent television route'.
8 My emphasis.
9 Stella Richman was in the US throughout the crisis.

Chapter 4

1 In June 1970, Wilson's administration was replaced by that of Edward Heath's Conservative Party.
2 In a newspaper interview which took place after she accepted the position, Guy Paine looms large over Richman's shoulder. 'If by taking out one programme and putting in another which we have originated the sales division are able to do a better job,' she noted, 'then we have achieved what we need to achieve'. She continued, 'One of the main purposes of getting the programme-mix right in your own time is to help the sales people with something that they can sell. Otherwise, how do you stay in business?'
3 Cyril Bennett strongly recommended Richman. Although he was fond of her and thought her an admirable producer, he did not believe her capable of running a large organisation. He told a friend on leaving LWT that Richman was his insurance policy: if she failed then he thought that he might be offered another chance.
4 Even with this series something went wrong. The ITC criticized one of the programmes for being too erotic.
5 LWT's and ITV's share of Peak Audiences, Saturday and Sunday, 1970

Month	LWT %	ITV %	Difference %
January	50	52	−2
February	52	54	−2
March	49	52	−3
April	46	51	−5
May	47	48	−1
June	43	45	−2
July	50	53	−3
August	48	53	−3
September	52	55	−3
October	55	56	−1
November	48	50	−2
December	46	51	−5

LWT's revenue declined from £12.1 millions in the period mid-1968 to mid-1969, to £10.7 millions in mid-1969-mid-1970.

6 Murdoch also picked up the shares of Peacock and several of the early programme-makers who had passed their shares on to LWT's brokers to be sold to the highest bidder.

Chapter 5

1   Montagu continued, 'Thank God they did not listen to me, because undoubtedly John Freeman saved the company'.

2   By coincidence at the previous ITA meeting, one of the members of the Authority had noted that LWT's problems would never have arisen if John Freeman had been at the company. Moreover, Lord Aylestone had Freeman on his list of possible successors to Sir Robert Fraser.

3   For example, Gary Cooper in *Mr Deedes Goes to Town* and James Stewart in *Mr Smith Goes to Washington*.

4   It is a measure of Freeman's impact that Churchill is reported to have wept with pleasure at the sight of Freeman, still in his uniform, making his maiden speech.

5   He rejoined the company officially on 25 May 1971.

6   Also present were Lord Campbell, Rupert Murdoch, David Montagu and Evelyn De Rothschild.

7   By 1975, when LWT was in a much healthier financial position, Thames complained vigorously to the ITA that LWT was being treated too leniently at Thames' expense.

8   He did operate with standard rebates; for example, there was a 40 per cent reduction on off-peak spots which had been booked well in advance, and peak-time spots were also discounted in advance or if agencies paid the account in full a couple of weeks after the campaign was over. However, these tricks of the trade did not undermine the anti-pre-empt strategy.

9   When Hardy resigned as Director of Sales Freeman wrote thanking him for 'saving the company from bankruptcy'.

10   They were 44 per cent down on fmcg spots.

Chapter 6

1   Now known as the British Academy of Film and Television Arts (BAFTA).

2   Jean Marsh won the US Academy of Television and Sciences EMMY award for Best Actress for her portrayal of one of the servants. Gordon Jackson was awarded the Royal Television Society Award for the Outstanding Television Performance of 1974 for his role as Hudson, the butler. The series itself won the EMMY for Outstanding Drama Series in 1974 and 1975 and the Foreign Press Association Golden Globe for Best Television Drama Series. In all, LWT's programmes won twenty-three significant awards for their 1974 output.

3   When Bennett was appointed to the Board one of the senior executives was widely reported to have said, 'Now we have a house Jew'.

4   Hill eventually left the company in November 1972 in pursuit of the kind of nationwide fame which the BBC could offer to him, and which the purely London-based *Big Match* could not.

5   Everyone claims to have spotted how successful *Upstairs, Downstairs* was to become from the first frame. Murdoch, according to Bert Hardy, thought that it would become the cornerstone of LWT's fortunes; Lord Aylestone had been present in the early stages of production and he inquired of John Freeman at LWT's reappointment whether the series would be made. Although everyone was convinced of its success, little credit seems to have been given to the woman who sponsored it – Stella Richman.

6   When one of the researchers on the Hitler play somewhat naïvely said to Bennett, 'You know, some of the things Hitler did were all right', Bennett growled, 'Yeh, he just had a bad press officer'.

7   LWT's contract, like that of the other contractors, should have been renegotiated in 1976. However, in 1974, the new Labour government instituted a wide-ranging inquiry into the structure and propose of broadcasting, under the Chairmanship of Lord Annan. The contracts were continued until 1979, while Annan's inquiry progressed; the IBA insisted, however, that it was still appropriate for the Authority to conduct its own review of the network's output. (The contracts were not renewed until 1981–2, by which time the original contract had run for 11 years. This had profound implications for the development of ITV which have seldom been explored.)

8   Taken from LWT's 10th Anniversary magazine. One story illustrates the strength of feeling for the company. In May 1975 the ACTT was on the verge of calling a national strike. The staff at LWT voted by 305 to 9 to break the strike 'even if the picket lines are out'. The cynical view is that LWT's employees' mouths were stuffed with silver, but there does seem to have been a genuine family atmosphere in the early 1970s.

9   The history of the former has been detailed in Michael Tracey's book *In the Culture of the Eye: Ten Years of Weekend World*, Hutchinson, London, 1983; however, the establishment of the series is germane to this story of the Freeman–Bennett programme strategy, and it helps to flesh out the bones of that scheme.

10   Frost's relationship with Bennett and with the station degenerated in 1973. Bennett and Frost exchanged increasingly acrimonious notes, each implying that the other was unreasonable and had lost his touch. Frost's contract was not renewed and, in 1974, he sold his shares to the company to finance his famous interviews with Richard Nixon.

11   The relationship between Frost and Birt continued with the Nixon interviews and with the Kissinger interview in 1979.

12   Another twist in the tale was that a few weeks after Cox's idea was accepted, and before it was known publicly, Clive Irving submitted virtually an identical idea. An embarrassed, and slightly worried, Bennett had to explain that they were already in negotiation with Cox and that they had not stolen any of Irving's proposals.

13   A second London-based series – *The London Weekend Show* – launched the television career of one of the most lampooned and most ambitious women in the medium – Janet Street-Porter.

14   Presumably named after the famous clown Joey Grimaldi.

15   They went on to update their characters in the 1978 series *Thomas and Sara* and appeared together again in the 1989 drama – *Forever Green*.

Chapter 7

1 It should be said that LWT's situation comedies – *The Fosters* and *Mixed Blessings* – attempted to play against the stereotype. Furthermore, in later LWT productions, such as *GlooJoo*, starring Norman Beaton, and *No Problem*, a cult situation comedy starring a collective of young black actors, LWT, or more precisely its most consistently interesting comedy producer, Humphrey Barclay, worked hard to create believable black comedy. Even *Mind Your Language*, which was widely attacked as being as racist as *Love Thy Neighbour*, started life as an anti-racist sit com.

2 Janet Street-Porter and her producer, Andy Mayer, conveyed much of what was happening in punk and youth culture in the mid-1970s, in the *London Weekend Show*.

3 This is not to say that ITV, and LWT, did not continue to make banal, trivial, uninspired and inadequate current affairs, drama, and light entertainment.

4 Cyril Bennett was the second. Tesler's career was marked by a number of 'firsts'. He was the first Director of Programmes to be appointed Managing Diretor of an ITV company – David Plowright of Granada was the second – and he was the first MD to be concurrently appointed Chairman.

5 Cyril Bennett's defection to LWT meant, of course, that there was no competition from Rediffusion for the post of Director of Programmes.

6 Another small irony: Tesler joined the BBC on the same day as Michael Peacock.

7 Tesler was still writing tunes – such as the theme for the variety show – *Talk of the Town* – in the late 50s.

8 *Sources of ITV's Top Ten Programmes by Years*

	ATV	Granada	LWT	Thames	Yorkshire
1969	11	28	2	3	
1970	9	34	7	38	
1971	3	38	10	36	10
1972	16	27	13	40	8
1973	14	22	3	47	7
1974	18	31	3	46	6
1975	24	21	2	45	9
1976	37	13	4	36	4
					5

Compiled by William Phillips from data furnished by the Broadcasters Audience Research Board (BARB). These data are based on the success of individual series of one-off specials rather than individual programmes. (If the latter had been the basis for comparison, Granada's long-running series *Coronation Street* would have unbalanced the figures.)

9 In the Autumn of 1976, eight of the BBC's fifteen top twenty programmes were broadcast at the weekend. LWT, by contrast, had not produced a top twenty show in the previous six months. This slump in ratings was intensified by a deal which guaranteed advertisers a certain audience for their advertisement and which required LWT to run the ad until the numbers had been achieved.

10 This hotel had been made famous by a speech by the leader of the Conservative Party, Edward Heath, in 1970, at which he outlined the Tories' future economic policies, which earned him the soubriquet – Selsdon Man.

11 At the inquest the coroner decided that Bennett's death was an accident. Dr Thurstone argued, 'There is nothing to suggest that it was a deliberate action and it appears probable that he was looking out of the window of his flat to see whether his car was in the yard.' Bennett had intended to go out that evening and had asked the chauffeur to leave his Rolls-Royce parked in the yard; instead, the chauffer had parked it around the corner where Bennett would have been unable to see it from the window. The coroner concluded, 'This is an unusually low window, and there was a lot of debris on the window sill which was not disturbed which would not have been the case if someone had endeavoured to climb on to the sill.'

12 On such a difficult issue as this, it would be entirely presumptuous of any historian who did not know Bennett to speculate on his actions. His death will remain a painful mystery to all involved. I have sought to present Selsdon as it appeared to those who took part and as it appears from the records and memoranda which led up to the meeting.

13 Birt was profoundly upset by Bennett's death, and he wept openly at the grave. Bennett was the first person to die whom Birt knew well, and the emotion of the event overwhelmed him.

14 Ron Miller and Russell Harty were away for the weekend at a sales pitch when they heard the news. They retreated to a private room with a bottle of whisky and told Cyril stories through the long night.

Chapter 8

1 As a gesture of affection, the company established the Cyril Bennett award at the Royal Television Society.

2 On the day before he began as Controller of Programmes, Grade went on to the set of a programme wearing a revolving bow tie and did the warm-up act. By all accounts he was terrible, but the staff loved him for it.

3 When George Bush chose Dan Quayle as his running mate for the 1988 US Presidential elections many commentators assumed that Bush could not face up to the pressures sharing the ticket with a fully qualified, aggressive partner who might put him in the shade. The same criticism could not be levelled at Tesler, whose reputation, position and self-confidence were secure.

4 Rex Firkin, who had been with the company since the late 1960s, and who had been responsible for several of its successes, left the company.

5   Highest-Rated LWT Broadcasts, September 1968–June 1989

Programme	Audience (Millions)	Date	
It'll be Alright On the Night	18.6	11 Jan	1985
Mind Your Language	18.2	10 Feb	1978
Lillie	18.2	26 Nov	1978
Blind Date	18.2	22 Nov	1986
The Gentle Touch	18.1	8 Jan	1982
It'll Be Alright On Xmas Night	18.0	25 Dec	1987
People Do the Funniest Things	17.9	11 Jan	1986
Maggie and Her	17.8	10 Feb	1978
Mind Your Language	17.8	17 Mar	1978
Mixed Blessings	17.7	17 Mar	1978

Compiled by William Phillips from data furnished by the Broadcast Audience Research Board (BARB).

6   *Love for Lydia* caused all sorts of problems. Bennett sacked the producer, the novelist's son Richard Bates. However, it did signal to the IBA that LWT was interested in 'quality' drama.

7   LWT's Top Rated Dramas, September 1968–June 1989

Programme	Audience (Millions)	Date
Lillie	18.2	Sun 26 Nov 1978
The Gentle Touch	18.1	Fri 8 Jan 1982
The Professionals	17.6	Sun 30 Nov 1980
The Seven Dials Mystery	17.6	Sun 8 Mar 1981
The Professionals	17.4	Fri 10 Feb 1978
The Professionals	17.3	Fri 3 Mar 1978

8   Its biggest audience for a single programme was 17.3 million, which places it at number 17 in LWT's highest rated programmes.

9   West Indian families were upset that although the parents in *Mixed Blessings* were West Indian, the daughter was clearly West African.

10 Specials planned before Bennett's death included *The Strange Case of the End of Civilisation as we Know It*, starring John Cleese and Arthur Lowe as a latter-day Holmes and Watson; *Come Spy with Me*, starring Danny La Rue; a Michael Crawford special, produced by David Bell who had been so successful with the *Stanley Baxter Shows*. A pilot comedy – *Clip Joint* – was written by the comedian Bob Monkhouse, produced by Bryan Izzard, and starred three of Britain's better comedy actors – Windsor Davies, Jack Douglas and Andrew Sachs – and yet it was universally regarded as a total failure, adding further proof to Bennett's dictum that the alchemy of success is mysterious and virtually impossible to manufacture.

11

Date	Network TVR	Individuals
7 Oct	29	14,529
14 Oct	25	12,605
28 Oct	21	9,994
4 Nov	21	9,717
11 Nov	19	9,577
18 Nov	25	12,681
25 Nov	26	13,325

12 In the classic style of LWT, the indication of major problems was accompanied by an apparent minor irritation. On the third show Bruce Forsyth had called Pam Ayers England's most prominent poetess, added, 'apart from Patience Strong and she's packed it in . . .'. A letter of complaint from Rubinstein and Callingham, Miss Strong's solicitors, followed. Miss Strong who, according to her lawyers, was still contributing to various magazines and publishing books, considered Mr Forsyth's remarks 'defamatory'. Forsyth had to apologise and invite Miss Strong on to the show before honour was even.

13 The consultants, TAPE, also recommended that LWT drop *The Worker*, introduce British guests to replace the Americans, and allow Forsyth the opportunity to use his *Generation Game* persona in audience participation programmes.

14 Alan Boyd, Forsyth's producer at the BBC and subsequently Head of Light Entertainment at LWT, believes that in the history of British Light Entertainment, the show will stand out as brave and interesting. In his mind, the problem lay with allowing a star – who was frustrated with his image as a host and who wanted to be seen as an all-round entertainer in the US style – to dominate the production.

15 In its annual report the IBA noted that *Bruce's Big Night* was a 'new and ambitious' programme which, after a bad start, was picking up audiences until a 'cynical and bitter' press campaign sabotaged the show.

16 Other changes included the 'promotion' of John Bromley and Tony Wharmby from, respectively, Deputy Controller of Programmes [Sport] and Deputy Controller of Programmes [Drama], to, respectively,

Controller of Sport and Controller of Drama. The announcements were made at the beginning of February 1977.

17 Geoffrey Hughes, whom Birt felt would not make the type of contribution necessary to modernize the department, and who was not part of his inner-group, was asked by Tesler, who wished to recognize his long service to the company, to become the first Head of the ITV teletext system.

18 Elliott and Birt had, in fact, lobbied hard for the new department. Elliott wrote a memorandum outlining the case for a unified Features department and indicating his willingness to become its Head.

19 As is the way with most of these seminal articles, several other people had claimed subsequently to have had a hand in the preparation of the piece.

20 This theatricality was at its most obvious during the tenure of the ex-Labour MP, Brian Walden, who was the programme's interviewer from June 1977 until 1986. Walden's powerful presence arguably gave the programme more years than many people felt that it deserved.

21 Of which Lord Palmerston, wrote, 'There are only three men who have ever understood it; one was Prince Albert, and he is dead; the second was a German professor who became mad; I am the third and I have forgotten all about '. Cf. An apocryphal story about Peter Jay. When questioned by a sub-editor about the meaning of an article on monetarism, Jay is reputed to have replied, 'This article is written for three men in England, and you're not one of them'.

22 Interestingly, *Mayerling* was produced by Derek Bailey who had produced Aquarius for two years before Bragg arrived.

23 ITV was ineligible in 1979.

24 Paul Fox, Managing Director of Yorkshire, grumbled 'funny way to promote ITV'.

25 Described by Allen as 'very unassuming and quiet, but a brilliant producer and a great unsung hero of LWT current affairs'.

26 In a *Sunday Times* article, 'Who Will Be Who in the 1980s', David Cox was described as one of the 'brightest young men in British television'.

27 Clive James went on to present and write a number of wry one-off documentaries about visits to, among other places, Paris, Las Vegas, and Dallas. He also presented the series *Clive James on TV*.

28 Although *Skin* had tiny audiences (in one LWT survey only 9 per cent of the London population claimed to have heard of it) the majority of people believed that it was a useful programme which contributed to the overall understanding of black life.

29 *Annual Hours Occupied By:-*

	1975–6	1976–7	1977–8	1978–9	1979–80
	52 wks	52 wks	48 wks	45 wks	
	28.25 hrs	387.25 hrs	367.25 hrs	365.25 hrs	273.75 hrs
	%	%	%	%	%
Off Peak, Specialised Cat 'A'	28.8	27.6	27	24.5	27.3
Peak/Off Peak Cat 'A' Drama and Ent.	27.3	31.9	27.9	34.1	38.1
Local Non-Networked Progs.	43.7	40.3	44.9	41.3	34.5

30 Both were eventually sold ten years later.

31 Hutchinson made a loss of £1.2 million in 1980 and despite radical restructuring of the company, of £477,000 in 1981.

32 One notable financial move connected with the company was Rupert Murdoch's decision in March 1980 to sell his non-voting shares for £4.8 million. Even allowing for inflation, the Murdoch's 1970 cash injection had proved to be a sound investment.

33 The contracts were then extended to mid-1979 and then, finally, until the end of 1981. What had started as a six year franchise ended up as a contract for thirteen and a half years.

34 August 1989. p. 00

Chapter 9

1 The Channel 4 consultants who advertised the post were appointed by the IBA to set up the new channel. In due course, the consultants became the first Board of Directors. Tesler was appointed by the IBA as a consultant and was in the interesting position of interviewing his Controller of Features and Current Affairs for another job. Tesler's recommendations helped to raise Birt's profile with the consultants.

2 Sue Stoessl left LWT to join Channel 4 and, over the years, she became one of Isaacs' staunchest supporters.

3 Tandem was created by Norman Lear, the producer of the comedy *All in the Family* which was the highly successful US version of the BBC's *Till Death Us Do Part*. Tandem was recognized as one of the most consistently effective producers of situation comedies in the US. Commenting on Grade's departure, John Freeman said, 'I was terribly fond of Michael, but I could see that he wanted to go and make his own fortune. If you are a Grade you have very strong feelings that you have to make good in your own right, and I think

that Michael had a very great psychological need to go out into the world and make his fortune or make his name'.

4 Alan Bullock was a biographer of the Labour party's first post-war leader, Clement Attlee.
5 This received a small but favourable review in the *Manchester Guardian*.
6 This included S4C.
7 The dispute was not settled until October 1984. Eventually, actors were paid 55 per cent of the ITV fee for Channel 4, and 37 per cent for TVam.
8 Brian Tesler, in a personal capacity and not as representative of LWT, was appointed by the IBA to sit on the Channel 4 Board.
9 In September 1983, the government announced that the IBA would be permitted to issue licences for Direct Broadcast by Satellite [DBS] channels. Initially, the BBC channels. However, when the BBC decided that it was too expensive and the IBA was invited to join a British Satellite Board the government insisted that DBS should use a British satellite which was considerably more expensive than an American equivalent. This resulted in the BBC and IBA inviting in other partners, which in turn resulted in a peculiar consortium of funders. This camel designed by committee fell by the wayside in June 1985. The IBA was then asked to review the situation. In early 1986, the IBA informed the Home Office that there was significant interest in DBS. The government then invited the IBA to offer three programme contracts for DBS services.

In 1986, LWT decided to join a consortium with Carlton Communications and to make a bid for the DBS franchise. However, this consortium decided that there were insufficient funds for a subscription-based service and, in their application, stated that the majority of the funding would have to come from advertising. At the end of 1986, the IBA, committed to the idea of a high technology, subscription-based service, awarded the contract to British Satellite Broadcasting, a company in which Granada had a major share-holding. LWT did join ITV's other satellite venture, *SuperChannel*. This was intended to be a 'Best of British' channel, which began transmitting to mainland Europe in January 1987; it was supposed to be an outlet in Europe for ITV – and BBC – programmes. It had difficulties from the start, and was eventually sold in 1988.

10 Whitney's previous contact with LWT had been through *Upstairs, Downstairs* in its early days. His company sold LWT the format.
11 Above-the-line programme costs were only recorded in LWT's profit and loss accounts when they were transmitted. By not transmitting *Mitch*, LWT did not enter it as expenditure and, consequently, it did not affect the company's profits. In short-term crisis, when the company wanted to shore up its profits and its dividends, it made sense not to transmit the most expensive type of programme – drama. This accountancy practice ensured that LWT had a considerable amount of drama in stock, and this badly hit drama production during the following few years.
12 He replaced it with a repeat of *The Professionals*.
13 This judgement has subsequently been confirmed. TV viewing has consistently declined over the past five years.
14 It took another year, however, before the first glimmerings of Gatward's intentions filtered through to the rest of the network.
15 The IBA also held a conference at Selsdon in 1983, at which it explored the future for broadcasting.
16 The seven day companies could make a drama – say an adaptation of a novel by Graham Greene – and then decide on which day they wished to schedule. Birt wished for a system which outlined the scheduling needs for, e.g., a peak-time Saturday and then satisfied them. If Nick Elliott had a drama series, it would have to meet these conditions.
17 In July 1983, when summing up the traumas of the previous eight months, Tesler pointed out the drawbacks with this strategy. 'They [game shows] are not so easy to repeat, and their overseas sales value is limited'. This latter was vitally important; LWT would not have been in profit in 1982–83 if it had not been for the sale of programmes to the US. Properly funded drama had to come back into the schedules at some point. However, it took another two years before this was achieved.
18 This last working party commissioned a management report from outside consultants which spoke of LWT 'loose' management structure and 'family' culture. They were, perhaps, two years out-of-date. Both the family culture and the management structure were undergoing a rapid, and unsettling, transformation.
19 Tesler penned on the side of Birt's note explaining these offers, 'let's hope the former'. His worry proved to be prescient.
20 When Birt became Director of Programmes it was pointed out to him that LWT was consistently making less than its NAR share of programmes. Instead of NAR being apportioned directly, LWT and Thames contributed not in relation to their NAR but matched the points which Central, Yorkshire and Granada would make for the weekend. If the contribution of these the three major seven day companies to the weekend was disproportionately low, then LWT's contribution to the weekend was also disproportionately low *compared to their NAR share*. LWT was in a double bind; it lost twice over, the weekend schedule was threadbare because the companies would not contribute their real NAR share to the weekend, and LWT could not compensate for this because it could not even make its NAR share. LWT argued successfully in the mid-1980s that this situation should be reversed, that three seven day companies had to match Thames' and LWT's contribution.

A new network system, adopted at a conference in Jersey in 1987 and called the flexi-pool, requires a degree in mathematics in order to understand it. Roughly, 16 per cent of the pot is open to offers from each of the fifteen companies. A committee consisting of representatives from the majors and the regional awards the programmes. The rest of the points remain in the hands of the big five. The system, once broken open, is now under constant review, and the flexi-pool may increase relative to the rest.

21 Gatward still wanted TVS to become a sixth major. His persistence, Dyke's terrier- like attacks on the Northern companies, and TVS's attempt to lead the other regionals destabilized the network and led, eventually, to a new method of bidding for programmes within the network, the so-called flexipool. It is arguable that the big five would have benefited more if they had accepted Gatward in the first place.

22 Birt had already convinced Channel 4 to accept *Credo* which provided him with more points to play with. This move opened up bitter charges of betrayal for those who believed that *Credo* was one of the few attempts made by mainstream British television to come to terms seriously with religion.

23 Birt and Dyke, although allies, disagreed about this famous quote. Birt felt that it hindered rather than helped the long-term argument with ITV.

24 Advertisers themselves rejected the notion that the new BARB figures had any effect on the amount which they spent on advertising.

25 See Chapter five for a description of pre-emption.

26 On LWT's Channel 4 time, campaigns aimed at housewives dropped to 13 per cent in 1985.

27 Curiously, *Dempsey and Makepeace*, a crash-and-bang police series which had been developed to replace *The Professionals* had a strongish following among AB men. Perhaps the presence of Glynis Barber had a little to do with its success. The show, which made a great deal of money for LWT in overseas sales, was not a success in the US and it folded after three series.

28 This theory was not without its critics. Two academics, Patrick Barwise and Andrew Ehrenberg of the London Business School, have long argued in their studies of the television audience that all programmes have similar demographic profiles. Birt, and many others at the sharp end of programme-making and advertising, felt that the Barwise and Ehrenberg argument confused a broad general truth, namely that television could not target as effectively as, say, magazines, with the more interesting argument about the very pronounced skews in audiences. It was clear to Birt, working daily with the ratings, that individual shows had different audience profiles.

29 In November 1986, LWT's share of London television advertising revenue reached 47 per cent, up 4 per cent from the previous year, and within striking distance of Thames. In September 1985, the trade journal *Campaign* remarked that LWT is 'undoubtedly the star performer *vis-à-vis* advertising. LWT consistently sells more of and commands a higher price for its airtime than any other station'.

LWT's status was helped somewhat by the almost complete chaos within Thames during 1984 and 1985. The company, which had always been regarded as safe and sensible, lost three sales directors in two years. Moreover, the managing director, Bryan Cowgill, had precipitated a major drama when he bought *Dallas* – then at the height of its popularity – from under the nose of the BBC. However, not only did he break the long-standing gentleman's agreement with the BBC over bidding for US series, he paid double the BBC's price without informing the IBA or his colleagues in the network. He resigned when his move was attacked from all sides and the support from his board evaporated.

30 In *Broadcasting Over Britain*, his promotional tract for the BBC, Reith designated 'people of education' as an 'élite' which would be enlarged as a result of the BBC's commitment to education.

31 Samuel Brittan was to write in 1989, 'To the extent that the government endorsed some Peacock recommendations, it is the letter that was accepted, and the spirit rejected. As the proposed fifth channel is likely to be financed exclusively by advertising, even the letter, in its up-to-date form, has now been rejected' *Freedom in Broadcasting* C. Veljanowski (ed), IEA 1989, p. xiii..

32 David Montagu, the last remaining member of the original London Television Consortium, and Freeman's great friend, was invited to take over as chairman. However, it was clear that Montagu's interests lay elsewhere. By and large, the offer was made for reasons of protocol and friendship. Montagu left the board in 1987 as the demands on his time increased as the result of taking on the chairmanship of the tobacco company Rothmans International.

33 Freeman summed up the relationship between a director of programmes and his chairman. 'If I were Director of Programmes, my ambition would be to make the best possible programmes. But, if I am Head of company with hundreds or thousands of employees, then my concern is to make money for that company. The relationship between the two should be one of creative tension; the job of the Director of Programmes is to screw as much money out of me as possible, and it is my job to see that he doesn't get away with it'.

34 Tesler had been appointed as Deputy Chairman of LWT in August 1982.

35 Others saw it somewhat differently. One board member notes, 'John was never one for dealing with anomalies in a ruthless way'. The board meetings of LWT and LWT (Holdings) alternate and Tesler chairs the first, with Bland in the chair for the second. Generally, they seem able to handle the difficulties inherent in the relationship. Nonetheless, the arrangement is awkward, particularly now that the Holdings company has divested itself of most of its non-television interests.

36 In 1985, Cresta World Travel, 70 per cent of which was owned by Page and Moy (Holdings) Ltd., was sold back to its original owners, and the executive directors of Sunspot Tours purchased a further 15 per cent of the company, thereby reducing Page and Moy's share of the equity to 40 per cent.

37 Century Hutchinson was sold in 1989 for a remarkable £64 million. LWT's share was £15 million compared to a book value of £4.3 million.

38 Bland also restructured the company. At the beginning of 1985 he introduced a scheme which gave votes to all shareholders. Holders of voting shares were offered five new shares for each one of their voting shares. At the end of this process the group had over 2,000 shareholders and no shareholder could own more than 10 per cent of the shares. 65 per cent of LWT's employees owned some shares, and the directors owned a substantial amount. The majority of shares – 58.4 per cent – belonged to 26 City institutions.

Chapter 10

1 Wharmby became a producer with LWT for a few years, working on *Dempsey and Makepeace* among other series. A director who worked with Wharmby recalls: 'Tony was a brilliant producer, he could sketch out an episode of *Dempsey and Makepeace* on the back of a cigarette packet. But he hated administration'.

2 Early in the following year, Jane Hewland became Head of Features, and David Cox moved up from *Weekend World* to replace Barry Cox as Head of Current Affairs.

3 Bell was so confident that he had Boyd, that the latter's name was inserted in LWT's internal telephone directory.

4 The idea for the *6 O'Clock Show* – one of the original names of which was *Friday Night Live* – had been presented by Barry Cox at Brighton the previous year. It was the seventh best ratings performer in LWT's history.

5 Tesler expressed concern to Birt about the first show. Although he thought the début 'excellent', he was 'nagged over the weekend . . . by a feeling that something . . . is missing from the programme. I think that it may well be that the show is determinedly light-*weight* as well as light-hearted: a sequence of tasty hors d'oeuvres with no main course. I wonder if an investigative Londoners' consumer spot is not the answer: a touch of *That's Life*'.

6 Street-Porter, called 'our favourite cockney' by a senior LWT executive, soon tired of the role. 'I was getting more and more depressed at the hideous cockney character they were trying to create. It was just more and more removed from reality. I went to John after the second year of the show and told him that I wanted out. He couldn't believe it. He told me that I was throwing away my career. I told him that I wanted to be a producer rather than a presenter and I felt much, much better'. The cockney character was important to the programme; Derek Jameson had been tried in one of the pilots, and Danny Baker was to take over the role when Street-Porter left.

7 It was also attractive to the audience. It sits just behind *Surprise, Surprise* and *Blind Date* in the list of LWT's twenty highest rated programmes since 1984.

8 Birt felt that there was too much drama on the stocks as it was. He was unhappy at producing more until he had transmitted the ones already there.

9 On reflection, Barclay adjudged that the show 'was a ramshackle venture venture which jolly nearly came off. The pity is that no one tried to follow it up'. Birt actually repeated it on LWT.

10 The average under Birt was ten hours a year. However, LWT made, on average, nine hours of situation comedies a year for Channel 4 between 1982 and 1987. p. 00

11 His resignation was announced in February 1983. Alan Boyd later remarked, 'Ironically, Humphrey's up-market sit-coms that were designed 10 years ago are probably more right today than they were when he resigned'.

12 John Thaw was greatly upset. The series looked dated, and it could have greatly harmed his career.

13 LWT produced, on average, three hours of drama a year for Channel 4 during this period.

14 This play, which featured young schoolboys wandering the red-light district of Amsterdam, picked up the highest rating of any ITV drama in 1985.

15 At the time of writing in 1989, *Sunday, Sunday* is still running.

16 At the end of 1983 she was poached by the BBC as a presenter of *60 Minutes*, the ill- fated successor to *Nationwide*.

17 The following year, Dhondy commissioned LWT to make *Club Mix*, a mixture of music and discussion.

18 LWT contributed fourteen hours of game shows to Channel 4 in 1985–6.

19 Gavin invented the opening sequence for the titles of the *South Bank Show*.

20 The first episode of 1985's *Game For A Laugh* attained its highest ever rating.

21 Only *It'll be Alright on the Night* and *On the Buses* performed more consistently.

22 Jane Hewland and Barry Cox, as LWT executives, sat on the board of the new company. Janet Street-Porter, to her great fury, was excluded.

23 Street-Porter became head of youth programmes at the BBC in January 1988.

24 In 1988, ten years after Grade's first attempt, ITV signed an exclusive contract with the league for live soccer. John Barclay, who was the last remaining programme executive from Peacock days, left the company in the summer of 1989.

Chapter 11

1 He has since returned to act as a consultant on a new series called *The Walden Interview*.

2 *Eyewitness*, Hewland's replacement for the *Weekend World* slot, began broadcasting in the spring of 1989.

3 LWT's permanent staff was cut from 1636 in 1982 to 1197 in 1989. Productivity increased from 712 hours in 1984 to 834 hours in 1988. Costs were cut by 13 per cent between spring 1988 and spring 1989, despite a summer pay increase.

4 Greg Dyke was further locked-in when he was appointed as Deputy Managing Director in 1989, and Managing Director in spring 1990. Dyke spent some of 1989 at Harvard Business School. Changed days.

INDEX